To Les & Pauline,

Best Wishes !

COLD FEAT

A journey to the North Magnetic Pole

Duncan L. Eadie

Jy 2009.

with a Foreword by PEN HADOW

Trafford
PUBLISHING

Order this book online at www.trafford.com/07-0616
or email orders@trafford.com

Most Trafford titles are also available at major online book retailers.

Note for Librarians: A cataloguing record for this book is available from Library
and Archives Canada at www.collectionscanada.ca/amicus/index-e.html

Printed in Victoria, BC, Canada.

ISBN: 978-1-4251-2215-7

*We at Trafford believe that it is the responsibility of us all, as both individuals
and corporations, to make choices that are environmentally and socially sound.
You, in turn, are supporting this responsible conduct each time you purchase a
Trafford book, or make use of our publishing services. To find out how you are
helping, please visit www.trafford.com/responsiblepublishing.html*

*Our mission is to efficiently provide the world's finest, most comprehensive
book publishing service, enabling every author to experience success.
To find out how to publish your book, your way, and have it available
worldwide, visit us online at www.trafford.com/10510*

 www.trafford.com

North America & international
toll-free: 1 888 232 4444 (USA & Canada)
phone: 250 383 6864 ♦ fax: 250 383 6804 ♦ email: info@trafford.com

The United Kingdom & Europe
phone: +44 (0)1865 487 395 ♦ local rate: 0845 230 9601
facsimile: +44 (0)1865 481 507 ♦ email: info.uk@trafford.com

10 9 8 7 6 5 4

Cold Feat
A journey to the North Magnetic Pole

Dedicated to my wife Niamh and daughters Rebecca and Olivia –
written with a love that no polar icecap could ever cool, and to inspire you to
cast your eyes on this great place of untouched wonder.

One life. Live it.

'A few toes aren't much to give to achieve the Pole.'

Robert Edwin Peary – (arguably) the first man to reach the
North Geographic Pole, 1909.

To mum and dad, for giving me the courage to venture over the horizon.

To those with dreams, who have the drive to make them reality.

Foreword by Pen Hadow

'If you dream of doing something, stop dreaming, get out, and make it happen.'

SIR CHRIS BONNINGTON, MOUNTAINEER.

was captivated from an early age by tales of adventure in the polar regions. The adventure described in this book, about how ordinary people cope in extraordinary environments, may captivate you too. I have been lucky enough to turn my polar dreams into reality, and eventually into a career, through the establishment of the Polar Travel Company. The founding goal of the Polar Travel Company was, and still is, to give an opportunity to a broad group of people, (not just high-performance athletes and special forces personnel), to experience the Arctic and Antarctic and some of its wonders. The experiences Duncan describes in this book are evidence of that aim being met.

I have found that each person gains something different from their experience in the polar regions. Every person I have brought to the Arctic, I suspect, has been left with a lifelong memory, and returned with a sense of achievement, and for some, wonderment. This doesn't seem to diminish with time or on subsequent visits – as I have found myself during many expeditions in this captivating region.

I first met Duncan on Dartmoor, on an English winter's morning in January, 1997. It was clear to me that he had a deep yearning to go to the Arctic, one which I was happy to have been able to help satisfy. The group of people he travelled with formed a great team, and we had a lot of fun on the ice, overcoming the daily challenges that we were presented with. When things got tough, as they did for all of us at times, just staring out across the bleak, but incredibly beautiful icescape, reminded us why we were there, and made all the effort worthwhile.

I hope this book gives you a desire to go to a place that is one of the last untouched areas on this planet. A place that has remained largely unchanged since man first walked the Earth. A grand celebration of wildlife that opens for six months of the year and then firmly closes with the onset of the long, cold Arctic winter, one that impresses on you just how insignificant a man is against natures might.

By picking up this book you have passed the first stage in getting your boots on Arctic ice. Whether you choose to do it in your mind's eye or find it within yourself to go there in person – go, breathe in the atmosphere, and experience nothing like you've ever seen before.

Pen Hadow 2006

Pen Hadow is the only person to have walked, alone and unsupported, to the North Geographic Pole from Canada. He is also the first Briton to have walked, without re-supply, to both the North and South Geographic Poles and as such is one of the country's leading polar adventurers.

Contents

	FOREWORD BY PEN HADOW	6
	PROLOGUE	12
1	DRAWN TO A COOLING BREEZE	15
2	GETTING ON BOARD	28
3	A FULL TEAM	48
4	TRAINING	56
5	PREPARATION	72
6	HEADING NORTH	88
7	AT LAST, THE ICE	122
8	THE LAST OUTPOST	157
9	POLAR BEAR PASS	184
10	THE MEETING	201
11	DUNCAN POINT	219
12	THE POLE, BUT UNDER DIFFERENT CIRCUMSTANCES THAN EXPECTED	240
13	CONCLUSION	263
	EPILOGUE	265
	ACKNOWLEDGEMENTS	268
	APPENDIX 1 -EXPEDITION LIST	269
	APPENDIX 2 -KOMATIK CONTENTS	269
	APPENDIX 3 - EQUIPMENT AND CLOTHING	271
	APPENDIX 4 - BIBLIOGRAPHY	274
	APPENDIX 5 - DATA CHART	275
	GLOSSARY	277

Figure 1 - The location of the major poles

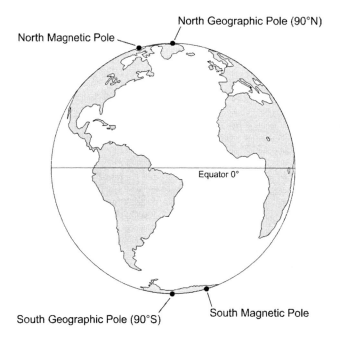

North Geographic Pole (90°N)

North Magnetic Pole

Equator 0°

South Geographic Pole (90°S)

South Magnetic Pole

Area of map detailed

····· **Arctic Circle**

Figure 2 - The North Magnetic Pole region and progress of the expedition

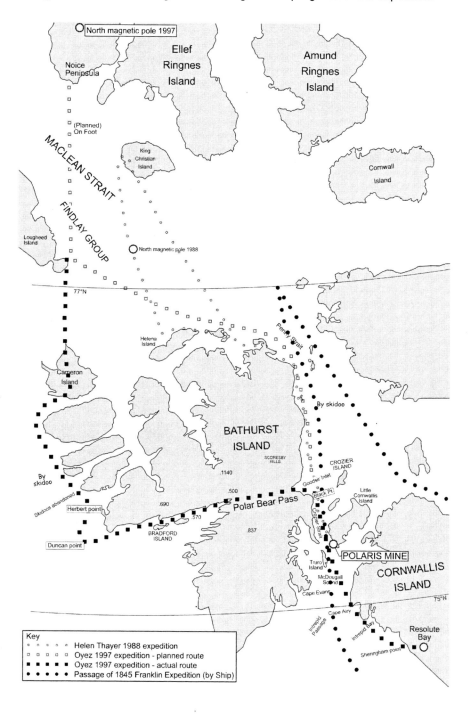

Key

o o o o o Helen Thayer 1988 expedition
□ □ □ □ □ Oyez 1997 expedition - planned route
■ ■ ■ ■ ■ Oyez 1997 expedition - actual route
• • • • • Passage of 1845 Franklin Expedition (by Ship)

Prologue

*'Had we lived I should have had a tale to tell of the
hardihood, endurance and courage of my companions
which would have stirred the heart of every Englishman.'*

CAPTAIN ROBERT FALCON SCOTT, ROYAL NAVY,
POLAR EXPLORER.

As a seven-year-old boy, in the early 1970's, I had been afflicted by a particular and, perhaps for someone of that age, peculiar dream. As I sank into my warm bed, with the winter wind and rain hammering at the windows, my young mind drifted like a snowdrop playing in the gale. The wind and cold around me were soon forgotten as I withdrew further into the depths of my bed, the warm sheets forming a perfect cocoon around me. As I slipped further into my slumber the darkness of my bedroom was no longer black but became a brilliant white, brighter than the sun. The lashing of rain at the window was no longer audible above the screaming blizzard wrenching at my clothes, the wind searching every crease of my clothing for entry, tugging at zips and snatching at cords as it tried to rip my clothes from me.

I was now standing alone on the Antarctic ice plateau, surrounded by the swirling white-out of the blizzard. Awkwardly, I searched the snow drifts looking for evidence of my target as I made my way about - as a blind man might stumble on a stormy rock-covered beach, looking for safety from the incoming tide. A grey image briefly revealed in the distance was nothing more than the driving snow playing games with my eyes. I struggled on night after night in the emptiness, looking for my quarry.

Finally, the blinding whiteness revealed a small dark shape drifting in and out of the blizzard. It was impossible to see how far away it was because the swirling rapids of snow rushing around me confused all perception of distance. I trudged onwards towards it, an eagerness in my pace, until I found the object of my search – a simple tent. Almost buried in snow, only a green cloth tip protruded from the frozen ice prison holding its inmates hostage. Inside I knew there would be three cold and exhausted men.

In my dream I was frightened to open the tent, for fear of what I might find inside. Gradually, I moved the snow aside and revealed a tightly closed entrance. The frozen ropes unwound in front of me, leaving the tent doors to flap wildly at the violent command of the wind. As the light gushed in through the opening, I looked inside and was just able to see three masses huddled together on the cramped tent floor.

Out of the darkness the light revealed three large brown sleeping bags lying among an overturned cooker, a notebook, a short length of rope, and other objects concealed by a dusty layer of snow. As I looked in further, one of the mounds seemed to move slightly until a leathery face slowly poked out. Were it not for the brilliant blue eyes floating on a forlorn face it would have been impossible to tell what this creature was. Cracked lips covered with sores washed in now-dried blood sat against a dirty black beard. This face conveyed utter exhaustion and desperation.

My heart began to pound, my lungs filled with air. 'Captain Scott, I've come to save you!' I shouted above the gale. No response came. The eyes looked forlornly through me.

'What is it man?' came another weary voice from the ground.

'The tent's blown open again,' came the reply.

'Will this devil wind rob us even of our death sleep?'

I screamed again and again at them with the passion, hope and naivety held by a seven-year-old child; 'I'm here to save you, it will be all right.' Nothing moved.

'Close the door, man,' came a murmur from the depths of one of the frost-encrusted sleeping bags.

The tent door gradually closed as the pair of dirty, bandaged, and split fingers tied the ropes, closing the entrance for the last time. I fell back just in time to hear a final murmur. 'Sorry Con, I must be dreaming – for I thought I saw a small child standing at the entrance.'

Then once again I was consumed by the blizzard of my dreams.

As each minute passed these men would come closer to death – and immortality. The men had braved everything that the Antarctic could throw at them. Captain Scott, Bowers and Wilson; their names were legendary, along with Evans and Titus Oates their fallen comrades, so much so that even I, a seven-year-old boy, wrapped up tightly on a cold winter's night - over half a century after their deaths, had been stirred to dream, night after night, of saving them.

I had been interested in going to the Arctic for a long time and, finally, in 1996, and now a grown man, I had found an expedition company that would transport me to the extremes of the planet, to the top of the globe, and for a sum that a mere mortal such as I could afford. Indeed, it was a price that many could afford. The trip wasn't going to be full of multi-millionaires who would use it as an excuse to cool down from the excessive heat of some Caribbean island, or full of scientists who would droll on about rocks and atmospheric patterns and how the science budget was too small. No, this trip would be full of ordinary people. People like me. Ordinary people who for once wanted to go somewhere extraordinary and see, and do, something unreal. And I was going with them.

1

Drawn to a Cooling Breeze

'Seize the opportunity of a lifetime in the lifetime of the opportunity.'

SIR CHAY BLYTH, YACHTSMAN.

'**W**here?' they would spout in disbelief.

The reply and expression were always the same. Their faces would show surprise, their eyebrows rise, their mouths open slightly. Their ears had heard but their minds could not believe the message that was passed to them.

'Where?!'

I would calmly, but enthusiastically, reply again, 'The North Magnetic Pole'.

'But why would anyone want to go to the North Pole for a holiday?' would come their response.

They had heard. There was nothing wrong with their ears – just their comprehension. Why go to the North Pole for a holiday? There were no bars, no nightlife, warm sunny beaches, or any of the usual holiday essentials. I was on the spot; why indeed?

I hadn't known what answer to give the first time. But soon the responses were so similar and predictable that I had the answers prepared.

'Where?' they would ask.

'The North Magnetic Pole,' I would reply.

'Where?!'

'The North Pole.'

'Why?'

'Well the desolation, the grandeur of icebergs as big as skyscrapers, seas filled with whales, the land trodden by the mighty polar bear, and the mysteries of adventurers such as Ross, Franklin and Amundsen.' After a few moments discussion, which I always got, as it wasn't Spain, France or Florida and merited a few minutes of their time, they would usually conclude with, 'Wow, I wish I was going.' So I wasn't crazy after all.

It had been on the way home in August, 1996 after another late night in the office, that I spotted the small article in the newspaper that started it all. Whilst squashed in the confines of a crowded London underground tube train I carefully manoeuvred the pages of the London *Evening Standard* so that I could read it in the dim light of the hot, packed carriage thundering through the dark tunnels beneath the streets of London.

The short article, wedged between the ravages of the latest political storm and the analysis of a disastrous football match result, proclaimed that a new company had been set up to take the adventurous traveller to the far, frozen reaches of the planet. North Pole or South Pole, they could accommodate you. It grabbed my attention. My hands steadied the newspaper as the train gently rocked from side to side above the clitter-clatter rhythm of the rails. In the hot, sweaty confines of the tube train my imagination had been awoken by the thought of escaping the crowded suffocating heat to the cold, empty wastes. It was the beginning of my adventure.

I soon received the company's brochure through the post. Pouring over expeditions to the South Pole, North Pole, Greenland, Svalbard and other such exciting and untamed places, my adrenaline soon stopped pumping when I saw the attached price list - which was quoted in US dollars and had lots of trailing zeros. My dreams hit the floor. The brochure was reluctantly relegated to collecting dust on a cupboard shelf, as my polar dream receded to the back of my mind.

Life carried on. I got married, moved house and found myself in a new role at work. However, like a large iceberg waiting out the summer months for winter, the dream failed to melt away. Re-reading the brochure again a few months later, I decided to phone the company.

'Hello, Polar Travel Company.' It was a well educated and organised sounding voice that answered the telephone. I explained my interest to Pendril Hadow, the owner of the Polar Travel Company. Pendril, or as I later found out, was known as 'Polar Pen' to his friends. He had a soft spoken upper-class accent that came across as confident, and friendly. Pen freely talked about his company and gave me the company background.

Formed to take advantage of the growing market for extreme activities, the Polar Travel Company was now in its second year of business. As we chatted over the phone an image was forming in my mind of what the owner of such a company was like. As well as being the owner, Pendril Hadow was an accomplished polar traveller, leading most of his company's expeditions. He was not only the brains, but also the workhorse behind his small company. As he spoke, my eyes passed over his credentials, listed in the inside cover of the company brochure. Harrow-educated, and listed in the Guinness Book of Records, for the furthest ever trip in an inflatable boat – from London to Greenland! He had also attempted to walk to the Geographic North Pole, alone and unsupported. He knew his stuff.

The brochure listed Pen as thirty four years old. I pictured a young Ranulph Fiennes in my mind, daring, adventurous and probably with a large debt on his shoulders, that might have been listed by his bank manager under 'Unusual' or 'Risky business'.

We chatted away and my interest gathered momentum. Pen was not a salesman, but then I didn't need to be sold, not on the concept at least. I desperately wanted to visit the polar regions and was looking for the right way to get there. It was towards the end of the conversation, after we had talked through the entire brochure, that Pen mentioned that his company also offered private expeditions tailored to individual requirements.

'I have a group walking the last sixty miles to the North Geographic Pole,' he said proudly, 'and another walking to the Magnetic North Pole.' That was it! Before he could explain anymore I knew I had found the way to satisfy my dream. I would walk to the North Magnetic Pole. I had just finished reading a book by Helen Thayer, the first woman to walk there alone, in 1988. The adventure she described both thrilled and frightened me. This was definitely the trip for me.

The Magnetic and Geographic North Poles are not to be confused. The Geographic North Pole is the point directly at the top of the world where all the lines of longitude meet at ninety degrees north; you cannot go further north. There is of course no actual stake in the ground at the North Pole – unlike the South Pole, where there really is a pole positioned in the ground - marking the world's most southern point. The Geographic North Pole is located smack in the middle of the Arctic Ocean, which is frozen all year round. The sea ice there, whilst solid, moves with the ocean, so even if you were to plant a stake or pole at the North Pole, it would soon drift away with the current.

The Magnetic North Pole on the other hand, is located approximately eight-hundred miles south of the North Geographic Pole, and six-hundred miles north of the Arctic circle. Located among the Queen Elizabeth group of islands high in the Canadian Arctic, there is nothing to mark this desolate spot. The location is a polar desert region, where temperatures can fall to -50°C. It is here, at the Magnetic North Pole, that all of the world's magnetic compasses point to when showing north.

This strange geographic anomaly is due to molten magma, rocks so hot that they are liquid, buried deep below the Earth's crust, effectively floating like bubbles, far underneath the ground. The magma is magnetic and due to its 'floating' nature and being heavily influenced by the sun's own magnetic activity, actually moves north east from year to year. On some days, depending on solar activity , its location can drift tens of miles far beneath the ground. Just like any magnet, there is a corresponding South Magnetic Pole at the opposite end of the planet, in Antarctica.

'So when is the 'Mag Pole expedition Pen?', my voice carried renewed enthusiasm.

'I'm taking them out there in March next year.'

'It sounds interesting,' was my understated reply.

Pen continued, 'They are a group of friends who every year do some sort of trip together. They contacted me a few months ago to put the expedition together and act as their guide.'

'So it was their idea?' I asked.

'Absolutely,' replied Pen. 'They came up with a proposal and budget, and let me arrange the details. I will act as the group's guide. They are a group of solicitors and quite an organised bunch.' Pen described how the expedition was planned to last twelve days and would leave from northern Canada. They would travel on skidoos, (a sort of motor bike that travels on ice), to gain some initial distance before walking the remaining one-hundred and twenty nautical miles across the frozen sea ice to the Pole.

All the equipment necessary for survival would be man-hauled, Captain Scott-style, in sledges. I had enough information. Pen had explained the objective and I responded enthusiastically, 'Pen, it's the expedition I've been looking for. How do I go about joining?' It was then he delivered the blow, in an almost apologetic manner.

'Well, actually Duncan I'm going to disappoint you here because they have a full team.'

I wouldn't be put down.

'There's room for a small one, surely?' I explained how this trip was the one I was looking for and I *needed* to join up. I was of course overstating many of the points, as I couldn't commit to anything yet. I didn't know whether I was physically fit enough to meet the demands of such an expedition and, crumbs, I hadn't even discussed this with my wife! But I needed to get my foot in the door, and left it with Pen that he would contact the group leader and ask if another team member would be considered. I put the phone down and sat in silence for a moment trying to contain my excitement. If I could get on such an expedition it would be great, I enthused to myself. But, I had to accept that Pen had just told me that there was no room. I decided to hope for good news and would call him again in a week's time.

The week went by very quickly. I was busy at work and there never seemed enough hours in the day. Unfortunately, the same was true for Pen. When I phoned him, he admitted that he had been too busy to take up my request to contact the group leader to ask for another member to be considered. However, Pen was meeting with the expedition members at the weekend and would speak to them in person then. I enthusiastically asked for the leader's telephone number so I could speak to him myself. I even asked Pen whether I could come along and meet them, but Pen declined my attempts to muscle in and said he would call me next week following the meeting.

The following week my mind kept drifting to the call I would have with Pen. Eventually he rang.

'Pen! How are you? Did you meet up with the expedition members?' His reply contained bad news.

'I met up with them and unfortunately they don't want another team member. Basically, as I said before, they are all close friends and have been doing these things together for the last twenty years. They get on very well and don't want to admit anyone outside of their close group.' He paused for my reaction. None came.

'Sorry, I did try.'

'Ah well, thanks for trying. Look, I'll keep in touch to see if anything changes.' I couldn't hide my disappointment, and sighed audibly.

The Polar Travel Company brochure found itself gathering dust once again on my cupboard shelf.

The months passed by, and my wife found herself in a new job, working for a New Zealand software firm. A trip to New Zealand to attend a training course saw her adding a holiday, which I flew out to spend with her. New Zealand, by fact of being one of the closest land masses to the Antarctic, is a supply point for many southern bases. Christchurch airport, on New Zealand's south island has a supply hanger for the American McMurdo base, the largest base in Antarctica.

Seeing one of the Hercules transport aircraft taking off for the great white continent set me thinking again about the Arctic. These thoughts were also re-enforced through visiting several polar-related museums and exhibitions that exist in New Zealand. I also had hidden a secret desire to search out Helen Thayer, the New Zealander whose travels to the North Magnetic Pole described in her book *Polar Dream* had inspired me in the first place. This was not to happen as I had learnt from Pen that she had moved to America. However, the spark still remained in my mind, the desire would not go away, I wanted to get to the Arctic.

On flying back to England in late November, with the chill winds of the English winter beginning to return, I decided to give Pen a call again as it was three months since we had spoken.

'Ah Duncan, good to hear from you, how are you?' Pen asked, with his usual polite and dignified accent. I cut straight to the point, asking again about the Magnetic North Pole expedition.

'I'm glad you called, you are still interested I take it?!' was Pen's response. It was less a question and more of a statement. 'You'll be pleased to hear that things are looking up.' My heart began to beat a little faster. 'One of the expedition members has dropped out, leaving just five in the group. I'm not sure why, I think he may have had other commitments. He went as far as paying for the flight.' I tightened my grip on the telephone, but before I could say anything, Pen said, 'They need another member to take his place.' He paused suggestively, 'Can I suggest to Mark, the expedition leader, that he give you a call?' At last things were moving, though it was luck more than anything else.

'Excellent!' I exclaimed, and heartily agreed that Pen should follow this course of action. For the rest of the day I felt as high as a cloud. I wasn't on the expedition yet, but the barriers were coming down. It would now be up to me to see if I could join this expedition.

Mark, the expedition leader, called earlier than expected. Actually he called me that same night.

'Duncan, Mark,' was the upper-class, loud, and very enthusiastic voice that greeted me on the phone. 'So sorry that we weren't able to meet before. Pen had mentioned your interest but the expedition was at that time fully manned,' his voice boomed. After Mark explained the nature of the trip it was up to me to explain my expectations and preparedness. Mark was particularly interested in my fitness and outdoor experience, and rapidly fired off questions at the rate of a machine gun spitting bullets.

I explained that I was thirty-one-years old, healthy and reasonably fit after years of practicing judo. I played ice hockey for sport and fitness and regularly attended the gym – generally sounding as positive as I could. Mark began to laugh out loud, 'Well, we are all old codgers in comparison, and will need to spend more time in training to keep up with you.' However I knew he was playing down his fitness.

I described how I had recently returned from a trip to Russia to climb Mount Elbrus.

'Wonderful, how high is Elbrus?' enquired Mark.

'Just over eighteen-thousand feet Mark,' I answered.

'That must have been quite a view,' was his reply.

'Well, unfortunately, I got within a few hundred feet of the summit and had to turn back due to bad weather,' was my honest answer.

Mark's reply was one better. 'We just got back from Aconcagua – hell of a trip, real slag of a mountain.'

Aconcagua at twenty-three-thousand feet was the highest mountain in South America, and the highest in the world outside Asia. I knew though not technically a difficult climb, like Mount Elbrus you could walk up it without the aid of ropes, it was high, and the loose gravel under foot was 'a real slag' as Mark put it. Mark was fit, there was no denying it.

'Look, let's meet up shortly – how about Saturday the fourth of Jan'. Come to my office. See you then.' The phone went dead as the conversation ended without Mark even saying goodbye. The whole conversation had lasted under four minutes. I felt quite drained, but exhilarated at the same, with the dead phone still buzzing in my ear. Mark seemed to be a bundle of energy. I replaced the phone and having now passed the first stage, I looked forward to meeting with Mark after Christmas, now only a few weeks away.

The next day I called Pen to let him know that Mark had phoned the previous night. He was not surprised. 'You'll find Mark very direct and fast moving. He has a very strong personality. He and the rest of his team are all solicitors and you'll find them quite a demanding group. It's one of the reasons why they were reluctant to let anyone in from outside.' He paused before continuing. 'You may find them a bit overpowering at times, possibly leaving you feeling a bit left out.'

I took his point on board, and looked forward to my meeting with Mark. Now that I had more confidence about my chances of getting on the team, I bombarded Pen with questions about the trip. I had never been to the Arctic and didn't really know how I would cope with the infamous low temperatures. However, I was sure that if I could get on the expedition I would somehow manage to cope. How cold would it actually be? What clothes would I need? How fit did I need to be? How fit were the others? The questions flew around my head.

My main worries concerned the cold, the presence of polar bears and whether I was fit enough to even attempt such a mission. Pen explained: 'We should expect to meet temperatures down to minus fifty centigrade, but with proper clothing this should be manageable.

I wasn't sure how my definition of 'manageable' compared with his. I had no idea what -50°C would be like; the coldest temperature I had ever experienced in my life was probably only -7°C during a particularly cold winter's morning in England.

'However, for much of the time,' he said, 'when pulling a sledge, the difficulty will be keeping from *over*-heating rather than just keeping warm.' This seemed hard to imagine. I wondered whether he thought he had scared me off by mentioning the -50°C deadly low temperature and therefore decided to counter this with a bit of sales spiel.

As for fitness, Pen stated that as a good measure I would need to be able to do an 'honest day's work on a building site'. A good analogy I thought, though the Arctic would be an unlikely place to suffer 'builders bum' – or an unfortunate place with potentially permanent scars if I did! I felt I was reasonably fit, however I had the soft hands of an office worker, and lungs that had breathed nothing but filtered, conditioned and purified office air for years on end. Would I be hard enough ?

'We may see polar bears, but they are unlikely to be a problem,' Pen confidently stated. 'They tend to be of more concern to lone travellers on foot.' When I asked whether we would be taking a dog for protection, to warn against such predators, Pen's reply was a definite 'No'. Dogs could be difficult to manage being his reason. I knew from reading Helen Thayer's account of her journey in 1988, along almost exactly the same route that Pen planned to take to the Magnetic Pole, that she had been harassed by polar bears for much of the way. She took a dog to warn her of the bears' presence, which was especially useful when she was sleeping or when she was travelling in fog. Without her dog 'Charlie' she would have never returned alive she felt.

'How will we protect against polar bears at night Pen? Post sentries?' The thought of standing about on watch duty in the Arctic cold was not appealing.

'That won't be necessary,' explained Pen confidently. 'I will carry a rifle for protection, but it's highly unlikely that a situation will happen.' I was not convinced, and 'highly unlikely' was not unlikely enough for me. Being woken by a seventy-stone hungry polar bear, on the other side of a few millimetres of tent canvas, was my idea of a living nightmare. However, Pen was the expert and experienced in dealing with polar bears, so I bowed to his knowledge and experience.

I have always been the sort of person who likes to know all the details. I suppose being a software project manager taught me that detail was all important. I knew that on an expedition it was the small things that would make all the difference. Once up in the high Arctic there would be no opportunity for buying any forgotten items. Correct preparation would be key to avoid problems that could result in arguments, delays, getting cold and perhaps worse. However, I wasn't on the expedition yet, so I focussed on getting on board first.

As I put the phone down to Pen, a large brown envelope shot through the letter box with a clatter. It was from Mark and its timely arrival re-enforced my first impressions of him, and what Pen had just said about the expedition leader. Mark was organised and moved quickly. Opening the letter I found a colour brochure that Mark had put together about the expedition. It contained everything I needed to know; including who the expedition members were, what they had done previously, and details about the trip.

Flicking through the brochure, I saw that everything was very well presented. Mark had indicated in a covering note that he intended the brochure to be used to gain sponsorship for the expedition. I carefully studied each page. The brochure introduced the trip as a 'private expedition'. Wow! I thought, a real private expedition, a one-off custom trip, not part of a scheduled holiday. It had the air of a Victorian adventure. The brochure clearly stated the expedition's objective :

> "To make a journey by snowmobile and by foot from the settlement at Resolute Bay, across the sea ice through prime polar bear country, to the North Magnetic Pole in 1997."

Of the three-hundred and sixty nautical miles between Resolute Bay and the Pole, it proposed that the first two-hundred and forty nautical miles would be covered by snowmobile. The remaining one-hundred and twenty miles would then be covered on foot, with our team hauling their supplies in sledges in the manner adopted by Captain Scott. Unlike Scott's expedition of 1912 though, we would have the benefits of modern clothing and equipment.

The front page of the brochure sported individual photos of the expedition team members in various heroic poses from their travels around the world. These included a shot of one of them jumping off an extremely high suspension bridge, another abseiling down a mountain, and others summiting various peaks. The text stated that this group of friends had also competed in the Fastnet sailing race, run the London marathon and various triathlons, rode the Cresta Run, sky-dived and, run the Pamplona Bull Run - as well as having climbed in the Alps, Andes and Himalayas.

They were all in their early forties and desk-bound most of the year. Mark's adventure résumé stated that he was from a military family and he had served in the 10th Battalion Parachute Regiment, territorial army, and the 63rd SAS, Signals, Territorial Army. I knew this meant he would be incredibly strong mentally. With this background, age wasn't really too relevant. If it was possible to get to the Pole, with a background like Mark's, I was sure he would get there. If I got the chance to join the team, I wondered if I was tough enough. I studied Mark's photograph whilst reading his stated outlook on life. 'My girth is expanding and my outlook on life is narrowing. The days of being able to run ten miles without being out of breath are probably over'. Mark was an impressive character.

Next to a photograph of a man camping in a snow hole at the top of Mount Blanc, was Rob's résumé. Rob was a partner in a local solicitors firm. He had also served with the 'paras'. I looked further down the brochure, hoping that the remaining members would not be so daunting. I was to be disappointed.

Geoffrey was the oldest of the group at forty-five. He had run a number of successful engineering businesses. Apparently, during a free-fall parachute jump, (the brochure said) Geoff was begged by the instructors to stop *terrifying them*! The brochure didn't state why – leaving me with wild pictures of Geoff in my mind.

The final member was Robin, known, according to the brochure, as 'Bunny'. He was also a successful solicitor, running his own law firm advising governments, particularly in the developing world. He wryly described himself in the brochure as 'going bald at the age of eighteen after only dabbling in the pleasures of the world, after which things went downhill'.

They were all very impressive, clearly highly motivated and professionally very successful. The brochure's closing line on the final page concluded 'More people have stood on the Summit of Mount Everest than have walked to the North Magnetic Pole, and none have walked to its new position'.

I took a deep breath and sat back for a while wondering whether I had bitten off more than I could chew. Perhaps this adventure would be as much a discovery of my own limits as it would be about seeing the geography of this northern part of the world. However, they did seem an impressive bunch of people to tackle such an adventure with, I thought to myself. I closed the brochure, my enthusiasm undaunted.

2

Getting on Board

*'You don't have to be a fantastic hero to do certain things.
You can just be an ordinary chap, sufficiently motivated.'*

SIR EDMUND HILLARY, MOUNTAINEER AND
POLAR EXPLORER.

Christmas came and went and my meeting with Mark, the expedition leader, soon arrived. The meeting, or interview, with Mark was going to be very important. It would also be different to any other interview I had attended. There was a lot at stake with this interview. I swallowed hard as I thought about it. It wouldn't be like a job interview where if you failed one interview there was usually another job at another company. Failing this one would mean not getting to the Magnetic Pole. I sat deep in thought, as the train brushed its way through a dull January morning, taking me to my meeting with Mark, at his office in Guildford.

The slight drizzle on the carriage window partially obscured the view of the Surrey countryside sweeping past. How could I convince him I was the right man to take to the pole? I knew lots about polar history and geography - after spending months pouring over books. He wouldn't be looking for a book-worm though, I knew that. I sat in the empty train carriage, running through all the reasons. I was fit, young, wanted to go, and knew a bit about the polar regions. I felt it wasn't enough. What was the edge I needed?

The train continued its way along the tracks. Soon the town came into view. Steeped in a grey mist, the angry clouds reached down to touch the tall buildings with their wet fingers. My concentration was soon broken by the booming of 'Guildford! Guildford!' from the tannoy as the train slowed as it approached the station. I jumped off quickly onto the platform and left the station. It was easy to find Mark's office, as it was situated on the high street.

I stood outside his office, glanced at my watch, and went in. The front door was unlocked and I found myself alone at the bottom of a set of stairs. I began to climb the dark stairs, which were adorned with old pictures. I could hear the muffled sound of a voice and walked towards it, until I got to an office door, whereupon I knocked loudly. The door opened quickly and a hand was enthusiastically thrust towards me. 'Duncan! Mark. Pleased to meet you.' He gave my hand a good strong shake, before gesturing towards a waiting chair, as he continued his phone conversation.

I took the chance to size up the situation. Here was Mark, ex-British paratrooper Territorial Army, climber of both the highest mountains in South America, western Europe (Mount Blanc) and many other adventures, as well as a successful local solicitor.

The first thing I noticed was that Mark had a beard, which wasn't present in the photograph in the literature he had sent to me. He was also reasonably small, at about five-foot-six, and looked, well, almost tubby – an appearance which I later found out gave him the nickname of 'El Porco'. Wearing training shoes and tight tracksuit trousers, he seemed out of place in the surroundings of his solicitor's office. Behind him, next to a row of dusty law books, was a large picture of a high mountain peak.

Mark's voice boomed into the phone's handset, as he spoke at a frightening speed, as if he were about to burst. The conversation soon ended, and Mark put the telephone down and turned his attention to me.

'Duncan, so good to see you, thanks awfully for coming along,' he said, as he sank into the dark red leather chair behind his oak desk.

'Didn't recognise you with the beard,' I replied.

'Oh, yes, it comes and goes – better protection for the weather ahead, don't you think?' Getting straight down to business and with a broad smile Mark continued, 'Now you've read the expedition literature and you look fit – tell me what you've been up to before.' I paused, ready to present Mark with a synopsis of my adventures, knowing that in comparison with the entries in Mark's brochure I had done very little.

'Well, let's see,' I drew a breath, 'a couple of years ago I went to Antarctica on an expedition ship. It was fascinating and stirred in me a passion for polar places.'

Mark cut straight to the chase. 'Did you do any walking or climbing down there?' I was afraid he would ask this. 'No, err, it was a trip along the coast of Graham Land. We stopped at several islands and wandered around, but only for a few hours on each one. It wasn't a physical expedition at all, not like the 'Mag Pole will be.' Mark sat in his chair patiently, the tick of a clock in the background counting the seconds, as he eyed me up and down.

'So you crossed the Drake Passage?' enquired Mark after an elongated pause.

This was the stretch of water that separated South America from Antarctica, a swirling expanse of Southern Ocean that had the fearsome reputation of being the roughest sea in the world.

'Yes, I sailed past Cape Horn and across the Drake Passage, it was-', my stomach turned audibly, 'as flat as a mill pond. I bet few people have seen that, eh?.' Mark didn't respond, but continued to eye me up and down in the quiet office.

I continued. 'Earlier this year, as I said on the phone, I climbed-,' I coughed briefly, 'or attempted to climb, Mount Elbrus.' This was obviously nearer Mark's own experiences and he homed in on it. 'And how did you find this?' 'Physically satisfactory,' I replied. 'I enjoyed the climb and the views. I had done a lot of training for it and basically climbed up without a problem until the weather moved in and cancelled the climb.'

'Well, we are always at the mercy of the elements,' Mark commented, his dark piercing eyes shining out from behind his thick black eyebrows.

'How did you get on with the rest of the climbing group? Did you know them before?'

'I didn't know any of the members of the Elbrus group before I joined the trip,' I replied, knowing Mark was drawing comparisons with his group, 'but I like to think I'm quite a sociable sort of bloke and get on pretty well with those around me. On Elbrus we all got on extremely well and had a very enjoyable trip.'

Before Mark could launch into his next question I concluded, 'In fact, equally with the Antarctic trip, I find not knowing people all part of the fun – by the time the expedition is up you know everyone and have made a new set of friends.' Mark was in agreement and went into the background of the group of friends he had enjoyed travels with over the last twenty years. 'This is likely to be our most physically challenging jape yet, and maybe even our last, now, that we are getting on in years.'

He paused, a little longer than before. I sat on the edge of my seat waiting for the next question. 'You know the cost of the trip – will you have any problem in obtaining the loot?' he enquired, with more interest than his previous questions.

'It's a lot of money,' I replied, 'but I can arrange the finances,' I assured him.

'Good,' said Mark conclusively. 'Well I'm happy with you. I'd like the others to meet you before we decide, but I don't see any problem. In fact Bunny may be joining us this morning. You'll find him quite a hoot.'

'Great,' I said, slightly more relaxed on hearing this result.

All of a sudden it seemed so quick and easy, as Mark had apparently made his decision. I would find out in the coming months that everything moved quickly when Mark was around. He would make decisions on the spot and just get on with the job in hand. There was no dithering on his part, all part of his military background no doubt. It was almost as if he had been born an hour late and had spent the rest of his life trying to catch up. I wasn't sure what I was expecting during the interview, but it wasn't this.

'We had planned and budgeted the expedition for six people,' Mark concluded. 'Bunny is taking the last vacancy up with a friend of his. Should this fall through I'm afraid the cost would rise.' (I was unhappy with this, because my budget was very tight, and I had been led to believe that only one person was needed to complete the team.) 'We'll leave it up to Bunny's persuasive powers, which are unusually awesome,' concluded Mark.

Right on cue the door to the room opened and in walked a smiling gentleman in blue jeans, white trainers and a sweatshirt covered by a rain streaked coat.

'Bunny!' exclaimed Mark.

'Hi Markey.'

'Bunny, meet Duncan.' I rose from my seat to greet 'Bunny' as he stepped towards me shaking off his wet clothes.

'How the devil are you? Awful day out,' pronounced Bunny as we shook hands.

'Has Markey extracted the torture tools from you yet?' he asked me as he eyed Mark with a knowing look.

'It all went very well,' said Mark defensively from behind his dark beard. 'You realise what you are getting into, don't you?' grinned Bunny. 'A whole lot of ear bashing from a bunch of lawyers. Most people go to the North Pole to get away from people like us!' he exclaimed before bursting into a loud chuckle.

I felt immediately at home with these two characters. Bunny had described himself in the sponsor's brochure as the 'Groucho Marx' of the team. He seemed full of fun. A blond-haired man, with golden skin reflecting his gleaming white teeth, and balding before his time, he had a ripe smile and a cheeky glint in his blue shining eyes when he spoke. Like Mark and Pen he also had an upper class accent – the sort where 'house' is pronounced 'hise'. Bunny's accent was even more distinctive – if you closed your eyes when Bunny spoke, you could swear Prince Charles was talking to you, it was most uncanny. I might be going to the Pole with Prince Charles, I thought.

'Right Markey what's next? I've just come from the gym and need a feed,' said Bunny, slapping his stomach.

'Splendid idea Bunny, let's toodle down for a bite,' agreed Mark enthusiastically.

Before I knew it they were both off out the door with me hurriedly putting my coat on before running down the stairs to catch up. Off we all went at a frantic pace through the streets of Guildford to find somewhere for a snack. It was a great laugh listening to Bunny and Mark as they hollered and chuckled, before we arrived at a tiny café. Inside we ordered coffees and sandwiches. Mark had already settled the bill before we seemed to get anywhere near the till.

Bunny asked me a few questions but I realised now that the two most important things to them were firstly, would I get on with the rest of the group? and did I have the cash for the trip? The answers to both questions were 'yes'. I seemed to have impressed on them that I was fit enough, or could be by the time of the trip's departure in just over three months. Between bouts of laughter I got a bit more information out of them as to their fitness and the previous trips they had been on. They were both accomplished mountaineers. Without a doubt they were very fit for their age and also very strong mentally.

'So what was climbing Aconcagua like then?' I asked, as they drank their coffees at an alarming rate. Mark, drinking espresso, quickly replied, 'Horrible, but we got to the top. But Bunny received a 'pin prick' on the way up.'

It transpired that Mark had got to the top of the mountain unaided, but Bunny had suffered from cerebral oedema, also known as serious altitude sickness, due to the mountain's height. This condition occurs when liquid or pressure forms on the brain due to the altitude, and unless the affected person is taken to lower altitudes quickly, will prove fatal, as pressure builds on the brain. 'Well I dropped to a lower altitude to briefly recover, before having a most unpleasant dose of steroids to get me to the top,' Bunny informed me in his most royal accent.

He was braver, if that's the right word, than I would ever be. I would have called it a day when this serious condition occurred. Mark got to the top through sheer guts as well. Some of the team members didn't get to the top. One, having burst a blood vessel in his eye and suffering general altitude sickness, retired from the mountain. It sounded like a hell of a trip and I hoped the one we were planning would be more pleasant.

As we drank our coffees I also discovered that Bunny was still on pain killers for a problem with an ankle. This gave me some concern and I commented to Bunny that this was not the sort of injury to have during what would mainly be an extreme cross-country skiing trip.

'Don't worry Duncan, I'll get a six monthly injection in it before I go, it'll be fine,' Bunny replied to my concern with a broad grin that was so disarming. 'You've got to realise,' chuckled Mark, as he swung back on his chair, 'that our friend Bunny here doesn't have the sense to feel pain.'

'Do you remember that time Bunny…?' Mark launched into a flurry of stories resulting in us all creasing up with laughter.

The few customers' conversations in the no longer quiet café were soon drowned out by the volume of our chatting. I looked round, slightly embarrassed by our noise, to catch the odd eye of a customer who had come in for a calm Saturday morning coffee. Mark was like a whirlwind, bringing a lot of noise and activity wherever he went.

'Now remember Bunny, we must enforce a strict diet from…,' he hesitated, 'from next weekend,' Mark proudly announced. 'And that includes drink!'

'You'll go mad Mark,' was Bunny's swift reply.

'I never said it would be easy. Come on, we start next week – so make the most of it now.' I felt that this last statement was for my benefit. Neither Bunny or Mark seemed as though they could keep to such a commitment.

'How about the sixth member?' I questioned, thinking if the cost went up it would be difficult for me to attend.

'Oh Markey, I spoke with Chris last night and he can't make it I'm afraid,' Bunny responded. Now that meant if I were included we were still one person short - making the trip not viable.

'Would any of your climbing chums be interested Duncan?'

'I'll see,' I replied, knowing that being asked the question by Bunny seemed to certify his acceptance of me into the group as well.

'So Mark, where do we go from here?' I said, as they emptied their coffee cups, whilst I had hardly taken more than a mouthful from mine.

'I would like to introduce you to the other members of the team, Rob and Geoffrey, so they can have their say. It will also give you time to ensure that you want to come with us on this jape.' I knew the answer to that question already. Pen was right: they were a strong group, mentally, physically – and verbally. They seemed never short of a word to say, but that is a solicitor for you!

They were both terribly good fun and we all seemed to hit it off very well. I was well aware that in the months ahead, possibly stranded in a polar blizzard, things could fray a bit, but with these first impressions I didn't think that would be the case. If the proverbial did hit the fan, then often a good sense of humour would carry everyone through, and there seemed to be ample of this in the group. Yes, I wanted in.

I returned to London on the train in high spirits, even the drizzly gloom of the day had now brightened up, with blue skies making way for a few rays of sunshine to bathe the wintry scene.

It had taken me some time, perhaps six months, to make up my mind to go north. There seems to be something in my nature that when I want to really do something I get very excited, and almost decide to go there and then, before something within me says 'hold on!' and gives me reasons - ranging from my lack of sanity to the more detrimental effect on my bank account - why the idea should not be acted upon. I then spend a period of inner turmoil whilst these two forces fight for control. This trip was no exception. It took me a couple of months to even tell anyone. My wife was the first to know.

We had only been married a year and going on an expensive, possibly dangerous, expedition would not be welcome. I would never approach her with a half-baked idea, or not knowing whether I wanted to go or not. Equally, I wanted to be prepared with details about the expedition for her questions.

It was over a Chinese meal I broke the plan to her. I showed her Mark's sponsors' brochure, which detailed the route, and descriptions of my companions. She responded with a 'oh here we go again' sort of look that I always get when a crazy idea takes hold. I can't imagine what sort of response some of the other ideas rejected within my period of silence would have been met with.

'Antarctica, Elbrus and now this,' she said in a rather lofty voice. I wasn't sure whether that was good news or not. 'So, this is the last one is it?' she enquired. I continued to describe the expedition further. She listened intently before saying, 'So you are going then?!' obviously feeling decidedly abandoned. I dearly wanted to go, and told her so. Niamh was not one for the outdoor life, and enjoyed her comforts.

As we sat in the calm warmth of the restaurant with good wine being poured for us, it seemed hard to imagine what I was attempting. But that was part of the point, I didn't want to just fall into a job, marriage, house, car and kids, and to spend my whole life managing domestic issues. All those things were great but I didn't want to complete my life without experiencing some of the remote and extreme parts of our amazing planet. Not the parts where 'extreme' meant that you couldn't get good room service. She understood this and a little reluctantly, gave her support, which was so important to me.

Why would anyone want to go to the Magnetic North Pole? After all, it's just a very cold place isn't it? Isn't it? It had became apparent to me quite early on that this was still a place of mystery. Even in our modern world of higher education, satellites, mobile phones and computers, the Arctic is still steeped in mystery. A work colleague admitted to me that she didn't really know where the Arctic was! Now I could understand if she didn't know where the Queen Elizabeth Islands in northern Canada, where the magnetic pole is located, are – but to dismiss the location of an area larger than that of Europe! My colleague knew it was cold, but that was about it. She wasn't alone; I was amazed how bad many people's sense of geography was.

Many people asked me where I was going to stay when I was there. What they actually meant was in which hotel would I be staying at the pole? Others asked me whether I was going with work, as if companies might have offices there. Another, wished me luck on getting 'to the top' of the Pole, thinking it was located on the summit of a mountain!

On telling people that there were no hotels, roads, or any other form of what we might associate with even the most basic holiday locations, I could see their faces contort and return once more to the 'But why are you going to the North Magnetic Pole for a holiday?' mode. I couldn't really blame them. What amazed me, and added to the attraction, was still how little people knew about these remote places.

The world nowadays is so accessible. You can travel to the other side of the world in a matter of a day, for less than the cost of an average month's salary. Only decades ago such a journey would take months by ship with a price tag that few could afford. Long distance travel is so much taken for granted now that it raises few eyebrows any longer. 'Where are you going again?' 'Fiji'. 'Nice,' the reaction would be. 'Mongolia for a two-week spell?' 'Sounds interesting,' would be the unsurprised response. 'The moon for three weeks.' 'Really? We've decided to stay closer to home this year – don't want to get any of those foreign bugs.' But that is progress and the miracle of our ever shrinking world.

But I wanted to go to the Arctic, as for the reason, why well I'm not absolutely sure – childhood dreams and adult demands of breaking out and doing something physically challenging, I wasn't really clear. Mountaineers climbed mountains, according to Mallory, 'because they were there'. Robert Swan became an Arctic explorer because, he said, 'it gave him something to talk to girls about at parties!'

For me, to some extent I was trying to find out more about myself, to find something that would give me an intense and exciting experience. I thought I had found this in my job in computers, idolising Apple Computer and their 'rags-to-riches' tale of setting up in a garage before becoming a leading company in the computer market. I liked their intense energetic work-all-night-to-get-the-job-completed mentality. Whilst at college I started writing software, had some programs published, and even sold a number of them. I never achieved the financial riches of my idols obviously – but I finished my education without any debts.

For me, the idea that in the sophisticated world where I live there are places where nature still holds absolute dominance over man, was fascinating. Looking out the window from my office across a sea of concrete I could see only a few signs of nature struggling against man's containment. A small grassy patch sat awkwardly next to a path, like a green island surrounded by a cold grey concrete ocean. Two trees fought for space, their trunks sprouting from a prepared opening in the hard concrete ground. They stood like prisoners of nature, forced to spend the rest of their days shackled to man's world, as the office blocks around them looked down condemningly.

I wondered what it would be like if the roles were reversed, if I was surrounded by nature for hundreds of miles in all directions. Everything that I had learnt in my urban life would be rendered useless. How to operate a computer, the underground travel map, and business contacts would be completely useless and seemed all the more petty as I thought about them. It all felt very cramped, controlled and messy in my world. I yearned for open spaces, and places where there was no sign of man's intrusion in nature, where nature was still undeniably dominant.

Every now and again nature would fight back into my urban world. A gale force wind would blow in a few double-glazed windows, or blow off the odd roof tile. But in my cocooned world it had become just an occasional annoyance, and we would continue to throw our poisons into the environment unopposed, and extend our cities - like unstoppable occupying armies moving into the countryside. The Arctic, above all else, would be a refuge from all this.

I'd like to think that I had some travelling genes in my blood and perhaps this influenced me. My dad had done some travelling in his time, leaving a future as a aeronautical engineer in Scotland for the Royal Air Force, just before the Second World War ended. On returning to a Britain recovering from the ravages of that war he found work as a merchant seaman. He would often say that when sailing towards the St. Lawrence Seaway in the fog you could smell the approach of an iceberg; such was the influence of large 'bergs on the locality.

He had also spent time in the jungle in New Guinea searching for oil, and experienced an earthquake where the land 'buckled and bounced like jelly' as he and his colleagues sheltered under a collapsed tin roof as all hell broke out around them. In the 1950's there were still men, deep in the jungle, who were cannibals. Dad had a photo of a native he had met who had feathers and a bone through his nose, that looked frighteningly convincing and most intriguing to a young boy. He often relayed stories of the jungle, and the very basic conditions that he lived in, that has put me off that hot and humid environment to this day.

Deep in the jungle, and in a makeshift camp, he told how rats used to draw the oil from his Brylcreem-laden hair when he was asleep. One time, during a flood he managed to get into a dugout canoe - that every insect imaginable seemed to settle on for refuge from the rising waters - some so bizarre and alien that they would stretch the imagination of even a very creative science fiction writer. Whilst these stories inspired me to look beyond the shores of Britain to find the wonders of our world, I knew that the last place I would venture would be a hot jungle. I would just find the chaos and multitude of life there too overwhelming. Hot jungles were off the menu for me, whereas cold deserts seemed strangely more inviting.

Dad finally settled in northern India for almost a decade before coming home again. He then hoped to go to South Georgia with Christian Salvesen, whaling, but meeting my mother changed that.

My own working life in London, in an IT job, couldn't have been further from his more wild and adventurous experiences. Whilst he never managed to journey to the Arctic, his brother travelled the gruelling and dangerous Russian Arctic convoy route to Archangel during the war, whilst serving in the Royal Navy. He saw a side of the Arctic I would never, thankfully, experience.

Dad's sister, was a nurse in North Africa caring for the broken bodies spat out in the fight to expel Rommel. On my mothers side, her brother had lived in India (which was how my dad was introduced to my mum) before emigrating to New Zealand. His son, and my cousin, had worked in the jungle of Borneo, conducting logging using local staff - until one night he had to flee for his life down the river after a dispute between tribes exploded into violence. All in all, the recent Eadie's had done a fair bit of hot and cold, wet and windy travel, so I liked to think I had some travelling genes in my blood too.

For me a career in the British Army was my desired future until, at the age of fourteen, and only two years before I could join up, a friend introduced me to computers in late 1978. I soon got hooked and this seemed to get approval from dad and his colleagues who, whenever this was mentioned, would slightly bewildered, nod quietly in agreement that 'computers were the thing of the future'.

It would be appropriate at this point, to describe the Arctic, so as to dispel your embarrassment - in case you too are one of the many who seem to know little about the area and were wondering which hotel I would book into on my arrival at the Pole.

The Magnetic North Pole is in an area of the world where conditions are most hostile to man. Temperatures can fall to -50°C and with wind-chill can drop to -70°C. There is little plant life, the nearest tree being banished to hundreds of miles south where conditions are more favourable. It is a barren world, ice-covered, and as featureless as the surface of the moon.

Surprisingly, in such a hostile environment there is life. It is centred mainly around the sea where temperatures are comparatively warmer. There the sea provides home to numerous species of whale and seal. These in turn attract polar bears and the scavenging arctic fox. Even the Eskimo, or the 'Inuit' as they are now more correctly known, find life that far north difficult, and few of those hardy people have any history of natural settlement there.

The Arctic is still a place where mysteries can hide. Only two centuries ago it was largely unexplored. Was it land? or just a sea of ice? Could one travel around this area to the Indies, or China? Was it inhabited by a lost people cut off from the world? From the fourteenth century men sent forth ships, to discover the answer to these questions, with fame, fortune and exploration as their goals. Many never returned. Those that did spoke of horrendous seas, intense cold and desolation. Everyone who travelled to this place and lived to tell the tale always returned with an intense view. Vowing never to return or being awe struck by its majesty, these were all common responses. Not exactly the stuff travel agents quote in their brochures!

Despite its climate, which in many places is not as severe as you might imagine, with the ice giving way to green lands in summer, the Arctic has been inhabited by man for at least ten thousand years. Currently the largest settlement inside the Arctic Circle is the Russian city of Murmansk, which, and perhaps you may be surprised by this, has a population of over half a million souls. Many of the people who live in the Arctic share more of a bond with their Arctic neighbours than their more southern companions, even if resident in the same country.

If you survey the globe from directly above, almost all the land you can see is in the Arctic. When looking at the world this way you can then appreciate how Arctic people who have spread horizontally across the world have a natural bond, rather than the more vertical view of peoples, usually employed when surveying maps. Issues of pollution, climate change, commerce, recognition of native cultures and land rights are all issues of major concern, whether you are Saami in Europe, Inuit in North America or Nenet in Asia.

It is believed that the Canadian Arctic, in which the Magnetic North Pole is located, was first populated by peoples crossing from Russian Asia across the prehistoric Beringia land bridge, to what is now Alaska. The seas gradually rose, as the glaciers melted and retreated at the end of the last Ice Age, to form what is now the waters of the Bering Strait. Here these hardy people found whale and seal, but it was a difficult existence, in a harsh environment. Many of these nomadic peoples continued south, until generations later they found the American plains, where they remained largely uninterrupted until the arrival of European settlers several thousand years later.

The whale and seal that the first Inuit people found eventually attracted Europeans, firstly the Vikings in the late Dark Ages, who had a settlement in Greenland, and eventually other European powers, most successfully headed by the Elizabethan English. Seal pelt became a fashionable item and whale blubber a commercial commodity, leading to wealth and fame for individuals like the Astor's, whose wealth developed from setting up a fur supply business in Arctic Canada, and organisations like the Hudson Bay Trading Company, profited immensely.

These early explorers and traders charted the lands, and gradually the high Canadian Arctic began to give up its secrets. Many such mariners took these secrets with them to their grave, as their small wooden vessels were battered by fierce seas, horrendous storms and dangerous ice floes. Some of these lands still carry the names of such brave men, enshrined in mountain ranges, passes, straits and seas; men such as Frobisher, Bering, Hudson and Davies to name a few.

Indeed even Horatio Nelson, as a fourteen year old boy in the Royal Navy, found himself in the Canadian Arctic in 1773. Here he had a lonely encounter with a polar bear. Fortunately, after his musket misfired, the ship's cannon fired to frighten away the bear. This saved him from a gruesome death and therefore, likely saved England from becoming a province of France some three decades later when Nelson won the Battle of Trafalgar. How little that polar bear knew of its potential part in Britain's fate!

As trade increased globally, with sea routes established from Europe to Asia and the Indies for spices, it was clear an alternative to the long and dangerous route via Cape Horn at the southern tip of South America was needed. Not only was the journey very long, as the Panama Canal was centuries away from being constructed, but the seas around Cape Horn were some of the roughest in the world, leading to many a lost cargo, as well as becoming a graveyard for seamen.

This single fact drove men for the next four-hundred years - to find a shorter passage across the top of Canada to India and China. Trying to find a passage west via northern Canada would be known as the 'Search for the Northwest Passage'. It would make and break commercial reputations, lives would be swallowed up by the sometimes cruel and unforgiving Arctic, but ultimately these expeditions would result in the mapping of the high Canadian Arctic.

The most famous Northwest Passage expedition was conducted in 1845 and led by Sir John Franklin. Franklin was an experienced Arctic traveller and he embarked with two well provisioned ships. As they entered the Northwest Passage their ships, as expected, became frozen in the ice over the winter. Unfortunately, the ships were not released in the summer and spent another winter marooned in the Arctic's icy grip. Eventually, as food ran out and they began to starve, they were forced to leave their ships.

They were never seen again, and all one hundred and twenty-nine men perished. When they did not return to England, concern grew until eventually, and over a period of the next ten years, the British Admiralty sent numerous ships looking for them. As hope died, ships were sent to look for their remains. The numbers of subsequent search expeditions were so numerous, in terms of numbers of people involved, that these formed humanity's largest expedition until they were superseded by the 1969 Apollo 11 Moon Expedition.

Over the ten years, to the mid 1860's, these expeditions revealed the coastlines and islands of the Northwest Passage and the Magnetic Pole region. One of the expeditions discovered the graves of three men from the Franklin expedition. The men were exhumed then, and also a second time, more recently, in 1984 – perfectly frozen, to the extent that their skin and even eyes were in the same condition as they were when buried by the Franklin expedition in 1846. It is believed that the ship's company suffered from lead poisoning from food stored in cans – a newly developed food storage method in those times. Other bones around the area revealed knife marks that suggested that the desperate crew had finally resorted to cannibalism.

The Northwest Passage was finally sailed in its entirety in 1906, by the Norwegian Roald Amundsen, the man who would beat Captain Scott to become first to the South Pole in 1911.

The problems and uncertainties to shipping of Arctic conditions in that northern part of the world, and the subsequent opening of the Panama Canal, meant that the Northwest Passage was not developed as a commercially viable means of getting to the Indies.

As people in the western world in the late twentieth century became more cocooned by their luxuries and home comforts, some people had the desire to rid themselves of this, get back to basics, and visit these remote places. This gave rise to the modern sports adventurer, whose drive was more for a sense of personal achievement, rather than the spirit of Edwardian or Victorian scientific gain. Most of the destinations had been explored. The geography could clearly be seen now from space, and measured and photographed accurately by satellite, without ever needing to go there in person.

The first commercial British expedition group to get to the Magnetic North Pole was in the previous year to our own planned expedition, 1996. The first solo woman traveller was Helen Thayer, who arrived there in 1988. The area still remains as cold, uninviting and desolate as when man first ventured there thousands of years ago. It is this fact that attracted many modern 'explorers' there.

A couple of days later I received a call from Geoff, another member of the expedition team. He wanted to meet me and I willingly obliged. We arranged to meet in a London underground station, where he would be accompanied by Rob. This would be my final 'interview'. After this the 'torture tools would be extracted,' as Bunny had put it, and a collective decision would be made about my acceptance. I now felt quite confident about my entry into the team as I knew that without me the team would be two men short and therefore unlikely to go ahead. I described my appearance over the phone so Geoff could spot me in the crowded underground station.

The next day after work I walked down to Blackfriars tube station. I carried a copy of Mark's expedition dossier under my arm, as Geoff requested, to help him identify me. Before I entered the crowded station I flicked through to the page in Mark's expedition brochure describing Geoff. His picture showed him wearing an orange balaclava, sitting in a snow hole at the top of Mount Blanc. With the balaclava on, it was not possible to tell what he looked like, and it was unlikely he would be wearing such attire in the middle of London. I arrived a couple of minutes early, and looking round the station could see no one obvious, as the crowds rushed passed me eager to get the next commuter train home.

After a few minutes I spotted a tall, distinguished-looking, red-haired man in a business suit, also apparently waiting. 'Geoff?' I confidently enquired. 'Yes, pleased to meet you Duncan,' replied the stranger. He then advised me that Rob had not been able to come. After the pleasantries we walked off to a nearby pub in Fleet Street. As we meandered down Fleet Street, avoiding the escaping office workers from their glass towers, we unexpectedly bumped into my wife, coming the opposite way. She joined us for a chat over a pint.

The interview went well and Geoff seemed both fit and friendly. I was impressed with his knowledge of the Arctic. As we talked, we sized each other up. Could I spend a good period of the next three months in close proximity to him and the rest of the group? I asked myself again. Geoff asked quite a number of questions, which I felt I answered without problem; it was more of a friendly discussion, than a question-and-answer interview.

Geoff was an amiable, intelligent character. Working for an engineering firm, he spent most of his time in London or in Singapore. Though at forty-five years old Geoff was the eldest of the group, he still shared the exuberance that I so admired in the other members of the team. He was tall, lean and fit and built like a runner, and towered over me. The meeting ended after an hour and we left the pub and warmly shook hands, before Geoff disappeared into the night.

I had a good feeling about the team. I was impressed by the knowledge they had of the Arctic, and polar exploration. Their adventures over the last few years had also shown them to have nerve, take training seriously and be able to have a laugh too. This last fact I knew would be crucial when the going got tough, as it undoubtedly would.

I turned to my wife, as Geoff disappeared out of sight. 'Well, what do you think?' Niamh explained she felt better about the whole expedition now that she had been party to our conversation, and met one of the team. She liked Geoff, and was beginning to feel part of what was going on. I also felt happy and determined and, under the glare of the street lights, with arms raised, determinedly proclaimed I would become the fittest of the group and be first to the Pole!

I went to work early the next morning. As I sat down, the phone rang. 'Duncan, Mark. I spoke with Geoffrey last night after your meeting. He was very happy with you joining our little adventure. If you can stump up the loot, I'd like to offer you a place on the team,' he said. This was it!

'Mark, it would be a pleasure,' I replied. I was going! One fiery demon inside me had been vanquished. After swapping e-mail addresses the phone went dead as Mark quickly put down his handset. My Arctic adventure had started.

Electronic mail, or e-mail, is now of course an essential part of modern life. E-mail allows computer users to send each other messages, by typing the message into the computer whereupon it is forwarded to the recipient in a matter of seconds, wherever they may be in the world. The person the e-mail is sent to views it from their computer. All of this can go on during work hours without disturbing those around you who, as they watch you hammering away at your computer keyboard, believe you to be furiously working away on the latest business plan, and not replying to an e-mail asking what is the underwear of choice for polar exploration! All of the team were on e-mail either at work or at home. It wasn't long before my computer bleeped to indicate that I had received my first e-mail from the polar team.

TO: DUNCAN   FROM : MARK

Welcome aboard the trip of a life time! I will give your email to the others on the trip so that we can all copy all emails to each other. We are still looking for the sixth member so if you have any ideas do tell me.

We are advertising in 'The Times' tomorrow and in the Saturday and Sunday Telegraph. I am seeing another chap in Guildford and if I think he is any good I will arrange for you and the others to vet him a.s.a.p. However, I don't think that he will come up to scratch because when I invited him out for a run he said that he could not come, because he was playing golf !! Bad sign.

It wasn't long before another e-mail appeared.

TO: DUNCAN
FROM: GEOFF

I enjoyed meeting you and Niamh last night. You seem to have a good grasp of the challenges of this trip and the difficulties it presents. The cold and the polar bears will be easy to cope with if you can put up with the rest of the team. You also seem to understand the group dynamics and I intentionally gave you an exaggerated view of what it may be like with our group. Having met you I am confident that you will fit in quickly and fit in well.

My polar dream had started. I would now focus on the next three months, getting the details right and my body and mind prepared for my polar adventure. I was now a member of the expedition, though the expedition was still not guaranteed to go ahead. We needed a sixth team member. This would be my next challenge, now that I was on the team.

3

A Full Team

'If you have men who will only come if they know there is a good road, I don't want them. I want men who will come if there is no road at all.'

DR. DAVID LIVINGSTONE, EXPLORER.

How do you find someone to travel with you to the North Magnetic Pole at short notice? It's not exactly a weekend jaunt in the country. Mark was putting notices in the national newspapers to find the final member, much like Shackleton and Scott had when putting together their own expedition teams to sail to Antarctica in the early part of the twentieth century. Shackleton's advert had asked for men to go on a 'Hazardous trip, low wages, cold and hardship, safe return doubtful'.

This generated a response from five-thousand applicants, none of whom knew the destination, such was the Edwardian spirit of adventure. This was the spirit I so admired in my forebears, and one I feared was becoming lost in our increasingly risk-adverse society. I hoped we would find our own Titus Oates, or Birdy Bowers, as Captain Scott had on his recruitment drive.

However, as a novice in the adventure game I had few contacts. But I wanted to be the person who found the sixth member. Not only would this increase my value to the team, but as I wasn't a well-paid solicitor I was the one most in need of the final member's financial contribution to the expedition.

My starting place was the expedition team that I had climbed Mount Elbrus with. After phoning each of them, one by one they declined. One was a teacher and could not afford the price, others had the money but couldn't take the time off. The teacher had attempted to cross the Greenland icecap on foot recently so his advice was helpful. Another was really into mountain climbing and was planning to climb a major Himalayan peak. His vision of travelling upwards would not be met by travelling across frozen sea ice, at just three feet altitude above sea level.

Finally, as my list of telephone numbers was exhausted I made the final call to 'WJ', a strong member of the Elbrus team, who was both fit and determined – an ideal candidate for the sixth member. It was late at night and the phone rang a few times before he answered it.

'WJ!, hi it's Duncan!' I exclaimed, glad to finally hear his voice after many previous failed attempts in contacting him.

'Duncan old friend, great to hear from you. It's a bit late – is everything ok?'

'Never better WJ, look I've got a great reason to call you.' (There was no reason to beat about the bush, so I didn't.) 'WJ, do you fancy coming to the Magnetic North Pole? There's an expedition leaving in three months' time and we need a final member. How about it?' There was no response. I paused before asking again, 'WJ?' I could then hear his roar of laughter in the background. He regained control.

'Duncan this is a call to remember, I'm lying in my bed with my wife, it's late and I get a call asking me if I want to go to the North Pole!' (I could see the funny side.) 'I've had a few strange calls in my time but this one takes the biscuit. Look, I'll have to call you back another time.'

He put the phone down, leaving me feeling a bit silly over the whole situation. I glanced at my watch, it was late and time for me to retire to bed too. As the funny side wore off, I realised that he was my last and best hope. I had probably just blown it.

A few minutes later the phone suddenly rang, its unexpected ringing causing me to jump. It was WJ. 'Look Duncan, tell me more.' He wasn't laughing now, he was interested. I could imagine the conversation he must have had with his wife in those intervening moments since my call. She would have asked what he was laughing about. He would have told her. They both would have laughed together and then sat in silence for a few moments. She would have asked whether he wanted to go. He would have explained that he didn't know enough about it. He would then have begun thinking about it, seriously. Umm the North Pole, I wonder....

When he rang back I knew he had taken the bait. I explained the details of the trip. He was interested, very interested. However, it couldn't have happened at a worse time. 'Duncan, you couldn't have called at a worse time. I am leaving for Argentina this weekend to climb Aconcagua. I'll give you a call on my return.' Though he was interested, he wouldn't be back for over three weeks - by which time we must have someone who was committed. I wished him well on his trip and realised that my best hope was dashed.

The next few days I racked my brain over who else I could contact. A work colleague who had recently left the army also put the word about among his friends, but to no avail. Mark put posters up at 21 Duke of York's headquarters, his old mess, still with no response. I was beginning to lose hope in finding our last member. I wasn't the only one, my computer bleeped as an e-mail from Mark flew in with equally desperate news:

TO: EXPEDITION TEAM   FROM: MARK

I feel that I have done enough 'cold calling' for one day.

I have:

1. *Spoken to Pen at length and filled him in on the current position, namely that unless we get the sixth team member then the trip is off. The deadline for the loss of the deposit is going to be extended to the 1st Feb '97 I think but we can discuss that further next weekend*

2. *Spoken to 21 Duke of York's and sent them an advert to put up in their mess.*

3. *Ditto to the Honourable Artillery Company*

4. *Fixed up to see a potential recruit on Sunday at 11.30. Only 50/50 chance I reckon.*

5. *Put in the adverts in Times and this weekend's Telegraph*

As I read the mail my heart began to sink. After getting this excited surely it couldn't end here? Just as I was getting gloomy, I received an uplifting call from my wife. She had been over to a solicitor client of hers and had picked up a copy of the company in-house newsletter. In a large picture on the front was one of the solicitors - on top of an impressive mountain in South America. He looked quite heroic, perched atop a snowy peak, clad in ropes, backpack and climbing boots, with a large drop to the side of him. 'Why not give him a call?' she suggested. Why not indeed? It was at the end of the day on Friday, and I had nothing to lose.

I soon got through to him. 'Hello Peter, my name is Duncan Eadie – you don't know me, but I saw a picture of you atop an impressive mountain in your company rag. I am part of an expedition and we are looking for a final team member, and you look like just the sort of person who might be interested in such a trip.'

There was a pause, as he took in this unusual and unexpected call. 'Um, and, err, where is this trip to?' 'The North Magnetic Pole, Peter.' I half expected a reaction similar to WJ's. It's not the sort of phone call you get every Friday afternoon after all. Before he could react, I continued. 'It's a solicitors' expedition to the North Magnetic Pole,' hoping that that element of the expedition may appeal to him more. I gave him a basic taster of the trip and offered to fax him details.

After a pause, which seemed to last a lifetime, he stated he was interested. Peter described himself as twenty-six, and a keen outdoor person who had climbed several mountains. It was too early to say whether he would fit in with the trip - but if he had the loot, he was in as far as I was concerned. I could now understand how Mark had made such a quick decision about me. We concluded our conversation and after faxing Mark's brochure to him I left work feeling hopeful.

The weekend shot by as always, and Monday morning found me on the 'phone again to Peter. He had digested the information in Friday's fax and was very interested. We met for lunch in a smoky pub in Tower Hill in London. Peter had an athletic build, was tall at six-feet, and had long blond hair groomed in a foppish style. He described how he had climbed many mountains, several over twenty-thousand feet, and had also instructed some climbing sessions. As we chatted it was apparent to me that he would be the perfect sixth member. On returning to my office I excitedly called Mark.

'Hi Mark, it's Duncan. I think I've got the sixth member.'

'Splendid!' Mark gasped. 'Send me some details.' The phone suddenly went dead, which was usual when speaking with Mark. He was at work and I knew as a property solicitor he made money through advising as many clients a day as possible. Time was of the essence to him and a social chat at work was almost non-existent. I quickly complied with Mark's request, gently tapping details of my "find" into my computer, and e-mailed it to Mark.

I soon received a reply from Mark, my computer making its familiar bleep as the message was received.

TO: DUNCAN EADIE   FROM: MARK

Great news about your solicitor friend. I have arranged to meet him in London on Thursday evening at the Climbing Shop in Covent Garden by the sleeping bags. I will speak to and email the others to see if they can come. I have met the other chap that I mentioned to you and he is really keen to come ...dependent only on everyone else thinking he is ok. The problem is he is 54 and looks just like Victor Meldrew. He plays golf three times a week but has done no climbing although he is a hill walker.

Nice enough bloke but I could not readily find his sense of humour and I must say I rather doubt his body is up to it. (But are ours?) My wife thinks he will be ok and he has certainly got the loot. He wants to come and meet us this Saturday on Dartmoor. Peter is much better qualified to share a tent with Bunny than poor old Victor. Apparently he has climbed some twenty thousand-foot peaks, leads HVS, has walked in the mountains since he was a kid and (talking of kids) just loves shagging old goats. He sounds ideal.

Mark had already contacted Peter and I could see that the wheels were now in motion. I felt satisfied that I had already made a valuable contribution to the team, thanks to my wife. Thursday night was to be the first meeting of the team. It was only the second time we had met. Unfortunately Rob could not make it so four members: Mark, Bunny, Geoff, myself and the prospective Peter, met in central London. We moved onto a small café at Mark's request, as it didn't sell alcohol. 'I'm in training now y'know' he announced proudly. We all suffered with him with our orange juice.

The questions were soon flying and it was quite apparent that Peter fitted in well with the group. The solicitors among the group were impressed by Peter's achievement in working for a prestigious London law firm, and with two Cambridge first degrees behind him he looked quite a bright young thing. I kept quiet regarding my own first degree – these were things that mattered not a hoot in the stark face of the Arctic.

As was usual, our small group made much more noise than anyone else. We talked loudly, laughed and giggled. It was all good team-building stuff. It wasn't long before Bunny was pleading, 'I could murder a bottle of rouge, Markey.' They were both tempted, but resolutely stayed away from the red wine. Geoff was already doing five-mile runs every morning, and the group was beginning to become competitive on the fitness front. This was good. My own appearances at the gym had become more frequent, but with three months training to go I did not want to become stale too early.

The absence of the health-threatening alcohol was counterbalanced at the café by large helpings of greasy chips. As the chips were delivered, Geoff warned the newcomers of Mark's ability to absorb any food around him. I looked down towards my plate to see El Porco's fork already helping itself to my food. Our eyes met over the hot, but still full plate. 'I'm so sorry, old man,' Mark apologised, 'but I thought one had lost interest in the meal, and I do hate to see good hot food go cold.'

He rapidly, and with some embarrassment, withdrew his utensil, but as others began to look at him he quickly explained in his defence, 'This is really nothing compared with Bunny's ability to absorb equipment.' His statement was backed by Geoff. They had been on many adventures when Bunny had turned up in less than the minimum equipment and then had proceeded to 'absorb' it from his colleagues. This was hotly denied by Bunny, who maintained he always had the highest standard of equipment.

We all agreed that special attention to individual equipment would be taken for this trip. Seeing warning signs approaching, I volunteered to take care of organising the group's equipment needs, which was agreed by Mark. Indeed, for the coming weekend we had arranged to meet with Pen at his home on Dartmoor, to discuss the training regime and equipment requirements.

I looked around at the group. We were all laughing, smiling, in deep conversation about the Arctic and how we might perform. We seemed to gel very well and I could tell that the team would work well together. I'm sure Peter felt that also, even at this early stage. I think we were both slightly in awe of the others – their military service and variety of expeditions over the years was most impressive. More remarkable was their outlook on life – to be running businesses, married with wives and children and to still have this boyish camaraderie and outlook on life was great. I hoped I would be like them when I reached their age.

In turn, they were slightly threatened by Peter and I. We were the youngsters of the team and they felt that the age difference between us would leave them at a disadvantage; I knew from the occasional poke at us that they were worried that we might show them up. I knew this wouldn't be the case, but I was happy to let them think that, in the spirit of the rising competition within the group.

Towards the end of the evening, with Peter obviously suitable as the sixth and final team member, Mark announced that Peter could become a member of the team if he so wished. Peter gladly accepted and we all toasted his entry and the group's success, with our orange juice. The team was formed, and we were on our way.

4

Training

'I run on the road long before I dance under the lights.'

MUHAMMAD ALI, BOXER.

In late January 1997, Pen invited the team to his house on Dartmoor for a 'kit weekend'. This would serve a number of purposes. We would be getting together as a team for the first time – Peter and I had yet to meet both Rob and Pen. We would also receive Pen's view on the suitability of our personal kit – and no doubt his view on our suitability to take such a trip. It was also time to pay for the cost of the expedition.

On Friday night, as I left the office wearing my weekend kit rather than my usual business suit I drew the inevitable stares. 'Camping this weekend,' I informed the growing number of tie and shirted colleagues looking on.

'In January? Somewhere warm I hope?' came the swift, slightly smug reply.

'Oh yes, Dartmoor,' I said. Winter on Dartmoor could be fairly grim, but it would probably be nothing compared with the far north. I fastened down the last buckle on my rucksack, and left the office with a hearty 'See you all Monday,' as the stares followed me out the door.

I met Bunny and Peter among the throbbing Friday night crowds at Victoria train station. We would all travel down to Pen's together. Bunny had offered to drive. It wasn't long before we had exchanged the crowds of people at Victoria Station for the crowds of cars on the M3 motorway. Bunny's Golf GTI, now full of rucksacks, hurtled along amongst the Friday night traffic. 'Steady on Bunny we want to get there in one piece!' Peter cried out, as Bunny switched between his foot being fully on the accelerator and then fully on the brake.

'Sorry chaps, bit of a speed merchant y'know'. With us hanging tightly onto the handles above the car doors, Bunny informed us that he had almost a full 'allowance' of speeding points. If caught one more time he would be banned from driving. 'I actually did get finally done six months ago,' he chuckled. 'I was driving home at full pace to see my kids after a spell abroad when I was stopped by a policeman.' Bunny recounted how he had been driving well over the speed limit.

'After being pulled over I knew things were not going to go well when I was asked the usual sarcastic 'Do you know the speed limit on this road, Sir?' by the smug police officer. I felt them closing in on me and let my frustration fly,' Bunny recalled.

'That's great! That's just great!' I roared at the policeman'.

'Go on book me,' Bunny continued, to his two nervous passengers, 'I'm getting divorced, my business is on the edge and now you want to take my license away!' Bunny said how he pounded his fist on his car bonnet before putting his head in his hands with all the passion of a man at the end of his tether. 'The policeman could see it was all getting too much, and what do you know?' said Bunny grinning from ear to ear, his eyes bulging, 'He let me off.' That just about summed Bunny up – Bunny the charmer. Undaunted, we continued into the night at full pace.

Just before eleven that night we pulled up at the Forest Inn in Hexworthy, a few miles from Pen's house out on the moor. Peter and I were really relieved to be there, having just spent five hours driven, at great speed down the motorway, and then, even more alarming, rally-style along hedge-lined country lanes in the darkness. The odd rabbit's eyes caught in the glare of

Bunny's headlights had matched the bulging eyes of Peter and I sitting on the back seat of the car. Eventually we left the night and entered the warm pub.

Bunny went straight towards the nosiest part of the bar, knowing that that's where the chaps would be. Mark already had a few pints standing by to welcome us, and booked rooms for us at the pub for the night. The team was at last together. Peter and I were introduced to Rob, the ex-paratrooper, still sporting a thin military-style moustache, and like the majority of the group a solicitor by profession. Rob was reasonably tall and looked fit and strong.

Mark had arranged for us all to rise early the next day and go for a run. After a couple of pints, Mark and Bunny's abstinence from drink now forgotten, we all retired to our rooms in the pub.

The next morning was dry and a little cold, perfect for outside activity. We all emerged from our rooms and made our way downstairs in various coloured tracksuit trousers and Helly Hansen tops. Bunny stayed in bed, complaining of a heavy week and the need of an extra hour's sleep.

The hamlet was quiet apart from the odd muffled dog bark and the occasional cock crowing. We began by running along the hedge-lined roads. They were covered in a thin layer of mud left by tractors. The air was heavy with country smells – flowers, dampness, mud, and of course the lingering smell of manure. A good speed was kept up by all.

The pounding of our feet and heavy breathing, interrupted by the odd cough, caused a number of startled crows in an adjacent field to take flight. The group was led by the plumper Mark, followed by the tall and long-legged Geoff, his crown of ginger hair hidden under a black woollen cap. Rob, Peter and I all followed immediately behind, narrowing into single file where necessary to avoid puddles and the odd slurry stream on the road.

Soon we were running downhill and then along various other narrow winding roads. After a few miles, and on our way back to the pub, we turned a blind corner onto a very steep hill. Our speed slowed down immediately, and our panting grew louder, but we all carried on upwards – so did the hill and it became very tiring. I sensed everyone wanted to stop, but I could tell no-one wanted to be the first to do so. We were still in the sizing-up mode, where everyone wasn't quite sure how fit they were in comparison with the rest of the group. I was just about to stop when someone else gasped, 'Bloody Hell!' and, with hands on hips, peeled off to the side. We all slowed down then and walked to the top of the hill.

The group's fitness seemed good, and there was also a healthy spirit of competition. The age difference between us didn't seem to matter. After a shower and a 'fat boys' breakfast of Full English all round, championed by El Porco, we were prepared for the day ahead.

We left the pub and drove the few miles over to Pen's house. The hedges soon gave way to moor land, the trees appearing more tortured and growing at unnatural angles after suffering decades of violent winds eager to uproot them. Pen's home was a lonely farmhouse at the edge of the moor. Hidden in a small valley with a gravel track passing by outside, it looked a beautiful but quite lonely setting. Pen would tell me later that good friends were soon made here, and the apparent loneliness of the location actually made people stick together more.

Our cars pulled up on Pen's driveway and it wasn't long before we were all greeting the man himself. Pen met us at his doorway, his border collie 'Baskerville' welcoming each of us with an exploratory sniff. The coffee was soon brewing, and we all spilled into Pen's rustic kitchen to gather around his large farmyard-style wooden table.

As we sat sipping his coffee, Pen outlined the brief plan for the day.

'Thanks for coming down chaps, good to meet with you all,' he began. 'The idea of the weekend is to get a feel for how fit you all are –', before he could finish his sentence Rob raised his hand and twitching his moustache, asked, 'This doesn't involve anything painful does it Pen?'

'No, Rob', replied Pen, followed by a pause, 'not on my part at least.'

'We'll also discuss training and diets, and review all your kit,' he continued.

'That won't take you long, will it Bunny?!' quipped Mark.

Having not seen a picture of Pen before and having only spoken to him on the phone before, he struck me as looking remarkably like Tony Blair, the leader of the opposition party in the UK at this point. It was uncanny. He was more solidly built and looked very strong but, with his dark hair and young-looking face, there was no denying that he was a Tony Blair look-alike. I chuckled to myself as I thought I was going to the pole with Prince Charles's sound-a-like, Bunny, and Tony Blair's look-a-like, Pen! As I examined Pen closer, my attention was drawn to the strange set of ears sitting under his full head of dark hair. His ears seemed damaged, with wrinkles and buckles at the top of them. My initial impression was that this may have been the result of frostbite.

As Pen conveyed to us, in his clear and dignified Harrow-educated accent, the plan for the weekend, my eye was caught by some photos stuck to his fridge door. A couple of photos showed him swimming among icebergs, and another one showed him perched atop a smaller 'berg that he was about to use as a diving board. An impressive sight, made all the more heroic as Pen was wearing nothing more insulating than a pair of swimming trunks. A few other photos showed polar bears. I looked closer at these and noticed how large the bears were in the photographs, and therefore how close the cameraman must have been to them.

'Gosh! Pen, is that you?' hollered Geoff, who had also just noticed the photos.

'The very same,' replied Pen quietly. The group then seemed to swarm around the pictures making various comments. 'Were you swimming naked Pen, or is the blue thing round your waist your trunks?' 'How much Johnny Walker did you use for antifreeze before jumping in?' After the usual jibes Pen cut in. 'Those were taken on the island of Svalbard, where I spent three months with a BBC camera crew, following and photographing polar bears. That was a seventy two day sledding journey without re-supply, across the archipelago. One of the longest journeys ever undertaken across the island.' The group were quieter now, giving Pen the respect he deserved.

After the coffee and briefing we all cantered out onto the moor, armed with raincoats and walking boots. Pen led the way, wearing an extremely unfashionable corduroy Breton cap, that gave him the appearance of a nineteenth century sea captain. We marched across a few paths before crossing some patchy grassland and then walked over a few peaty brooks and some marshland.

We continued to make our way across the moor, sometimes in single file to negotiate boggy parts. I stuck by Pen and fired off question after question about all aspects of the trip. My main worries were dealing with the cold and of course polar bears. Pen was very relaxed about both subjects – saying that neither would be a problem; the correct kit would resolve one issue and he was very experienced with the other.

I also questioned Pen about how he found himself in such a strange business. As a boy, Pendril was heavily influenced by his nanny, Enid Wigley. She was previously the nanny to Sir Peter Scott, son of Captain Scott of Antarctica. Pen was brought up from an early age on a diet of stories of polar adventure. He had ice in his blood as it were – or as Robert Peary would put it 'polar fever'.

Pen was a keen sportsman at Harrow and found himself looking for greater physical challenges once he left. This resulted in his world record-breaking voyage from London to Greenland in an open inflatable boat. A feat that Pen openly advised people 'would not be a wise thing to try and beat'. Pen was gathering a set of field skills: endurance, navigation, and the ability to survive on his wits in extreme environments. He then made an attempt to become the first person to walk to the Geographic North Pole solo and unsupported from Canada.

The hours rolled by before we reached the foot of a large tor, where we had a brief lunch. Wild horses roamed on the horizon and the conversation moved away from the Arctic. It was then that I realised that Pen's 'frost bitten' ears were probably the result of years of playing rugby rather than coming off the worst in a brush with the Arctic. This was much more comforting.

As we sat on the rocky ground, Mark recounted how on army training courses he liked to be last along the exercise trail, as he would pick up on all the faults of the troops before him. Citing the example of ambush practice, he said he would see empty shell cases on the ground, thus alerting him to the fact that an ambush had taken place ahead with the other troops. He would be ready when they tried to jump him; clever old Mark.

Our little march was very enjoyable and not at all strenuous. But before we all began to think that Pen was soft, he informed us that he would usually run the whole course with a rucksack full of rocks! It was a few more hours before we were in sight of the track leading back to Pen's house again. By now it was about four p.m., dusk was only half an hour away and the air began to take on a damper, colder feel as night beckoned.

Finally, we made our way up Pen's stony drive, ready to take off our muddy boots and enjoy a hot coffee. Pen, with a strange grin on his face, disappeared into his barn. He returned moments later with a set of two huge tyres. The two tractor tyres were linked to a harness. Without looking for volunteers Pen spoke to Geoff, who was the nearest. 'In you get Geoff.' We all gathered round as Geoff tied the harness around his waist, and with the tyres attached began to trudge up the hill to the top of Pen's garden. Baskers the dog was lying on the ground, tongue out, watching – he had seen it all before. It was obviously very hard work, the veins on Geoff's head looked as though they were about to burst, as he strained to keep moving slowly forward. After less than two minutes effort and only halfway up the garden Geoff was knackered.

'Gentlemen, this is the best exercise to simulate sledge pulling,' announced Pen. 'I suggest that you incorporate such an exercise into your training routines.' By now, with Geoff still catching his breath, we were all queuing to show that we could do better. I was next in the harness. Once strapped in I leaned to move forward, only to find nothing happened. No movement at all. The weight of the tyres was considerable. On my second attempt, using all my strength and with the appropriate demonstration growl, I managed to move forward a few inches. Wow!, this was hard work. I was determined to get to the top of the garden, which I did, but only just to the strains of 'Pull!, Pull!' from the rest of the group. As I watched Rob getting strapped in, I hoped that our own sledges would not be half as heavy. There was no way any of us could move such a weight for more than a few yards, let alone one hundred miles. I had read how Sir Ranulph Fiennes on his epic crossing of Antarctica started with a fully loaded sledge of 485 pounds. He could also barely move his sledge. Without saying anything I put the exercise down to Pen attempting to shock us about fitness – it worked! We all decided that tyre pulling would be good exercise material.

After the tyre test we put our tents up in Pen's backyard before going off to the Forest Inn for dinner. After a grateful refuel at the pub we headed back to Pen's house for the kit inspection. Once back inside we gathered around a giant old oak dining table, a family heirloom, which Pen insisted was 'not to be written on'.

We pulled our differing sizes of personal bags of equipment into Pen's dining room, before taking our places round the table. Pen sat at the head of the table. Baskers sat at his feet underneath. 'Ok chaps, let's talk about the expedition - kit and diets,' announced Pen, followed by a snigger from Rob on the mention of 'diets' whilst pointing to El Porco's fuller figure. Pen paused a moment while waiting for the group to settle, and Peter quietly tapped Rob and nodded towards Pen.

Pen began to talk through the details of the expedition route, pointing out various places on the large map of the magnetic pole area spread out in front of him. Though we all knew the route, as most were now reading Helen Thayer's account of her journey, it was appropriate for Pen to go over it again.

'We will travel by skidoo from Resolute Bay on Cornwallis Island up the east coast of Bathurst Island,' he said, with his finger moving up the map, 'until we reach the Findlay group of islands.' His finger pointed to the small group of islands outlined on the map. 'All our equipment and food will be carried with us, and there will be no re-supply. So remember everything that we bring,' Pen looked around the room at the number of bags spilling over with clothing, 'we'll need to man haul – so no kitchen sinks please.' His finger moved up and down the map. 'We will travel on the sea ice throughout the whole trip. The sea will be frozen to a depth of approximately three to seven feet – thick enough to land a Boeing seven-four-seven on!'

Tapping the map at the point marked 'Penny Strait' at the top of Bathurst Island, he emphasised that there were great currents moving here as the sea was pushed between Bathurst and Devon Island. 'We could meet open water here and lots of jumbled ice.' Pen continued, 'Once at the Findlay group of islands, which should take about three days on skidoo, we'll leave the skidoos and travel north on skis for the remaining one hundred and twenty nautical miles. Then, after ten days of man-hauling our sledges, we should arrive at the Magnetic Pole, off the coast of the Noice Peninsula just north of Ellef Ringes Island but, as I said before, please don't make any firm commitments for your return date.' We were all aware of the uncertainties that the Arctic could introduce to any well planned schedule.

'Once at the Pole we will be picked up by an aircraft, which will have dropped some men on the way, to drive our abandoned skidoos back to Resolute. So that is the essence of the expedition. I'm not aware of any other expeditions this year, therefore you could be the first to stand at the Pole in 1997. Any questions?'

'Polar bears,' Peter piped up. Pen moved his hand in a circle over the whole map. 'We'll be in their backyard. Many of them move through Polar Bear Pass on Bathurst Island, which we won't be visiting.' He stressed again, 'won't be visiting.'

'Are we likely to see any bears?' prompted Peter again.

'There is a good chance,' said .Pen, 'but I'd be more afraid of the ones you don't see.' His attempt at humour was lost on the group, for which this was a serious subject. I moved my hand to the map pointing out our skidoo route that would pass the eastern end of Polar Bear Pass, 'Helen Thayer met up to three bears a day in this region,' I said, questioningly.

'That would be highly unlikely, and I wouldn't believe everything you read,' countered Pen, 'that sort of news sells books -' Mark cut in before Pen could finish, 'That sort of news also stops people going on trips to the Arctic,' hinting that Pen had his own interests to protect too. Rob, as ever, spoke up at the right moment, and in a low lawyer-like, almost threatening way, twitched his thin military-style moustache and murmured, 'Let me just check the get-out clause in our agreement with you Pen before we proceed.'

'Be a shame to go that far and not encounter a bear though, wouldn't it?' said Geoff.

'Yes, you have your encounter,' said Rob, 'and make sure you take a couple of photos so we are sure that it was a polar bear that ate you.'

'Seriously Pen,' said Mark getting the conversation back on track, 'this is one of the highest populated polar bear regions in the world. What will we do at night?'

At that high latitude there was almost twenty four hours of sunlight, so total darkness would not exist. We would still need to sleep, and that would be when we would be at our greatest exposure to inquisitive and hungry bears.

'Standard procedure: leave the food sledge a few hundred yards from the entrance to the tent, and have an alarmed trip wire around the encampment.' I looked around the room, wondering how comfortable the others felt about this.

'No dog to warn us?' I asked.

'No dog!' replied Pen firmly. I was uncomfortable about this, but Pen was the expert.

Many people think of polar bears as lovely playful creatures, which they are. But not when you are in their back yard, in the cage with them, as we would be, rather than just looking in through the metaphorical bars. My wife summarised polar bears as the 'Great White Sharks of the land – but with much better PR'. The facts speak for themselves: the polar bear, *Ursus Maritimus*, is the world's most formidable land predator and is at the top of the Arctic land food chain. It has no natural enemies, except man. It is a powerhouse of muscle, teeth and claws. Surrounded by an insulating layer of fat, polar bears don't feel the cold. They can cover a hundred miles in a day and can run faster than a man. Each of their front legs are the size of a large man's waist, terminating in a set of razor-sharp claws. Their powerful paws can easily crush the skull of a seal with one fell swoop. When standing on its hind legs an adult can rise over ten feet tall, and a large male weigh almost half a ton.

They have excellent hearing and vision and, according to the Guinness Book of Records, have the best sense of smell of any mammal on Earth. Indeed one was tracked walking in a straight line for twenty-three miles, at the end of which was a carcass whose odour the animal had picked up all those miles away. They can smell seals resting under three feet of ice in their breathing holes. They are also excellent swimmers and spend much of their time in the water chasing prey.

A fishing trawler spotted a polar bear swimming eighty miles off the coast of Greenland, the nearest point of land. They are true survivors, often going for long periods without food. They will eat anything that comes their way: birds, fish, seals, walrus, whales, scrub, fauna – and explorers, or even each other. As such I would be lower in the food chain than them, something that slightly dented my human pride.

In fact, a bear cub's biggest danger is being eaten by other polar bears – surviving in the Arctic does not mean having a conscience about cannibalism. Not the sort of image that comes to mind to consumers of greetings cards, posters and cartoons that regularly portray these animals as fluffy and cuddly creatures.

Polar bears have a curious nature. Driven by hunger, and, because they are top of the predator pile, they know little fear. They make a formidable adversary. A daunting animal that any explorer may have to contend with in these regions – a region where one doesn't even have the option to hide up a tree in moments of danger!

We questioned Pen for perhaps another hour about every aspect of the trip – the route, bears and temperatures, before we cast an eye at all the equipment bags around the room.

'Everyone knows the Arctic is cold – and it is, but with the right clothing we'll be ok.' With that signal from Pen, we all began opening our equipment and clothing bags. Pen's dining room was soon covered in trousers, tops, gloves, boots and all sorts of other items. Baskers, with tail wagging, quickly left the room amid the explosion of colourful clothing.

With a pile of clothing in front of each of us, some piles larger than others, some piles neatly stacked and others strewn in a random fashion, Pen began his inspection. Looking at each person, like a general inspecting his troops, Pen walked along the line of us.

Mark had his full mountaineering duvet suit out. This was an impressive piece of serious kit, despite it's purple colour. With a one-piece duvet suit covering his head, arms, body and legs, Mark would be very warm indeed. He had used the suit when climbing Aconcagua and therefore it was tested. Pen duly signed it off – 'acceptable!', and along with most of his other equipment, to Mark's great delight.

My turn soon came around and the pride of my equipment, my down jacket, was rejected by Pen as 'Not warm enough'. My Gore-Tex jacket was also rejected and Pen made an example of this. 'No Gore-Tex please gentlemen, not in the polar regions. Any moisture will freeze on the inside, before it can pass through the jacket, and you'll get very cold very quickly.' I had a pair of gloves that just about passed, but other than that I would need to equip myself properly.

Peter was next to have his prized piece of kit rejected. His down jacket also being labelled as 'not warm enough'. To add insult to injury, his sleeping bag – a borrowed one at that, was also rejected for the same reason. Rob had a smattering of army kit, which Pen labelled as 'Not suitable for Arctic use Rob, but may be of interest to an army museum'.

There was growing anticipation in the room as Pen finished his inspection of Geoff's equipment and came to the last in the line. Bunny nervously twitched around his equipment pile, the smallest in the group. Having seen Pen's rejection of my Gore-Tex jacket and knowing Bunny's reputation for never having the right equipment, but never admitting this, we all fell strangely quiet.

'And what do you have here for me Sir, in that rather undersized package?' Pen jollily sneered, in the politest way possible.

'I only thought it necessary to bring the items that may be questioned,' Bunny cleverly retorted. 'The items that are suitable,' he looked at Mark, 'the majority of which I might add, were left at home.' Pen opened the bag and picked at it's contents, 'Gore-Tex trousers and Gore-Tex jacket – unsuitable!', to which the room erupted in laughter. Knowing his rouse was completely seen through Bunny sighed, 'I think a kit-buying frenzy is in order,' to the continued shouts of 'Unsuitable! Unsuitable!' from the ever rowdy onlookers.

Pen gave us all five minutes to pack our assorted varieties of clothing, before beginning a lecture about what we should be taking. Pen could supply some clothing, down jackets and boots, but the rest we would all have to buy ourselves. We were led through all the equipment. Starting with undergarments, known as the 'base layer' that would wick away any sweat from our bodies and pass it towards the next layer to keep clothing next to the body dry and warm. It was all quite serious and detailed, until I couldn't resist taking a photo of Pen, as he raised a pair of example underwear above his head – his retort 'Bastard!' shot from him almost as quickly as the camera flash lit the room.

Cottons and other natural fibres were definitely out as they tended to hold moisture, which would then freeze. Polyesters had not been 'in' for the last two decades back home, but in the Arctic they were the only things to be seen in, the height of practical fashion.

Pen told us about multiple layers of gloves, head and foot wear. A three-layer glove system was necessary, which made me wonder how this met Pen's 'the problem will be trying not to overheat' statement a few weeks previously. Two balaclavas were needed to keep the head warm. The outer one would cover the whole face except the eyes, with a hole for the nostrils and a gauze covering for the mouth. Strong sunglasses or goggles would top off the head gear.

Though Pen supplied a full kit list, I was busy taking notes in my role as equipment officer. I didn't want any of the group getting up north to then find they had something sub-standard. The lecture continued. Velcro, not zips, as zips could become clogged with ice. Windproof, not waterproof clothing. Loose-fitting, not tight-fitting (to let warm air circulate). The list went on and on.

Lastly, we got down to sleeping bags. Pen brought out the largest sleeping bag I had ever seen – was it for us all to sleep in? 'Definitely suitable!' he exclaimed as we all gathered round. 'An Ajungilak Denali bag, rated to -55°C,' he announced. It was indeed impressive, and looked like a giant cotton wool cocoon. When closed, only the sleeper's face protruded. The manufacturer named its company after the Inuit word *Ajungilak,* which means 'sleep well'. The bag and sleeper would then be placed in a Gore-Tex outer bag and both would be on top of a two-inch thick foam mat, acting as an insulating layer to protect the sleeper from the cold ice. The Gore-Tex outer would stop any moisture in the tent penetrating the sleeping bag. Keeping moisture out of clothing would always be a top priority.

We spent the next half an hour on training guidelines. Pen realised that we all spent most of our days deskbound and therefore our muscles needed toning up and strengthening. This would best be met by general cardio-vascular exercise such as running or swimming to get our fitness levels up, before concentrating on exercises that would emulate our specific activity up north. Tyre-pulling would be the best way to achieve this, together with skiing simulation. We had to bear in mind that we would each be pulling more than our own bodyweight on each sledge, for at least eight hours every day.

Pen warned us, 'For anyone who thought that pulling a sledge over ice would be like dragging a weight across a flat ice rink with the sledge merrily skittling along behind, you should think again. Think of it more like pulling a dead weight over sand.' Whilst we all knew this from our reading, the group intentionally raised a steady groan, broken only by Rob stating in a hushed but intentionally audible tone, 'Lets hope Mark doesn't snuff it – I don't want to be dragging *that* dead-weight anywhere!'

Pen then spent the remainder of the evening describing the diet that we would be fed during the trip. He began by explaining that the body was like a complex chemical factory with a large furnace that needed firing to power and warm the body. During our normal daily lives about two thousand calories would be enough to fire this furnace, however the demands of our expedition would raise this to six thousand calories a day, almost the maximum the body could process.

Our calorific need would be met by feeding us high calorie foods, mainly sugars and fats in the form of chocolate, rice and pasta, dried meats, fruits and nuts. Everyone would also be allowed to bring some of their own treats. Pen gave us a list of food and suggested that we all begin to eat this two weeks before the start of the expedition to ensure our bodies became accustomed as 'There is nowhere less inviting to be caught short with diarrhoea if the change of diet upsets you.' Not a pleasant thought and definitely good advice.

After a farewell coffee and a flurry of cheques to Pen to settle the finances of the expedition, we all trudged out into the darkness where our tents awaited us. Geoff and I shared a tent. It wasn't long before we were both asleep. During the night the January weather closed in and a downpour turned into torrential rain. We were camped on boggy ground and a small damp patch in the middle of the tent grew to become what felt like a small stream. Growing amounts of water entered at the head of the tent and flowed between Geoff and I to escape through the bottom. I wriggled in my sleeping bag, attempting to find refuge in the few remaining dry patches, and managed to get back to sleep comforted by the fact that such miserable wet occurrences could not happen in the Arctic.

The weekend was soon over and it wasn't long before we were heading back to London again. This time a little more tired, and with a couple more bruises than when we had come out. Pen kindly lent us an audio tape of Robert Swan, the Antarctic traveller, to listen to on our journey back in Bunny's car. On this tape Swan described how working in extremely low temperatures in the Antarctic was very difficult and how his team members had to look after each other and keep a sense of humour when things got difficult.

This was tested to the full when a team member of Swan's had their heel come off in their hand, when taking off a boot. We all wondered how cold it would get up north, and how strong our sense of humour would need to be. Now the emphasis was on the team to deliver. We now had three months to prepare, and become super fit so that we were ready for the Arctic.

5

Preparation

'There is nothing impossible to him who will try.'

ALEXANDER THE GREAT, SOLDIER

fter the weekend at Pen's we returned to our homes and reflected on what had been said and what needed to be done. Obviously training and gaining the correct equipment formed the bulk of what we needed to do. We had become more serious now as the Arctic beckoned from a closer distance in time. On the surface everyone was still happy and bubbly, but the talk now was about fitting in training schedules with busy professional and family lives.

It seemed to me, from reading various books and accounts, and speaking with those in the know, that successful polar explorations relied on three things all in equal measure: physical fitness, mental durability and lastly, a dose of good old fashioned luck. I would spend the next few months trying to hone the first two of those success criteria, and would hope that the latter would prevail.

With the advice from Pen ringing in our ears and our date with the north getting closer, the training schedule went up another gear. E-mails from Geoff and Mark arrived:

TO : ALL TEAM   FROM : GEOFF

A good weekend, with lots of useful information from Pen. We now have a complete team and a strong one - I feel.

I have just been on a 50 minute tyre pull (with 1 Land Rover tyre and 2 car tyres) and have done 2 laps of the field at the back of my house. I offer the following observations:

1. It is very hard work

2. Over accentuated arm movements with poles help

3. It seems to be very hard on the back, shoulders and groin muscles. Must start doing sit ups am. and pm.

4. Hopefully we can avoid a hernia - my harness is transferring the load at my hips - is this right?

Obviously it needs to be worked on to build up the duration.

Mark quickly responded:

TO : ALL TEAM   FROM: MARK

Great weekend.

I am super impressed with your T P effort on your return home. I went for a two hour walk and then an hours TP with only one tyre and thought that I had done really well.

I am really pleased with the team we have now got. We all seem to get on well. Obviously there will be times when everyone is pissed off with one or all of us but I am sure that the stormy rows will be forgotten and we will work really well together and get our objective.

I attended the gym regularly, often running there and back, and used weights and exercises to strengthen my legs, back and arms. As Pen had mentioned we were to be long distance people – not sprinters, and so endurance rather than speed was important. I gave up ice hockey, whilst I had never suffered a serious injury in seven years of play, it was too risky to continue as an injury could slow my polar training, or even stop me going on the expedition altogether.

I had an extensive examination by a dentist to ensure my teeth and fillings were in good order. These were some of the bones that would be subjected to the greatest extremes, with air entering the mouth at, say, minus forty followed by a mouthful of almost boiling hot tea, which would put pressure on fillings that could see them pop out. Indeed just the reaction to cold air often caused explorers' fillings to shrink and so be more liable to cracking. An early dentist's examination helped ensure my teeth were in the best state that they could be, given that an over-enthusiastic Australian dentist had left me with a mouthful of mercury by the time I was eleven years old.

I acquired a number of old car tyres from a car depot for my own sledge training. This was not as easy as I had expected because a suspicious salesman needed to be convinced that I wasn't going to put the tread-free tyres on an old car. Eventually I had to tell him that they were for exercise, to which he became even more disbelieving. 'Can't see how Jane Fonda could use these,' he quipped. I ultimately had to put a hole in the tyres there and then, thread the rope through and give him a mini demonstration before, slightly bewildered, he let me take them away.

The first pull of the tyres across the heath near where I lived taught me that unless I wanted to attract all sorts of strange stares and the sort of 'Oi, mate! Do you know you are being followed?' type of comments, that this exercise was best carried out at night, to save embarrassment. I found the nightly tyre pulls across the local heath particularly enjoyable.

I also needed to replicate the skiing part of dragging a sledge for eight hours a day. Whilst the tyre pulls were good for neck, back and leg muscles I knew that when conducted on skis different muscle groups would be used, something I needed to build up before I hit the Arctic. I invested in a skiing machine made by a Norwegian company. It was basically two skis tied to a wheel with some arm supports emulating skiing poles. This enabled me to use a skiing motion without going anywhere, moving my arms and legs in harmony against the variable resistance of a wheel. I set this up in my lounge against a white wall which I tried to convince myself would be like skiing in an Arctic blizzard as I faced the featureless white wall for hours on end. This exercise was incredibly boring, but nonetheless helped certain muscles to develop. I even managed to keep it up for five hours one day before the monotony, and I must admit a twinging right knee, caused me to call it a day. Some of the other team members also got these machines, after my recommendation, and found them equally demanding.

As we would be travelling over relatively flat, sea ice I wasn't worried about down hill skiing techniques. I was however, one of those lucky people, having gained a good sense of balance from ice hockey and being generally sporty, who successfully tackled their first black ski run three days after putting on skis for the first time.

Gaining inspiration from Pen running his moor land wilderness course with rocks in his pack, I decided to buy a big bag of cement, and placed in it my rucksack. I then conducted some tyre pulls with the added weight of the cement in my backpack. I also started long brisk walks with the cement pack, with the specific aim of strengthening my back and legs. This momentous weight was probably more likely to cause injury than anything else so it wasn't long before this grand, and somewhat eccentric, fitness scheme was dispensed with. Jane Fonda wouldn't have approved of this technique.

I was very confident about the strength of my legs anyway, to be honest, as they had never let me down. They seemed naturally strong. Years of running, judo and ice hockey had strengthened them and prepared them for a mission like this. Indeed I was always rushing around or so everyone thought, but I wasn't actually rushing at all – it was just that I normally walked at least twice the speed of the majority of the population. Every walk down the street was conducted as though I was driving in the fast lane, passing everyone by. Even as a child I seemed to speed through the crowds. No doubt this came from my mother who also possessed this fast paced momentum, as did my younger brother and sister who had to learn to keep up with her or be left behind. Visitors never seemed to be able to keep pace with the Eadies. Despite this, I admit I wasn't the greatest runner in the world – Mark's ten miler description in the expedition brochure *would* have caused me to break into a sweat, although I had proven more than once that I could march thirty-five miles in a day, no problem.

A few weeks later, and with hours of private tyre pulls behind each of us, the team met up again for a full day's collective tyre pull. We all gathered on the South Downs with our different shapes and sizes of tyres and dragged them across muddy fields, narrow paths and over wooded hills.

It was still early and the morning sun tempted the valley mists from their slumbers. The countryside was quiet, disturbed only by the man-made sound of tyres dragged across wet stones and foliage, and the occasional panting and wheezing of their masters. This strange herd of six mud- spattered men, each with ski poles, rosy cheeks and enough tyres to tread a small fleet of cars, wound their through the countryside, occasionally causing the local wildlife to flee in horror.

After two hours we came across a clearing in the woods occupied by a group of army tents and vehicles. 'What sort of a bloody army is this?!' bellowed Mark, breaking the silence of the wood, disgusted that they were not up at dawn, hinting that the enemy would have been. Rob was equally disgusted and instructed the rest of us to load our tyres into one of the lonely army Land Rovers, which he would hot-wire and save us a few miles of more 'sledging'. It was this loud prompt that caused one of the tents to open and a weary eye peered out. Bunny followed up in his best Russian accent, which was terrible, that we would then drive to Westminster and, disguised as British solders, destroy Parliament and take over the country. 'Come Comrades!' was his rallying call as we trudged off into the woods again. It. was particularly satisfying to feel that we, apparently, took our training, at least on this occasion, more seriously than these soldiers.

As the hours passed and the surroundings changed it was clear that our tyre training regime was not varied enough. We had all been pulling tyres in fields of one sort or another. Today's travels through the woods exposed us to the tyres getting caught in ruts, hooked on roots and all other manner of obstacles. Rather than walk back to the obstruction to free the tyre we would simply heave at different angles from the far end of the rope to release the snagged tyre. This placed differing strains on the back muscles but would undoubtedly be representative of pulling a sledge over ice, with its cracks, breaks and bumpy surface ready to unbalance the sled. I resolved to incorporate more back strengthening exercises into my gym sessions, to ensure my back was prepared properly for the Arctic sledging.

At one point on the Downs the mud path changed to a sandy track, which was presumably used for horses. This new surface was much harder going than the slippery mud and wet grass, the drag from the sand being considerable. I recalled how Pen had always said that pulling a sledge over ice was like pulling a dead weight over sand.

As the day wore on, we bumped into ramblers, horse riders and other travellers. A horse rider, upon seeing us and our rubber flock of tyres, asked us simply 'North or South?' Clearly he knew what we were doing. A well deserved pub meal completed the day.

In trying to get ready for the Arctic there was one area, and a major one, that would be difficult to prepare for in London's early spring – low temperatures. Ranulph Fiennes, the famous British polar adventurer, had tried to acclimatise for the polar regions by arranging to sleep in large refrigeration stores. He also used this to check the suitability of his equipment. If it was good enough for him, then I thought it only right for me to do the same. I approached my local supermarket and local butchers to see whether they would oblige. The supermarket eventually refused, after my unusual request had travelled up several levels of management, saying recent EU legislation meant humans could not occupy the frozen meat store overnight. At the other end of the scale the local butcher exclaimed, 'But, it drops to minus twenty in my store!' to which I replied 'Brilliant!' He probably thought I was a nutter and made some excuse why I shouldn't spend a couple of nights locked up with his pork joints.

Without the advantage of sleeping in a large refrigeration store I embarked upon a campaign of placing all equipment into my home freezer. My wife would often open the freezer looking for something to eat only to find it full of all manner of polar gear on test.

We had set the freezer to maximum cool, bringing the temperature down to minus twenty degrees Celsius. I knew that temperatures at the Magnetic Pole would drop by double this amount. It became clear that some items, especially plastics, would completely change their characteristics in low temperatures. Some chocolates became rock hard – tooth-breaking hard. Some plastics became very brittle. I didn't want to arrive in the Arctic to find that my fork froze to my lip, or my eating bowl develop a big hole in it when it was used. I recorded the results of my tests and passed them onto the team. My wife became very interested in these tests, and before I knew it she was telling me that she had found fruit bars that remained chewy at minus twenty, had a great calorific to weight ratio, and had bought a truckload of them for my consumption.

Having taken the role of the group's equipment officer I was to determine the best kit for us all to bring. I did a lot of research, quizzing Pen for advice, reading kit lists from a number of recent polar expeditions and talking to a lot of manufacturers. The devil would be in the detail and I wouldn't have a chance to test all of it myself. I wanted to ensure that we had the best possible equipment. There was no point us putting in all this training only to be let down by sub-standard equipment or, just as crucially, not having something that was needed. In essence the challenge was to take equipment that would not be too bulky, too heavy or too expensive. We would need the equipment to be able to cope with air temperatures down to minus forty-five degrees Celsius and dropping to minus sixty when travelling by skidoo, with the associated wind chill caused by the speed of travel.

This balance meant we had to get the latest clothing technology to ensure that we had the warmest, lightest clothing that would also allow our bodies to breath. At odds with this need for space-age clothing was Pen's recommendation for vapour barrier socks. These were needed to stop the sweat from our feet from getting into our boots, where it would ultimately freeze and reduce the effectiveness of the boot.

'I strongly suggest that a simple supermarket carrier bag will suffice,' said the polar expert. 'Simply placing the foot into the carrier bag, and then in turn placing this into a sock will keep any moisture at bay and keep your feet warm.' I was stunned.

'Is this a joke?' said Rob bewildered.

Bunny just laughed.

'Anyone's will do?' questioned Rob sarcastically, 'I bet Pen gets his carrier bags from Fortnum and Mason!'

Most of the group thought this hilarious whilst I was having convulsions over how I would determine whether a Tesco, Asda or Sainsbury's carrier bag was best suited. We all eventually bought professional mountaineering barrier socks – apart from Bunny who, not to be outdone, insisted that his supermarket carrier bags were best value. 'They are supplied by Waitrose,' he announced, and with tongue firmly in cheek proclaimed, 'Whilst they cost ten pounds each, each carrier bag does come with a free bottle of red wine!'

I put all the smaller items into my freezer to test their robustness. A couple of cups fractured after they had endured -20°C for 24 hours and then had a boiling hot drink poured into them – potentially disastrous on the trip. Another bowl was rejected as it couldn't take the punishment of being sat on once cold, something that you could imagine it wasn't designed for but an occurrence that could easily happen once packed in the sledge or lying around in a crowded tent.

A few weeks later I had a full kit list. Pen was providing the food, tent, communications and cooking equipment; this mainly left clothing and bedding for us to provide. Each person was to bring three sets of sunglasses or goggles, and three hoods or face-masks. There was a set of layered clothing and then an outer shell. Three sets of gloves with 'wristlets' to keep the exposed area between glove and wrist covered.

Whilst Pen stated only one pair of underwear was required per person I advised this be increased to two. This luxury was needed, I felt, as if anyone had a stomach problem arising from the high calorie diet the extra pair of underwear would be appreciated all round. The underwear of choice was Helly Hansen's patented 'wind proof' underwear. It took me a while to see the funny side of asking a sales assistant in a shop if they had 'Any wind proof underwear?', some of whom undoubtedly thought I was trying to wind them up or that I expected to find a cure for flatulence in their camping store. This underwear also had an additional and unique protector over the genitals that added further protection against the cold. No one argued against the choice of underwear.

We had a number of, as Bunny called them, 'kit frenzies' in Covent Garden camping shops. Typically our loud team would descend on a store and simultaneously seem to try almost everything on, with the richer lawyers saying they liked this or that and with me dictating that they couldn't buy it because it didn't meet the standard we needed. In one shop Bunny, blinded by a particularly large hooded jacket, managed to trip over Geoff who was tightly wrapped up in a sleeping bag on the shop floor. Bunny's loud and silly but highly infectious laughter quickly filled the whole store as he rolled around the ground uncontrollably. Among the highly paced and seemingly chaotic scenes that seemed to follow our group everywhere eventually, over a period of six weeks, we acquired everything needed. Even Bunny had all the right kit.

Swapping tips and advice we often made some personal amendments to equipment. I added some string to my outer gloves that would wind around my neck, like Captain Scott, so that I could take them off and not lose them in the wind. Also added to all trouser and coat zips were elongated draw strings so that the zips could be pulled without having to remove our large clumsy gloves and exposing our hands. To speed toilet activities, as I would be wearing trunks as well as the genital-protecting Helly Hanson wind-proof briefs, I decided to cut out a section of the trunks so just pulling down the briefs would allow me to more quickly have a pee.

Whilst diet was important, Pen had not seen the obvious marketing opportunity for his business in creating a new fad: the 'Polar Diet'. After all, what could be better or more attractive to many people than to eat as much chocolate as they wanted?, indeed to be actively encouraged to eat it, and to still lose weight! Ok, you had to go to the Arctic to do this and pull a heavy sledge, but that could be covered in the small print. The thought of herds of dieters roaming the Arctic wastes pulling sledges overloaded with chocolate brought a wry smile to my face. The polar bears would also, if asked, lend their support to this diet – after all two fat dieters and a sledge full of chocolate a day would keep most of them happy too!

Whilst Pen specified and provided the food for the trip, we each had to bring our own personal pack of rations – treats that we individually favoured that would be consumed during rest periods. As with all the equipment I took a survey of snacks and passed them through my freezer test. I emailed the results to the team, slightly more tongue-in-cheek than usual:

TO : TEAM   FROM : DUNCAN

Taking a night off training and needing something to occupy my mind I thought I would conduct a scientific experiment , the results of which may be of interest to the hungry polar explorer. I hope to have these results published in 'Which' – 'Arctic Chocolate Bars'!

We will all no doubt take a personal supply of snacks (you'd better, you're not getting any of mine!) to help us on our way. But which ones? and how do they perform at low temperatures? This question has occupied science for many years, so armed with my trusty freezer I got to work.......

Leaving each bar in the freezer for 24 hours (the temp gauge read - 25C) the following results were found. Listed in energy rating order (per 100g):-

Bar Name	Energy (Kj) Per 100G	Energy (Kj) Per Bar	Result
Cadbury's Dairy Milk	2195	1065	Highest energy count! Easy to break off in chunks.
Twix	2073	1201	Easily broken in hand due to slimness of bar. Surprisingly high energy.
Fuse	2030	1005	As recommended by Ran Fiennes' nutritionist! Ok to break. Bit tasteless. High energy.
Fruit & Nut	2030	1005	Easy to break as in chunks. Tasty. High energy.
Picnic	1985	960	Very hard. Caramel frozen solid.
Mars Bar	1899	1234	Caramel frozen. Can't be bitten into. Breaks by hand into lumps too big to place in mouth.
Milky Way	1895	494	Ok. A Bit bland.
Fruseli Bar	1809	604	Tough to eat. caramel freezes. Nuts hard. Not worth the hassle.
Turkish delight	1425	730	Jelly centre doesn't freeze! Easy to bite into. A bit different.
Dried Fruit	1273	630	Tasty. Doesn't freeze. Snax
Fruit Pastilles			Lots of taste. No need to break with hands (but need to have unwrapped previously).
Snickers			Caramel freezes solid. Can't be bitten into.

Summary

The criteria for a successful snack would seem to be:

1. High energy content. Hit list is:

    i. Cadbury's Dairy Milk

    ii. Twix

    iii. Fuse/Fruit & Nut

2. Easy on the teeth - Don't pick a bar with thick layers of caramel - it turns to concrete at low temps - a teeth shatterer!

3. Prepare your favourite snack by cutting it into bite-sized chunks BEFORE getting onto the ice! This will avoid the hassle of unwrapping bars with gloves on and snapping it into chunks too large to place in the mouth. Hold 1 day's ration in a little plastic bag. Mix up contents for variety. Wonderful!

Hope this information has been useful. My next task is to tackle the equally interesting scientific problem of 'Which- Arctic Beer'!!!!!!! I may need a few assistants on this one!

By now I had read Helen Thayer's *Polar Dream* at least five times, each time finding another tip or suggestion that would need following up. Her solo journey to the Magnetic Pole was indeed spectacular, but as the months got closer to my own trip, more and more of what she described became less of her description and more of what I too was likely to face. It was difficult to imagine exactly how cold things would be. Some nights I imagined sleeping in the freezer compartment of my fridge, with my head rested against a large ice cube. The Magnetic Pole would be at least twice as cold as the environment my frozen dinners were exposed to.

Helen Thayer also wrote of severe Arctic storms and blizzards, thin ice, and of being tracked by polar bears eager for an easy meal. They would often approach her in a blizzard, where their sense of smell could track her, and where she could not see them in the conditions. Without her dog, who had similar senses to the bears, she would have met a grizzly end many times over. We however wouldn't have the luxury of a dog.

I decided that I needed to work out what the boundaries of my fears were. If I met a polar bear what would I actually do? I wanted to play the various scenarios in my mind before I went to the Arctic, in the hope that should the occasion arise I would be a little more controlled, prepared, less panicky, and hopefully increase my chances of survival. Whilst I knew the expedition would enable me to discover more about myself, I couldn't help but try to work out my boundaries before I left England. Each of us on the expedition no doubt dealt with the uncertainties in our own way. Geoff for example, didn't even tell his employer where he was going, fearing they may object.

I was very aware of my previous experience when I climbed Mount Elbrus in southern Russia. On the final day of that expedition when we attempted to reach the summit of the mountain, things had got a bit dicey. To get to the top quickly, after a blizzard forced a late start giving us less time, we had decided to climb with minimum equipment - which meant we would carry less weight and therefore have more energy to reach our goal. We had aimed to get to the top of the mountain and back to base camp within the day.

During the final climb a storm came in, bringing freezing temperatures and strong winds, which eventually produced a complete white-out. The climber following me collapsed, with a combination of light altitude sickness and fatigue; his lips were blue and he wasn't making any sense. I couldn't see or hear him, until the person behind him, seeing him stumble from side-to-side, blew a whistle. The conditions at this stage were getting silly. The group made a decision to split in two, one group deciding to call it a day and accompany the sick climber back to base camp, a separate group deciding to attempt the final five hundred feet to the top – we were that close. I decided to remain with the summit group and go for it, as I felt strong and determined.

However, none of us had our sleeping bags or tents with us, because of our equipment-saving regime to help speed us to the top. The summit group huddled together to finalise the plan as we were blasted with snow. The guide was now getting worried about avalanches, given the amount of snow fall, and shouted against the gale that we were likely to have to dig snow holes and remain on the summit overnight. Someone shouted back, 'What would that be like?' to which he screamed back in his thick Russian accent, 'Probably the worst night of your lives.'

Stuck on Europe's highest mountain at over eighteen thousand feet in a blizzard, with no camping equipment, all of a sudden seemed like utter madness. I looked around and quickly decided to change my mind and join the party descending to base camp instead. However, in the intervening two minutes since they had left, the storm had swallowed them up, and they were nowhere to be seen. My only option was to remain with the 'worst night of your lives' group. After ascending another two hundred feet, which took an hour but seemed a lot longer, we decided to abandon our summit attempt and descend to base camp through the blizzard, which we eventually did.

I don't believe that my life was ever at risk, but what did weigh on my mind was how I had taken the wrong decision at a crucial point. Dominated by my desire to get to the top of the mountain, and being in good physical condition to complete the climb, I had not taken sufficient account of the developing situation. I wanted to ensure that this didn't happen again. Indeed this focus to obtain the goal was common to many Everest climbers who overcome everything to reach the summit – but then don't live to tell the tale. The climbers mantra being 'getting to the top is optional, getting down is mandatory.'

I ran through as many scenarios that I could imagine that I might encounter on the Magnetic Pole expedition and determined for each what I would do. For example, how would I cope if I fell through thin ice into the cold ocean below? or if the entire expedition took place in dense fog? or if we suffered equipment failure near Polar Bear Pass and were being shadowed by the infamous boys-in-the-white-coats?

I tried to determine what my limits were and how close to them I would allow myself to get. This mental preparation was important to me and this made itself felt in all sorts of curious forms. As I lay in bed at night I would often imagine the gunfire-shot-like sound of ice cracking in the distance, or the low groaning and mumbling of ice on which we might be camped, moving beneath me.

I liked to think my hearing was very good and I tried to train it further by listening intently to the sounds of the night. I studied pictures and videos of polar bears so I could recognise their shape from any angle, even among littered and broken jumbles of ice. The conclusion of all this thinking was that whilst I wanted to get to the Pole I wouldn't risk my life – I was far too inexperienced to push myself that far, and I also decided I wouldn't risk losing a finger, toe, or other appendage however non-life-threatening these would be. I established this as my baseline around which I could weigh up situations and risks and make decisions against.

Meanwhile, Mark had arranged that we all join the Wimbledon ten kilometre run one Sunday. Whilst being a short run, which would tend towards the speed rather than endurance profile that Pen had asked us to concentrate on, it was a good opportunity for everyone to test their general fitness.

I definitely wanted to finish first in the group, so did Peter, the other youngster. Mark was expecting to win. Bunny was testing out his recently injected ankle. Rob looked confident. Geoff had a target finish time. The spirit of competition kept the group on their toes, and fear of getting left behind ensured that I attended the gym and used the ski machine regularly.

A gun went off to announce the start of the run and the three hundred or so runners began to move. The team all started as a group and jogged at a brisk pace. After about five kilometres I decided to set a higher pace and broke away from the team. It wasn't long before I had lost them among the other runners. I continued my pace, breathing heavily, in order to ensure victory.

Within the last quarter kilometre, and confident of being the first across the line from the group, I casually looked over my shoulder to see Rob hot on my tail only a few paces behind. With a big grin he panted that he was 'keeping the honour of the old boys intact'. We crossed the line together. Within a few minutes the rest of the group crossed. Our general level of cardio-vascular fitness was now pretty high. We had all done well. Bunny did not seem to have any issues with his ankle. After collecting our medals, we all left for home happy with both our individual and the group's performance.

Now with three weeks before we left for Canada, we had all reached the peak of our exercise regime. I was attending the gym up to three times a day – before work, during lunch and after work. The tyres were regularly exercised during our night-time excursions on the heath, the skiing machine less so in front of the white wall, and my wife Niamh was beginning to complain that she didn't see much of me now.

Individually we were all looking for funds or equipment to be donated by the various companies we worked for. Peter managed to get funding for a down jacket from his employer. I had managed to gain several thousand pounds' sponsorship from my employer. I wanted to use my participation in the expedition to raise money for the Royal National Institute for the Blind, in memory of my late Aunt Dorothy, who was sightless her entire life.

Mark was still looking for sponsors for the team as a whole, and had circulated his expedition sponsorship document which detailed our objectives and opportunities for sponsorship, to numerous companies. We each received a pleasant call one day from him stating that, *Oyez*, the legal stationers would sponsor us and take the expedition title. This was great news; the cash injection reduced the cost of the trip for all of us. We became officially known as the 'Oyez Solicitors' Polar Expedition 1997'. This was secured with an Oyez flag which was to be hoisted, and photographed at the Magnetic Pole, various press engagements and a bag of Oyez branded logos that were to be applied to all relevant clothing.

Shortly after this we had a sponsor's meeting, where an Oyez photographer took publicity shots of us pulling tyres in preparation for the event. Mark insisted we all attend in similar coloured equipment, which he specified. We attended as detailed, while Mark promptly turned up in a different colour scheme all together, as was his privilege, being the expedition leader.

The London *Evening Standard* said they would feature us in an issue; as did *Maxim*, one of the popular 'lads' mags', which even thought about sending a journalist out to Resolute Bay to cover us as a feature.

Individually we each carried out our own private charity sponsorship. The Royal National Institute for the Blind provided a photographer from the local *South London Press* and, most bizarrely, an RNIB branded vest. Providing a vest really proved to me how little they understood about what I was attempting, or perhaps they had a good sense of humour – 'Where? The North Magnetic Pole? Send the poor guy a good vest, he'll need it!'

6

Heading North

'I believe that the Good Lord gave us a finite number of heart beats and I'm damned if I'm going to use up mine running up and down a street.'

NEIL ARMSTRONG, ASTRONAUT. FIRST MAN TO WALK ON THE MOON.

Finally, the last day at work before we set off came around. Waiting in the queue for the bus in the morning seemed to take longer than usual. I was in a hurry for the day to finish. The usual faces were in the queue awaiting our transport. Faces that I had grown to know over the last year, although the relationship ended there. In the commuter culture of London it was an unwritten rule to not talk to anyone who you had not been introduced to. I had not exchanged a word with any of the people that I had queued in the rain, wind, sun and snow over the last year. Not talking would have been acceptable, if we had exchanged the occasional smile, or made some indication of each other's existence. But the highest rule of the London commuter was not to be broken, and I for one would not be the first to break it. We all sat quietly in the shelter waiting for our transport.

People began to stand up quickly. I rose with them, accepting the flock-like indication that the bus was about to arrive. Drawing to a halt with a shudder and squeal of the brakes as the red doors opened, we all silently stepped aboard. The views out of the window, a newspaper, or the odd novel, were all preferable to starting a conversation. So off we all went, beginning the day together, before we split up into our separate lives, until the same time tomorrow. I often wondered what the people around me did for a living. The man with the dapper suit glancing at his watch might have worked for a clothes shop. The young woman with her head in the magazine, with a dress cut overly low for the time of the year, stereotypically portrayed her to be a secretary out to impress her boss. Or so I imagined. None were chat show hosts that was for sure. But then neither was I.

The journey was short but enjoyable. Over Tower Bridge we sped. Peering through the grime-stained windows I could see the Thames sweeping past a grey HMS Belfast moored in the Pool of London. The Tower of London surveyed us from its cold, unfeeling walls. The building had been standing there for close on a thousand years. Much had changed around it since then – the City skyscrapers behind, the erection of bridges, and the embankment of the River Thames.

What did not change was the overpowering aura of the Tower. Built as a symbol of Norman rule over the vanquished English by William the Conqueror in 1086, it still carried its spell, made all the more sinister by its bloody past. A garden behind the Tower marks the location of the site where various rogues, political and religious prisoners, publicly, as an engraved tablet describes marking the spot, 'suffered'. In nice weather people now eat their lunches in these gardens, the bright sunshine disguising the horrors of the past. Only a nearby pub, named the 'Hung Drawn and Quartered" carried any reminder of the victims' agonies.

The bus pulled up to the stop at Tower Hill, tooting at a pedestrian who was hailing a cab to get out of the way. The pleasant part of the journey was over. I would now join the rest of the London working population underground.

As I entered the tube station as one of the throbbing hoards, I passed a sign warning 'Beware of slipping! - Wet floors due to adverse weather conditions'.

As I arrived on the concourse a loud speaker announced, 'Unattended bags may be destroyed,' followed by a second informing the reluctant listening population, 'Trains can arrive unannounced, stay clear of the platform.' Boy!, was I looking forward to escaping the dangers of the city for the safety of the Arctic!

This morning I stepped onto the tube train with a new spring in my step. The doors closed behind me on a wet and grey London day. The doors remained closed, the train did not move. No one spoke, no one made eye contact. The temperature began to rise. Someone further down the carriage tutted their disapproval as they thought they would be late for work, again. Still the train did not move. A muffled announcement informed us of the delay. 'De train at platfarm 'tree will shortly be movin', awaiting a train to clear de tunnel.'

Closing my eyes I could imagine I was in the Caribbean as the lilting accent of the driver wafted over the intercom, the sound waves cutting through the hot air. 'Awaiting a train to clear de tunnel, de train at platfarm 'tree will shartly be movin.' He was well groomed in London Underground speak, relaying the message once, and then again backwards - in London Underground speak he was well groomed! Starting with a jolt we were off, bringing me back sharply from the Caribbean shore of my dreams to the crowded, grimy underground carriage. Bouncing off people in the crowded rush-hour train, avoiding feet, bags, and the uncaring stares of passengers, that you become used to after years of travelling in the tube environment. The passengers swayed from side-to-side as the train thundered through the tunnels. Sweat was beginning to form on my back in the crowded and humid confines, even at that time of the year.

The train ground to a halt at Blackfriars station and my heart began to rev a little faster as my eyes watched for the slightest movement of the doors beginning to open. I was off! Past the bewildered elderly man stepping off the train and looking for the exit sign. Past the woman clutching her handbag and the man furiously stuffing his newspaper into his briefcase. First onto the stairs I charged upwards to the ticket barrier. Unfortunately another train had just entered the station from the other direction and had already spewed its human cargo onto the platform. I met with them near the exit.

Ticket in hand, heart slightly pounding, I could feel other people close behind me, the click-clack of their shoes on the stairs announcing their presence. I joined the queue to the exit. Such was the life of a commuter in the rat race. No doubt this was being repeated all over London, and indeed in every large city across the world.

My short daily spell as a mole travelling underground was over, until this evening at least. Finally I was into the open air – London air, which was made up of the noxious fumes from taxis. As I stepped above ground I glanced at the cross on top of St. Paul's Cathedral's massive dome, which was no longer golden but a dark syrupy colour. The greyness of the day surrounded me as I skipped over another puddle and then, accidentally, I bumped into a man coming the other way. His appearance mirrored the day. His grey wet hair unmoving after the impact. An apology would merely have aggravated the situation. The dull eyes of my prey saw through me as he mumbled something before moving on again.

Rising buildings enclosed me as the population moved around on the ground, watched from fluorescent-lit windows high above, by the early shift. I passed occasional figures huddled into small doorways, shivering in the cold. Dressed in only a shirt some workers' overwhelming need for a cigarette forced them into the street, without even the time to protect themselves against the weather. Oh, how the Arctic wastes would be a welcome respite from this mass of polluted humanity!

My last day at work passed uneventfully. A meeting to discuss the project I was working on raised a few smiles when someone asked where I was going for the next few weeks. Before I could answer a colleague jumped in enthusiastically, 'Penguin poking!' As they all laughed I pointed out that there were no penguins in the part of the world I was going to, only polar bears. 'Perhaps there was a connection,' someone said. 'Maybe that's why people don't live there either.' 'The polar bears ate them too,' voiced another before bursting into a loud laugh. I laughed a little less than the rest of them.

'How cold will it be?' asked one of my teasers.

'Could be down to minus forty or even lower,' I replied.

'Oh dear', came the response, 'I was in Canada once and it was minus thirty, simply dreadful, freezing, most uncomfortable.'

'How long were you in those conditions for?' I replied, looking for some useful information.

'Oh about ten minutes, I was waiting for a taxi which was delayed, I almost froze to death. How long will you be out in minus forty?'

'I'll be living, working and sleeping in those conditions for three weeks,' I replied bravely, knowing one of us was about to look very silly. The room fell silent.

After a few more jollities at my expense one of them realised that the journey would involve me walking through prime polar bear country. 'Are you mad? – that's like being in an open zoo. I know a friend of a friend,' she explained, 'who knew someone working on research up there. He stepped out of the tent one night to go the short distance to another tent. Never got there – they found the remains of him amongst polar bear tracks a few hours later.' She didn't need to be told that there were no hotels at the North Magnetic Pole. She knew her geography. Here was the first person who knew something about the place – and she was telling me I was mad. I laughed it off, knowing deep inside that the possibility of a bear encounter would be the worst and perhaps best part of the journey. It certainly had the potential to leave the most lasting impression.

My work colleagues took me out to the pub for lunch where I was deluged with questions. Some in their laughter thought I had obviously lost it, others asked detailed questions about the expedition. I was presented with a gift-wrapped box of plasters, some cold sore ointment and, of all things, a blow-up sheep! They all insisted that I took this to the North Magnetic Pole as, they said, it was an essential going-away gift for any serious polar explorer. It always amused me that anyone going to the polar regions was automatically labelled a 'polar explorer'. Though I wouldn't be discovering anything, the term showed how the Arctic was still a place of mystery and, perhaps, romance.

I was happy to be a 'polar explorer' on a private polar expedition. It all added to the sense of fun and adventure that had built up inside me. My participation in the expedition generated a lot of interest among the women too, enabling me to empathise with Robert Swan's reason for choice of career. It all felt like a leaving do, which I certainly hoped it wasn't. I was surprised by everyone's attention and kindness and left work on a high.

I spent the night of the 21st March, 1997 conducting final packing and checking and rechecking equipment, with a nervous anxiety. Over the previous weeks I had been constantly taking out equipment from my kit bag and re-evaluating it. I wasn't quite at the stage adopted by many mountaineers who would even cut toothbrushes in half to save weight, but I knew every pound packed would have to be dragged around on my sledge. I laid all my equipment out on the living-room floor one last time and did the final pack; everything correct and ordered. A good night's sleep didn't happen, as I was too excited.

The next morning brought one last worry – my insurance certificate had still not arrived, despite multiple phone calls over the previous days. The bags were packed into the car, filling the boot. I phoned my mum who wished me luck and a safe return. Dad was out so I couldn't have a goodbye chat to him. Just as my wife and I drove out of the house I spotted the postman up the street and virtually accosted him! He passed over all my letters, amazingly enough my insurance certificate was with them.

Gatwick airport was the usual chaotic scene, but I spotted the others quickly enough, as we were all wearing our white sweaters provided by our sponsor Oyez sporting their logo. Bunny and Rob had grown beards to prepare themselves going north, though they didn't yet have the thickness and protection afforded by Mark's facial bush.

Alarmingly Bunny had brought a pair of crutches! As I hastily stated that these were not official equipment he assured me that he had brought so little equipment he had wanted to bring something to help make up the weight. I wasn't sure which of those two facts I should be more alarmed about. Meanwhile, Pen had already travelled ahead of us and was at Resolute Bay in Canada awaiting our arrival.

Amongst the mountainous bags of equipment were each team member's wife and family. We played out the same scene that thousands of other travellers at this and other airports were all playing, as we kissed and wished each other a safe journey, before we went our separate ways. Out of the blue came my own father, a pleasant surprise and one which was typical of his sense of humour, and the reason why he wasn't able to come to the phone earlier.

We all split up to spend a few last moments with our families. It wasn't long before Mark began making noises that we should get through the gates now – despite there being ample time. My wife Niamh wished me luck before passing me an extra goodie bag of rations as a present. Her final words as she looked me in the eye were simply, 'I love you. Take care.' Dad shook my hand tightly, before the 1997 Oyez Polar Expedition went through to departures. We were now officially on our way.

Our journey would take us from London to Canada, to Ottawa, and then the next day onto Edmonton, before catching a third flight to Yellowknife, then a fourth flight on to Resolute Bay.

Whilst we all sat on the first plane, high above the Atlantic, Mark was buzzing and getting more concerned by the moment that there was very little transfer time at Edmonton to catch the Yellowknife flight. A plan soon hatched, with Rob encouraging Mark's frenzy, that we should continue on to Edmonton that night instead of waiting until the next day. The first group meeting was thus held between rows twenty three and twenty four at thirty thousand feet. However, getting to Edmonton that night, rather than waiting until the next day, would cost an additional couple of thousand pounds, so was rejected by the rest of the group, then everyone went back to reading their newspapers and books, whilst Mark continued to fluster.

We landed in Canada, in Ottawa. This introduced the first snow of the expedition. We all left the hotel to find a big Canadian steak-house where large quantities of wine were consumed, and the majority of a beast. We all knew that this would be the last proper feed in civilisation before the alcohol-free Resolute Bay. It was also likely to be the last place we would see, and even consume, warm red flesh for a while.

The daylight flight to Edmonton enabled us to see the Canadian countryside, which was truly awesome. From our satellite-like view we passed over a manicured landscape of tightly patched fields making perfectly formed squares, for seemingly hours on end. Each field no doubt produced some wonderful crop. The sheer size of the country which we were flying over was breathtaking, as it rolled past for mile after mile.

We devoured everything that the flight crew handed out, and often asked for more, as our calorie-hungry bodies had yet to realise that the day wouldn't be spent in arduous training exercise.

Our leader Mark was still concerned about flight times and the tight window that our arrival at Edmonton would leave us to board the Yellowknife flight. From down the aisle you could hear the growing volume of the conversation between Mark and Sylvin, our male air host.

'What we need you to do is to radio ahead to keep the connecting plane waiting for us,' insisted Mark.

'Relax Sir, all will be ok.'

'Look, my good man, if we don't make the flight because this aircraft is late arriving it's nine months training down the drain.'

Should we miss the connecting flight to Yellowknife, we could have been delayed by up to a week, because onward planes to Resolute were very infrequent. Mark in his flustered state was, however, exaggerating the situation.

'Just relax Sir, we are on time,' our host responded, not the slightest bit intimidated by our overpowering leader.

Mark stormed back down the aisle, to Rob's accord of 'Relax, relax.' We then immediately had another meeting, with Mark raising options to plan for the worst, and to see who was for hiring another plane. The group agreed to wait and see what happened.

The hours rolled on as we flew over Canada at an altitude of almost seven miles. We read books, ate, slept, and ate more if we could persuade the steward to provide us with extra rations. At times I was able to look out of the window; the deep blue of the stratosphere contrasted sharply with the white fluffy clouds underneath. It was easy to imagine the white clouds as ice; their ripples represented barriers, their darkened shadows cracks in the ice and the odd ice forms that I knew I would shortly encounter once at sea level. The stark contrast between the dark sky and meringue-white clouds was beautiful.

We arrived in Edmonton on time and ran to the next gate, jumping the queues and running past everyone in the departures queue, who looked at us in utter disgust. A group of lawyers had never shown such bravado! Before takeoff the plane's wings were hosed down with anti-freeze by men on a cherry picker hovering over each wing and spraying gaily.

The next change was at Yellowknife in the Northwest Territories, just north of the Great Slave Lake. At sixty-three degrees north on the map this was still south of the Arctic circle but, according to the temperature sign at the airport, it was -18°C outside. I remembered seeing Yellowknife on the world map as a child and had often wondered what it was like there, with it having such an intriguing name, and strangely remembering the fact that it was built on permafrost.

I took the opportunity to satisfy my childhood curiosity and had a look outside the airport as we awaited the final flight to Resolute Bay. Passing the Yellowknife youth football team, who were gathered in the departures lounge, I took a ten minute stroll outside in the bright sunshine. I concluded that -18°C, and the lowest temperature experienced so far in my life, was 'no problem'.

We again changed planes, this time for the last time, for the final leg to Resolute Bay, which would also see us stop at the settlement of Cambridge Bay, just over six hundred miles further north. As we flew further northwards the large open plains disappeared, consumed by forest, before they too withered and gave way to the white snow covered mass below us.

Before landing we circled the Cambridge Bay settlement. From on high, Cambridge Bay appeared to be located on an island, surrounded by a frozen white sea, with grey dotted houses forming a perfect circle around the edge of the island. The surprisingly large settlement of almost a thousand souls looked like a final outpost of humanity clinging onto life.

This time when we landed the runway was made of ice, and it threw up a cloud of frozen particles as we touched down with the jet engine screaming into full reverse. The plane pulled up behind a large radar dish whose purpose in the Cold War was to monitor any incoming ICBM's that might be fired by the Soviets from across the North Pole. These dishes were spread across the whole of the Arctic from Alaska in the west, across northern Canada, and right across the Greenland icecap in the east.

Whilst the area of Cambridge Bay had been an Inuit hunting ground for some centuries and known for its good hunting of swan, caribou, musk-ox, fox, arctic hare and geese, it was when it became a supply station for the Cold War early warning systems that it took a permanent foothold, in the middle of the twentieth century. The majority of citizens in Cambridge Bay were Inuit.

Once we landed we had a chance to get off the plane and, as we were in the Arctic for real now, we took it with some excitement.

After the months of training, and a lifetime of dreams, I was finally there! If the history and geography books had enticed me with tales of grandeur, heroism and hardship, my initiation to this cold world was no less awe-inspiring.

As the doors of the aircraft opened, the Arctic air rushed in and embraced us tightly with its icy grip. The air invaded my nostrils, and plunged rapidly downward into the depths of my lungs, and violently expelled the warm blood from my hands and face. I wasn't alone. As we stepped outside the warm confines of the aircraft, the temperature dropped in moments by over 40 degrees Celsius. Someone gasped in a tortured voice from behind me, 'Bloody hell!' We were bathed in bright, bright, sunshine – yet our bodies were telling us to get into survival mode quickly. I didn't expect the Arctic to welcome us, for this wasn't a place for men – this was somewhere where men trespassed temporarily, and cautiously.

By the time we had walked to the aircraft hanger – 'passenger terminal' would have been too grand a word for the pre-fabricated hut that greeted us, everyone's nose hairs had frozen. For anyone who doesn't believe they have nose hairs, just stand in an air temperature of -24°C, (as the temperature sign there announced), and you will discover that you have. The cold was literally breath-stopping, yet it also felt very pure. It wasn't the damp cold I had experienced all my life in England, instead it was pure, undiluted, and crystal clean frozen air. I wasn't now quite so confident as I had been standing in a 'balmy' -18°C at Yellowknife, six hundred miles south. It was going to be much colder than this where we were going, suddenly it really hit home what we were attempting.

Rob's nose started involuntarily bleeding. 'We have a casualty,' he muttered, with his handkerchief drawn tightly over his nose. I hoped his blood wasn't a bad omen. Inside the terminal warning posters were displayed on a wall. Back home, such posters would warn the newly-arrived of the dangers of pickpockets or being ripped off by taxi drivers. Here, the dangers were of a different, more serious nature and they advertised the danger of polar bears, written in English and Inuit – represented by a strange series of squiggles.

At last we were on the final leg of the journey to Resolute Bay. At this stage all the passengers were flying to Resolute Bay, so we began talking to each other to find out what brought our companion travellers this far north.

A group of athletically-built men were, on investigation, from Holland and, like us, on an expedition to the North Magnetic Pole. Another gentleman was on his own, 'Because I can't get anyone else to go with me.'

During the flight we all went up to the cockpit, where the captain warmly welcomed us, and gave us a weather report, supplemented by an interesting insight into flying this far north. The aircraft was approximately fifty per cent given over to cargo, so as we left the passenger area and walked through to the cockpit we had to pass through the cargo bay of the aircraft. Most supplies went to Resolute by ship once a year during the brief Arctic summer, when conditions usually allowed sea travel.

The bright clear blue Arctic skies became clouded over as we made our final approach to Resolute Bay. Peter and I tried to look through the grey clouds and eventually spotted something unexpected far below us. 'Look Peter, it's a car!' We looked at the black dot moving along a grey line in the snow. The airport was located approximately one mile from the hamlet of Resolute Bay and this grey line formed the only road, of course an ice road, for hundreds of miles around.

Finally, we touched down at our destination, after two days of almost constant travel, again on an ice runway that welcomed us with a shower of snow and ice crystals that flew up as the engines went into reverse to slow our progress along this unusual runway. Resolute Airport was a single runway, bordered by snow ridges at the edges, with a single terminal hut at one end.

After leaving the aircraft we entered the hut with our fellow passengers, who were now wearing their Arctic coats, all blazoned with a variety of big name high profile sponsors badges, that made our legal stationers' singular patch look very small-scale. Posters adorned the walls in English and Inuit, all warning travellers not to approach polar bears under the dramatic title of 'Warning! Death Lurks Nearby'. Another poster showed a picture of the Polaris Mine base, which we would pass on skidoo during our route to the pole. A ship was shown in the mine's harbour floating in a still, blue sea that looked positively Caribbean.

Pen, who had travelled ahead of us to Resolute, appeared, and a round of handshakes, smiles and cheers ensued. He presented himself in a large red smock and black trousers – there was no Breton cap on his head this time. Finally we were all together at 75 degrees north. Pen introduced us to Terry, the owner of the Resolute High Arctic Hotel, where we would be staying. We collected our bags before driving the short journey down the road from the airport to the hamlet of Resolute Bay, whose population was just under two hundred, of which about half were Inuit.

Resolute Bay is located on the south west coast of Cornwallis Island and is surrounded by the frozen waters of the North West Passage. It is the second most northern Canadian community, Grise Fjord being the most northern, just over two hundred miles further north. 'Resolute is not the end of the world, but you can see it from here,' the saying goes.

Resolute Bay takes its name from HMS Resolute, one of the nineteenth century ships that searched for the lost Franklin expedition in the mid 1800's and wintered there for one year. The area was first surveyed by Sir William Parry in 1819 – though the settlement has only been in existence since 1947 when it was set up as a weather station and airfield. Inuit from the surrounding areas of Pond Inlet, Port Harrison and Quebec were moved there by the Canadian government to populate it, to some extent to stop the Americans laying claim to the territory. The area around Resolute Bay has been known as a hunting ground for some centuries and evidence of an Inuit settlement has been found in the immediate area dating back to 1200 AD.

Resolute Bay has now become an important staging post for the Magnetic North Pole, as well as Geographic North Pole, expeditions. For many years it was the headquarters for the Polar Shelf Operation of Canada which carries out ocean research. Now the tiny airport services the Polaris Mine which, located just over seventy miles further north is the highest latitude zinc and lead mine in the world.

We reached the hotel, after a brief drive on the only road, but we were thankful for the ride, as I looked across the barren wasteland between the airstrip and the hamlet. The large, but old and battered, American four-wheel drive we were using pulled up outside the hotel. On arrival we jumped out into the cold. Pen parked the truck and then took an electrical lead from under the car's bonnet and plugged it into the hotel wall. This powered a small heater that kept the engine from freezing when it was off, an unusual but necessary accessory in this extreme environment.

The hotel was a prefabricated building, like all buildings in Resolute Bay. It looked like every other building, not being particularly welcoming and entirely functional. It had an exterior covered in snow and ice, and paintwork that was chipped and bleached, after years of being ravaged by the Arctic weather.

We entered the hotel through a battered outer door caked in ice, and stepped into a different world. The heat of the room was both overwhelming and welcoming. The floor was laid with the deepest pile carpet I had ever seen. Once we had removed our shoes Terry, the hotel owner, invited us to sit down and offered us a hot drink. We swam through the glorious shag pile, pushing our cold toes into the depths of its pile as Terry assigned our bedrooms. The main reception area was square with a library of polar books on one side, and pictures of all sorts of polar places and people adorned the walls. Doors off to each side of the living room led to the bedrooms where guests shared two or four to a room.

After our introduction to where things were, and saying hello to a few of the other residents, followed by a welcoming warm cup of tea, we decided to take a quick wander outside. Having sat for the best part of two days, and although early evening, our body clocks told us it was the middle of the night, we decided that we needed to go outside to have a stretch and get a view of our new surroundings.

With an average yearly temperature of -16°C in Resolute, the sea is usually frozen over, or at best ice strewn even in the short summer months. In the height of the summer much of the snow withdraws from the island, leaving dirty brown bare ground where little grows. In the summer of 1962 a record high temperature of +18°C was recorded, four years later a record low of -52°C was recorded during the winter of 1966. It is a town of extremes and was described by British polar explorer David Hempleman-Adams simply as 'Hell on earth'. It would be interesting to see what sort of people lived here – was this somewhere the residents had escaped from the world to? Or somewhere where the world had left them?

We escaped the warm, but by now suffocating, heat of the hotel and plunged into the other extreme outside. The hotel was surrounded by a hamlet of about forty buildings. Occasionally someone would dart from one building to another. Beacon Hill overlooked the settlement. The sky was by now beginning to darken, although the sun never actually sank below the horizon at that time of year. It was a strange place with a real 'one horse town' feel about it. Most of the buildings were wooden bungalows covered in layers of ice, with the obligatory wall of blown snow stacked up hard against the leeward side.

Many houses were painted green or yellow, to make a break from the sterile white surroundings. Some of the houses had battered four-wheel drives or skidoos sitting outside. Telegraph poles marked the small snow-covered track that twisted through the tiny community, where telephone numbers were only three digits long. Various oil drums, pallets and other assorted items covered in snow surrounded most of the houses.

'So, what does everyone think?' Mark asked inquisitively, his breath forming a light steam in front of his face as he spoke. We surveyed our new surroundings. A variety of responses came back to him: 'Let's get the next plane home.'; 'Don't think much of the night life,' to the more predictable. 'Frightfully cold, what?' concluded by Geoff. 'Frightfully cold?! – I'm fucking freezing!' gasped Peter with red .cheeks and rubbing his hands. At this last point Mark held his hands up and shouted, 'Look chaps, let's have no annoying 'I'm cold'. It *is* cold, we know it's cold. Discussions about the cold are off the menu until we get home, okay?!' Everyone agreed. What started as a joke could begin to dampen spirits, and the temperature that dare not speak its name was banished south. The first snowball, or ice ball, was launched immediately after Rob asked, 'Mark, could I just borrow your gloves then please?'

We wandered through the hamlet, which was generally still and quiet. As we walked past each house I wondered how the inhabitants found themselves living this far north. Many of the houses had large fur balls outside, that on approach would reveal a watchful eye as we went past. The local dogs had to keep warm outside. They weren't pets after all, but working dogs built for this environment. The husky dog had joined man when he arrived from Asia via the Bering land bridge around ten to twenty thousand years ago. Many Arctic communities did not allow any other breed of dog, to ensure the husky blood remained pure. Occasionally, it was known for a polar bear to wander through the hamlet, and the dogs would offer a good warning of this – before the inhabitants would come out to kill and then skin the bear. Each dog eyed us suspiciously as we walked past. None of us made a move to go over and pat them as you might ordinarily do on seeing a dog. These dogs were hard, like their owners, and tethered on large steel chains that clinked when they moved in the still air.

We soon met a couple of kids who were playing outside with a large black dog, which I supposed was some sort of husky. The dog looked rather gruesome so our chat to the boys was brief. Peter noticed that another dog was following us at about twenty feet distance. It looked particularly mangy, and I didn't fancy it coming much closer. It was difficult to know whether it was someone's pride and joy or whether it might end up in the pot as food for the other dogs.

We wandered towards a small church, which stood out with its green roof, and looked typical of small, corrugated roofed churches that existed all over the world. It was comforting to know that God visited even this desolate place. A nearby signpost directed us to the North Pole, alongside other major cities that were listed, including balmy Mexico City, quoted as being some three-thousand miles south.

Just as we decided to call it an evening and go back for tea and warm up a bit, Geoff took an almighty slip. His half somersault would have made many a circus artist proud. He landed with a great thump that seemed to shatter the stillness of the evening. He looked slightly ridiculous once we all noticed that he was wearing his Oxford brogues. Shoes that would have been the perfect attire in any merchant bank in the City of London, but a very dangerous combination of soft leather on ice here. Before we could make light of the situation Geoff moaned that he was hurt, which actually sent more of a cold shiver down our spines than the -25°C ambient air temperature. He hadn't broken a leg, but would likely have a decent bruise on his hip, as a souvenir of Resolute. We soon had him up and he hobbled back to the hotel to nurse himself.

After a good meal back at the hotel, Pen arrived. Our equipment had been placed into a garage, where we could unpack properly and prepare tomorrow. We all congregated around a table where he spread a large map of our route. Pen took us through the route again. There was a moment of silence when he unexpectedly stated, 'We are going to have to change the route. There are reports of thin ice, caused by strong currents, at the top of Bathurst Island. It may be dangerous, and more likely time-consuming, to try and navigate around the thin ice, and possibly large pressure ridges with the skidoos, so I'm changing the route.'

His finger moved across the map from the top of Bathurst Island to the middle of it. 'We are now going to go across Bathurst Island via Polar Pear Pass.' This sounded like bad news, and raised all my fears of the previous months. It was around the entrance to Polar Bear Pass that Helen Thayer had had trouble from bears stalking her. It is one of the routes these animals travel (hence the name) across the island. Indeed there were so many bears in the area that an observation post had been setup in the Pass to watch their movements. But to actually travel through Polar Bear Pass and spend the night in the lair! I swallowed hard at the thought.

We spent another hour going over the chart, details of kit, and the outline for tomorrow, when we would spend the day packing and checking equipment before sleeping in the tent overnight as final acclimatisation before leaving the next day. 'Get a good night's sleep tonight gentlemen in your soft, warm beds,' were Pen's parting words as tired, a little excited, but not quite ready for sleep, we retired.

The next morning my eyes slowly opened, bringing me from the depths of my sleep as the world around me came into focus. I sleepily made out a bright light streaming through the curtains. 'This isn't my home,' my awakening brain thought before I realised, on drawing back the curtains, that I was in Resolute – the ice on the *inside* of the window confirmed this. It wasn't a dream after all, I *was* going to the North Magnetic Pole. At this hour of the day Resolute's Inuit name of *Qausuittug* which meant 'place with no dawn' became apparent – it was bright all the time, dawn didn't make an appearance here.

Geoff was still asleep, his feet sticking out of the end of the standard size bed as his tall frame overflowed it. My watch told me it was early, four a.m. Canadian time. The silence around me was disturbed by a buzzing sound coming through the thin walls from the next room. I then remembered that I had heard this sound most of the night. Someone next door obviously had a computer and was using a modem to send information across a telephone line.

It wasn't long before sounds of movement were emanating from other rooms as the newly arrived people awoke fresh from their time-zone jumping flight into the Canadian morning. Not being able to get back to sleep and not wanting to queue for a shower I was soon up. Motioning to Geoff as he awoke from his slumber I headed towards the shower. The door of my neighbour's room was ajar and I could make out a room crammed with computers and cameras struggling to compete for space in the small confines.

I spent longer in the shower than normal, taking the time to enjoy each warm drop of water as it ran over me. Many polar explorers stop washing a week or two before they get on the ice, allowing a thin layer of insulating body oil to build up on their skin. I found that the final hot shower was more enjoyable for me, before I entered the cold wastes.

Soon the place was buzzing as the newly arrived people began to wake up and make for the breakfast room. The residents of the High Arctic Hotel were lured by the magic of the Arctic from all corners of the Earth. British, Dutch, French, American and Japanese were all present. We sat down and began to chat, as strangers do when they are away from big cities. A few complaints about the noise coming from my neighbour during the night were voiced.

My neighbour – Dave, was a free-lance photographer on assignment who had travelled up to cover the David Hempleman-Adams expedition to the North Geographic Pole. On hearing the complaints he apologised and admitted the noise was caused by him. Dressed in an expedition top with slouched trousers and fluffy socks he looked more settled than the rest of us. He explained that he wired his photos via computer to the London newspapers. This meant sending them through the night.

On mentioning his sponsor's name the tone changed and his audience became more interested in Hempleman-Adams's progress. The British adventurer was out on the ice attempting to get to the North Geographic Pole unsupported, with the Norwegian marine Rune Gjeldnes.

Hempleman-Adams was very well respected in the adventure business, although he was not a household name yet like his contemporary, Sir Ranulph Fiennes. Hempleman-Adams had successfully walked alone and unsupported to the South Pole, and was one of only a handful of climbers to have climbed the highest mountain on every continent. Dave the photographer again apologised for last night's noise but explained that this was due to him covering a story of a lone British adventurer having a lucky escape from death.

The traveller in question, Alan Bywaters, whilst attempting to walk to the North Geographic Pole alone and unsupported, had fallen through thin ice into the freezing sea. He had managed to pull himself out, and as the water began to freeze his clothes solid he realised that death was not far away, particularly as his equipment was now sinking to the sea bed some two miles below. Miraculously, among the frozen ice floes he found a set of footprints which he followed, after some hours they led him to Hempleman-Adams tent, where he collapsed outside suffering from hypothermia. Adams and Gjeldnes brought him in and managed to warm him up with soup and lying either side of him to share their body heat. They saved his life. Bywaters was then rescued from the ice by plane. He would live, and luckily would likely keep all his frost-bitten appendages.

Dave the photographer had travelled up on the rescue plane to get an exclusive on the story. The room was by now quiet with all around the table putting their breakfast to one side and listening to the latest news. Now Dave had everyone's attention he explained in his strong south London accent that 'Adams was furious over the episode. It meant looking after Bywaters for a couple of days waiting for good weather so the rescue plane could land,' he explained. This could have affected Hempleman-Adams's own chances of reaching the Pole, as during this period of inactivity as nurse-maids with Bywaters, the ice was flowing back to the shore from where they had begun and away from the Pole, to say nothing of the carefully rationed fuel they had used in keeping Bywaters warm.

The arrival of the rescue plane also potentially compromised their unsupported status. Many of the guests around me were heading up to the North Pole in various expeditions, so were concerned for the man, but were also looking for clues as to what the ice conditions were like.

Dave had been in Resolute for some four weeks now and was bored to tears. 'Anyone got any drink?' he requested in a half begging fashion, as befits a man locked in a dry hamlet without any form of entertainment. No one had, but it was worth the attempt. He had been head photographer for a major UK newspaper, liked the lights and the big city stories – so being up here in Resolute was initially unique, but now seemed like a major punishment. I'd never met a professional photographer before so we had a quick chat. 'You can't learn it,' he enthused, 'You've got it or you 'aint,' said the man who had turned professional at seventeen. He wasn't wild about the hotel being full up now, because he used the communal bath to develop his prints.

The Dutch were the main group going for the North Pole. Already up there in addition to Hempleman-Adams was Pen's women's polar relay team, and a Japanese man supporting an explorer attempting the crossing from Siberia.

We all ate breakfast to full capacity, not knowing when we might be eating next. After breakfast and it still being early, our group went for another walk around Resolute. The temperature outside was 'about twenty five' according to the cook. That meant twenty five below freezing. It was never necessary to say 'minus' when quoting temperatures in Resolute as this was assumed. It was very still and quiet outside, and I suspected that this was always the case in Resolute and not due to the early time of the morning.

Peter, Bunny and Geoff decided to walk up Beacon Hill, which overlooked the settlement. I took a quick walk around with my camera, taking photos of the school, the church, and from a very safe distance various husky dogs who, though chained to the ground outside their masters' houses, always kept one cautious eye on me. I met Bunny and Peter about an hour later and captured on camera their now quite red faces sitting, under their blond hair and ice-strewn hoods. We made our way back to the hotel, pausing to take a photo of a mileage sign that declared the North Pole to be one thousand and eighty six miles away, with my home city of London over three thousand five hundred miles to the south east.

Back at the hotel we had only just got changed into our indoor clothes again when Pen turned up. He quickly said good morning to Terry, the hotel owner, (and widow of a famous Arctic traveller), before motioning to us to get our stuff. It wasn't long before we were all attempting to climb into Pen's borrowed and battered four-wheel drive. Luckily for us it was American and therefore so much bigger than its European counterpart, big enough to fit all seven of us into the cab, with all our equipment stowed in the back. The four litre engine coughed, then growled into life, and after a moment's pause we jerked forward onto the ice-covered road. Resolute was still quiet, though to be honest I could not imagine it ever being anything else. The growl of our engine shattering the silence only caused the odd sleeping husky to open a tired eye.

After circling the hamlet we arrived at 'The Rookery', Pen's headquarters in Resolute and so named after Penguin Biscuits, the sponsor of his women's North Pole relay team that was currently on the ice. The Rookery was a large insulated shed on the outskirts of town. It had a feel akin to Captain Scott's Antarctic base, with a large Union Jack on the wall, four bunk beds to one side, skis and skiing equipment in various states of maintenance seemingly all over the place, and a map of the far north with progress lines drawn over it.

There was no deep pile carpet, just an insulated wooden floor. Every now and again there would be a buzzing noise from one of the rooms with the muffled voices of radio communications bouncing across the Arctic airwaves. Pen's two assistants Nobby and Mike introduced themselves, both with accents to match Pen's. Mike was a yacht sailor and well over six feet tall. Nobby occasionally wore glasses, that together with his slighter frame gave him a bookish appearance.

Pen gathered us all around. 'Right, firstly I'm going to give you your kit, namely outer jackets and boots, then we'll attend to your smocks.' At this statement both Nobby and Mike jumped up as we took our smocks off. Pen had purchased some real black bear fur in Canada to line the outside of our hoods. Synthetic materials were not as good as genuine fur as they tended to catch the moisture in your breath which would then freeze, thus clouding visibility. The bear fur didn't suffer this and Mike and Nobby soon had the sewing machine running and attached the fur to the hoods of the smocks. They also sewed on the sponsor's patches to our jackets. These had fallen off as we arrived at Resolute as the glue lost its tackiness in the cold conditions. As this activity was going on in the background Pen gave us a quick tour of the Rookery, his HQ. He showed us where the tea and coffee facility was, the water, and of course told us to take as many Penguin biscuits as needed as they were placed everywhere in large amounts, having been provided by their generous manufacturer.

Once we got to the toilet he demonstrated a most peculiar device. As storing waste materials was difficult this far north, as drain pipes would freeze and pumps would be needed to move the effluent away from Resolute, he simply didn't bother. All waste materials were vaporised in his toilet! He demonstrated with a couple of tea bags. As they went down the steel loo, he flicked a switch, closed the lid and the whole unit made a humming noise. This noise increased until there was a loud 'whoosh!' by which time the heat had built up to such an extent it completely vaporised the contents. Everyone was amazed by this, but Pen countered by saying if you were just going for a pee it was simpler to go outside. This device was immediately named the 'Hell Hole' for obvious reasons.

When the noise of the sewing machines stopped Mike and Nobby reappeared, this time with two large cardboard boxes. One box contained boots, the other down jackets. Soon we were all lying on the floor trying on the different sizes of boots. These were known as *Mukluks* – Inuit for boots. They were the modern version of Mukluks, made of cloth and polystyrene, and had thick rubber soles to stop the cold getting through to our feet. As there was no leather to break in and the boot was very pliable there was never any worry about blisters. They were also rated down to -100°C, which was very comforting to know.

The down jackets were synthetic rather than stuffed with the feathers of the eiderdown bird. Whilst eiderdown feathers were regarded as the best insulator, they could become difficult to keep dry, and wetness was always one of the greatest fears for any polar traveller, knowing anything wet would soon freeze solid.

After another cup of tea the final preparation began and we gathered around a workbench in the Rookery. Pen showed everyone how to use the communications equipment. We were taking two devices, a radio and an Argos beacon. The Argos would be used each evening to transmit a set code, our latitude and longitude position, and the current temperature. The codes would be manually set by us and each code would mean something different. For example, 00 – 'All well', 01 – 'evacuation urgent'.

Twenty different messages had been coded that we could transmit without uttering a word. The radio was much simpler to use but required the use of an aerial and needed better atmospheric conditions to be able to send and receive. Thus the two devices complemented each other. Our call sign on the radio would be 'Resolute 269' so as to quickly identify us from other expeditions operating all over the Arctic. Mike and Nobby would man the radio at set periods of the day back at the Rookery, our base camp, and we arranged to speak with them every other night at seven p.m. Resolute time. We also alerted the airport at Resolute to our identity, as they would serve as a backup to our own radio operators.

Pen's lecture moved onto defence. The room took on a more serious atmosphere as he brought out a very large but old-looking rifle. Mark gasped at the sight of it – 'Are we hunting elephant, Pen?!' Before Pen could answer Rob stated, 'That's large enough to be a danger to small aircraft.'

'This is only to be used in extreme emergencies,' announced Pen sternly.

Pen also stated that he would be the only one to use the gun, for safety reasons, even though many in the team had adequate shooting experience. I felt comfortable that the weapon was adequate protection against a gang of lawyers. He outlined our polar bear procedure, which was basically to stand together – to create a larger shape, and make as much noise as possible by shouting and banging pans. Pen explained that most polar bears had never seen a man before, but were very inquisitive animals. He described this by comparing them to the way sharks are sometimes thought of. For example, they sometimes don't intentionally kill people, but knowing that they'd take an investigatory chunk out of you to find out what you were, wouldn't really make you feel any better.

Bears also knew little fear because they were the master of their territory, and have no competitors apart from man and other polar bears. Pen underlined this by describing how he was once on an ice-breaking ship that had stopped in the ice when a polar bear made a bee-line for the vessel. The bear was not at all intimidated by the size of the ship, walked up to it and hit it its steel side hard with its paw, as if to say 'get out of my way.' Truly a powerful creature with an ego that would probably humble even most lawyers.

He described the best angle to shoot a bear: basically kneeling down and aiming to shoot into its chest, just under its nose, so the bullet would pierce its rib cage, killing it. It wasn't really advisable to wound a bear, as a wounded bear on the rampage would be very frightening and dangerous. Given the thickness of its skull it was possible, apparently, for a bullet to be deflected from its head – so aiming correctly was very important. Also in the unlikely event that we had to kill a bear, the expedition would have to stop and the authorities be alerted. The authorities would then send someone out to us to ensure that we had had no option but to kill the animal. 'Unless you basically have claw marks down your face,' Pen explained, 'this would be very difficult to prove.'

The reason for this was that the Inuit had a certain number of bears that they could legitimately kill each year, and often they would sell the permission to do so to other people (usually Americans). Such a big game activity could command tens of thousands of dollars hence it was necessary to ensure that every Tom, Dick and Harry wasn't blasting away, saying that they were in mortal danger.

Pen stressed again that taking a shot really was the last option, and that he had never had to fire on a bear in all his years in the polar regions. If you had to shoot, it would usually be to kill, because the sound of a warning shot might not frighten the bear away as cracking ice made a similar and familiar sound and was therefore unlikely to deter it.

Pen's lecture went on to cover emergency procedures and we all listened intently. As well as the radio and Argos, we would carry an emergency device called an EPERB. Should this be triggered it would send an internationally recognised distress signal that would be picked up by airliners flying over the pole. They in turn would alert the emergency services who would race to our rescue.

'Make no mistake everyone, this should only be used in dire circumstances – major haemorrhaging, or generally expected loss of life. Once that beacon goes off all hell breaks out and the EPERB can't be switched off,' said Pen. The resulting cost of a rescue had no upper limit and could easily come to quarter of a million dollars. Pen placed the pin securely back in the device, and looked into each of our eyes in turn to ensure we understood and would comply. No games now, 'Only in dire circumstances,' he reiterated.

We then moved onto testing our outdoor equipment, with Pen lighting up the camp stove on the bench. Mark was named as cook, for which there was no challenger. Mark loved his food and we would all benefit from his culinary skills being applied to the variety of freeze dried food that we would be living off. Lighting the stove was more difficult than expected because the fuel had to be pumped up to pressurise it, and just enough fuel let out into a collector before a match was applied to ignite it. Mark stood back as Geoff willingly showed us how it shouldn't be done, as a huge flame spewed out into the room, to everyone's surprise and alarm, given the small size of the equipment.

Finally the major pieces of equipment, skis, poles, and sledges (known as 'pulks'), were given out. With so much kit around the three-room Rookery it was now very cramped. Each person was nominated a colour and coded their equipment with plastic tape in their designated colour so that they could quickly identify what was theirs. Speed was important in the Arctic as no one wanted to mess around in the cold trying to work out if, for example, the almost identical white skis outside the tent were their white skis for their white boots, or someone else's.

We checked our skis to ensure that they were the correct length for our height. They were Norwegian armed forces skis, and had special bindings to work with the soft Mukluk boots.

Pen issued each of us with two long adhesive strips of synthetic seal skin, each two inches wide, one strip to be applied to the underside of each ski. This would give the ski some grip when walking on the flat ice. We would after all each be pulling a fair weight over mainly flat ground rather than down hill Alpine skiing.

The next thirty minutes were spent skiing outside the Rookery, making sure our bindings fitted correctly and pulling our pulks for the first time. As the pulks were empty they easily bounced along behind, occasionally trying to overtake us or banging into our heels. Each pulk was about six feet long, with a hard fibre glass bottom and two runners underneath. The top part of the pulk had a cloth cover with a zip that ran the length of the pulk to enable access to the contents.

In these pulks we would be hauling everything that we needed to survive: tent, stove, food, fuel, blow up plastic sheep, communications equipment and so on. No kitchen sinks though.

We took the pulks over to a larger shed where Pen introduced us to Gary, 'My right hand man, and a major Mister Fix-it.' Despite all the leg-pulling, everyone had the highest regard for Pen and so our respect for Pen immediately spread to Gary, given Pen's introduction. Gary lived in Resolute and his house was next door to the Rookery. He worked at the power station that provided heat and light to the settlement. He also organised everything for the Polar Travel Company when Pen wasn't around, taking in supplies and generally making sure everything ran smoothly.

Speaking in his soft Canadian accent, Gary introduced us to the Bombardier 375 skidoo. We would use the skidoos for the first 2 to 3 days of the expedition to get us quickly over the first two-hundred and seventy miles of the route, to the northern tip of Bathurst Island. We would then sledge the remaining one-hundred and twenty nautical miles to the pole.

The skidoo had a long flat seat that was large enough to take two passengers. It had two skis at the front, an engine in the middle, and a large caterpillar track at the back under the seat. It was controlled by a pair of handlebars similar to those found on a motor bike. The caterpillar track drove the vehicle forward. These machines had had a major impact on Inuit life, with a four-day hunting trip now being able to be carried out in a single day, due to the hunter now driving to his hunting ground at up to 40 mph on the skidoo.

We would have four skidoos on the expedition: three two-seaters and a smaller, lighter, single-seater for Pen. Pen would use his lighter, more manoeuvrable skidoo to scout in front of the convoy and look for ways through the ice. Each of the three larger skidoos would pull a large wooden sledge, called a komatik. The komatik would contain all our equipment including the pulks that we would use when on foot later in the expedition. Pen was the pathfinder and we were the juggernauts, following behind.

These large cargo sledges, or komatiks ,were very heavy and made entirely of wood. The wood gave them a flexibility that modern plastics or metals could not offer in this environment. Interestingly, wood was as foreign a material as plastic this far north with both materials having to be imported. The komatiks were lashed together with nails and rope and each one would be pulled by a skidoo. They had a large central box, big enough for a man to sit in, where most things would be stored, and two long runners to guide them along the ice. There was space in front of and behind the central box of the komatik for extra storage. Jerry cans of diesel were loaded in plus the other paraphernalia for the expedition.

The silence of the settlement was broken by the wail of three skidoos all starting up on Gary's cue. Clouds of white exhaust rose into the atmosphere and the air was filled with the sweet, thick, smell of diesel. We broke into our pairs and roared off, to become familiar with the vehicles. Peter and I enthusiastically tested the speed and stopping power. I managed to turn the skidoo over and pull the windshield out of place – these vehicles were not as stable as I had imagined. After fifteen minutes we formed a convoy and were joined by Pen on his scout skidoo whereupon we all followed him out onto the sea ice. The start of the sea ice was marked by an almost invisible crack, separating the sea ice from ice covering the island from the beach.

The sea ice was as hard as concrete and the skidoo's suspension offered no absorbance as we bounced along. We drew up with the front of our skidoos pointing towards a small iceberg, which was stuck in the ice, now unable to move until the middle of the summer thaw. As our engines stopped, the deafening Arctic silence returned again, Pen continued the lessons. 'Don't go too close,' he pointed at the motionless iceberg. 'The sea current rocks the iceberg from underneath so the ice can get soft around its edge. Get too close and you could fall through.'

The moon was behind the 'berg, which added to the eeriness of the landscape that was still bathed in the full light of an Arctic evening. 'This is the sort of place where you might see a polar bear,' Pen announced. 'Broken ice reveals sea water, water means seals, seals mean bears.' Another reason not to get too close to an iceberg.

We continued on until we were all very comfortable with handling the skidoos, taking them over small ridges, a variety of bumps, and some soft snow. We turned and left the sea ice. Because of the cold air and the added wind chill caused by our velocity, we were all sinking into our jackets in the frozen air which was looking for any weakness in our covering. Our breath quickly froze in the cold air and soon even my balaclava, especially around the mouth, was frozen solid as all the moisture from my breath trapped there turned to frosty concrete-like ice.

Back at the Rookery, we prepared the equipment that we needed to spend our first night outside. Staying outside for a night would serve as a final test of our equipment before we moved away from the settlement and onto the Pole. The tea machine and Hell Hole were in full operation. Each time we left the warmth of the Rookery the cold air took our breath away.

The expedition would use one large tent, and we erected it not far from the Rookery. It was important that everyone had a job to do, not only to get the tent erected quickly but to avoid standing around, since anything less than full activity meant getting cold very quickly. To achieve this, routine was all important, which meant the organisation had to work smoothly.

Peter and I crawled under the tent which was lying flat on the ground. We crawled in the tent and held it up from the inside, so the others could work underneath us to put the poles in place and lift the roof. Bunny was soon inside the newly erected tent with the snow brush, brushing out any snow from the floor so it did not turn to water later when the cooker was operating and heating the tent. Mark zoomed in and got the cooker started before Peter and I exited and placed snow around the valance to keep out the wind and secured the guy ropes into the ice via ice screws. Rob was caught not doing anything for a moment, and Peter and I looked at him with suspicion. He simply replied to our cold stares from behind our goggles with 'I'm, err, overseeing this,' before disappearing, slightly embarrassed, into the tent.

The more organised we were the quicker things ran, when they didn't run like clockwork we all got cold, very quickly. No one could stand around for more than a couple of minutes without something freezing, so when we got going it was a big hive of frantic, exaggerated activity.

Any period of inactivity produced a strange sequence that we named the 'ice dance'. The arms would swing round and round in wide circles, forcing the blood back into the hands. The feet would stamp up and down forcing the blood back into the toes. Each person had their own slight variation of this technique, but it worked and every single person, even Pen, hardly went an hour without spending time on the icy dance floor.

Various shouts and orders kept the operation moving, 'Where's this?', 'Where's that?', 'Bunny! A spoon please.' The cooker fizzed and spluttered before beginning its more rhythmic roar. Soon everyone congregated inside as the air began to warm. Setting up the tent and stove had been slightly disorganised, but it was a good effort for our first time in our real environment.

As the evening wore on the sun began to sink, and turned the sky from a bright blue to a reddish hue, which reflected off the ice, reducing its harsh colour. The temperature also dropped to approximately 'thirty'. The stars pushed themselves through the night. The Hale-Bopp comet was blazing above us, and while this world-wide phenomenon was also visible in the day, it commanded much more of the sky in the fading light.

The sleeping bags were moved into the tent, occupying most of the space inside. There wasn't going to be much room for us, but it would do. It was clear that we would all be in bed early, for once activity stopped, the cold attacked, and the best place to be was in a sleeping bag. Mark cooked up some great stew and we began our first night under the stars with the sun still on the horizon. After wrestling for space – 'Do you mind? Your knee is in my face,' and 'That's not my knee, that's my foot,' – we all slowly but surely fell asleep.

I woke early in the morning to find that the inside of the tent had been delicately painted with ice and frost. There was a particularly thick piece of ice along the back wall of the tent, that looked like a small waterfall had been frozen in mid-torrent. There was a light sprinkling of snow all over the sleeping bags and their occupants' face masks. It was still bright, due to the never-setting sun at that time of year, which managed to cast an orange glow through the tent walls.

I was cold but had nothing to complain of in my sleeping bag, wearing some long johns and a balaclava. My head of course poked out of the bag and exposed itself to the minus thirty air during the night. It was very tempting to bury my head in the sleeping bag completely, but this would have filled the bag with moist air from my breath, which would freeze when the bag was in the pulk on the komatik and eventually affect its insulating property. Each of us would lose almost half a litre of water through our breathing during the night, and this combined moisture had collected on the tent walls, where it had frozen.

We were all beginning to wake at about the same time. 'Could you get your foot out of my face?' - 'It's my knee.' Mark was first up, jumping out of his sleeping bag into the super cooled air. As he moved he created a snow shower inside the tent as his head banged into the roofing. Everyone complained as small snow flakes rained down on them. Given how full the tent was, only one person could get up at a time. Each person quickly launched themselves into the air and, balanced on their sleeping bag to avoid their comrades, as they put on their salopettes, over top, gloves and then boots as quickly as possible.

We each left the comparative warmth of our sleeping bags in a rush to put on our day clothes, without trampling on our complaining tent companions, before we froze. When I had put on my clothes, I left the tent and was blasted by the Arctic light. It was an intense bright light, blue, pure, and despite the air temperature, made me welcome the day, as my lungs filled with what must be some of the cleanest air on Earth. It was intoxicating. After packing the tent away we retreated to Pen's Rookery for hot tea and muesli. Pen assigned to each of us final jobs for the morning as we prepared to leave.

The remaining pieces in the puzzle were put together, and with our camping experience of the previous night still fresh in our minds we focussed on the small details that would make everyone's lives quicker and more comfortable during the trip. As Mark put it, 'According to an old soldier's saying, any idiot can be uncomfortable.' How true that was.

Back at the Rookery, and with the map out, we went over the route one last time. Pen gave us the latest weather report from a satellite image which we all peered over to see whether we could determine where was good and bad ice, or solid or broken ice. Pen was still determined that we would go through Polar Bear Pass.

We all set about our final jobs. Each person gathered their own equipment. These were then loaded onto the komatiks. Each person went about their jobs, returning to the Rookery to get more instruction from Pen. All the coming and going caused the handle on the Rookery's entrance door to become a bit loose, which Nobby quickly rectified.

One by one, as we each completed our tasks outside, we congregated in the warmth of the Rookery. The tea machine was in full swing, with the occasional whoosh of the Hell Hole sounding in the background.

'All done Peter?'

'All done boss.'

'That fuel all loaded Rob?'

'All measured and loaded Pen. No smoking near my sledge chaps, ok!'

'Where's Bunny?'

'In here Pen, putting my final thoughts down the pan,' came Bunny's chuckling voice from behind the modesty curtain hiding the Hell Hole. There was then a soft whoosh – not the usual deep vacuum sound generated by the Hell Hole, but a much softer, almost apologetic, whimper – before the lights flickered twice and then, after what seemed a long pause, went out altogether. Despite the brilliant sunlight streaming through the ice strewn windows of the Rookery, the hut was plunged into darkness. The temporary silence that always follows any power loss was broken with Bunny nervously muttering, 'Have I just done something wrong?'

Within moments a curtain of very hot air, with an overpowering smell of acrid burning seemed to visibly drive itself across the room, to contaminate the whole Rookery. Powered by the half vaporised contents of the Hell Hole it was truly overwhelming. The Hell Hole was well named. Peter was first to the outside door, wildly pulling at it, only to discover that Nobby's door handle fix had actually somehow locked everyone in! He turned, about to explain this before the next desperate person attempting to leave pushed him aside before they too discovered the same problem. With no exit everyone then charged, coughing and spluttering, back the other way to the Hell Hole to see what could be done at that end, ignoring Bunny's embarrassment as he sat on the pan in the darkness. With hands over our mouths each of us desperately yanked at the flushing system, but to no avail.

Moments later Geoff appeared behind us all. 'Crumbs! what's that awful stench?!' as the wall of musty heat hit him almost instantly.

'Geoffrey where have you come from?!' demanded Rob.

'Err, just come in from outside, where else?' replied Geoff, somewhat surprised by what seemed to be a stupid question. 'What the hell *is* that smell?' he demanded again.

'I thought the door wasn't working?' wailed Rob.

'It isn't,' Peter protested, seconded by Mark. Just as they answered, Gary opened the door and walked in. Everyone, all in unison, all determining what the problem was at the same time, shouted, 'Don't shut the door!'

Too late – Gary was in and had closed the door behind him. He too was then involuntarily and automatically forced to express his revulsion at the stench that he had just walked into. 'Nobby your bloody door fix lets people in but not out!' cried one disgusted traveller from the darkness.

The expedition couldn't leave and would probably quickly die, due to the stench and heat produced by the Hell Hole. Not a noble end, or even start, for the 1997 Oyez Solicitors Polar Expedition.

Fortunately, the door handle was soon sorted out – it had to be before the occupants broke the door down. Power was restored, and Bunny's contribution to the atmosphere was vaporised and sent to hell for a second time.

7

At last, the Ice

*'Polar exploration is at once the cleanest and most
isolated way of having a bad time which has been
developed.'*

APSLEY CHERRY-GARRARD, POLAR EXPLORER.

F inally, at eleven o'clock we all left the Rookery, cheered by Nobby, Mike
and Gary, who waved a Union Jack vigorously to see us off, its warm
red colour cutting through the frosty air. We waved back in exaggerated
motions to our well-wishers.

Earlier we had organised ourselves into pairs, so that there were two
riders to each skidoo, with Pen riding his skidoo alone and pulling a smaller
and much lighter komatik. Each pair of riders mounted their skidoo, which
pulled a large wooden komatik containing our sledges, skiing equipment,
fuel and survival provisions. We were all fully clothed in preparation for the
temperature to drop significantly, caused by the added wind chill once we
began racing over the ice on the skidoos.

Mark had a particularly smart all-in-one plastic suit, which would deflect
the wind, covering his purple mountaineering suit. I had on not one, but
two down jackets – the main one and the one rejected by Pen as not warm
enough. We each had on three pairs of gloves, two balaclavas and a set of ski

goggles to protect our eyes from the cold wind and the glare from the ice. It was now that we realised when Pen told us months ago that our prized kit was 'unsuitable' that he had been right – this was no place to be mucking about with your health with inferior equipment. The Arctic would not be forgiving of anyone's mistakes.

Almost immediately as soon as we took off on the skidoo my fingers froze, and my soft velvety balaclava quickly became as stiff as thick cardboard as the moisture in my breath froze it solid. It wasn't long before an impressive icicle began to develop on the outside of my balaclava, hanging down from my mouth area like a strange fang. I shivered under the multiple layers of clothing and found my head recoiling into my neck, and that in turn towards my chest as I sunk down into warmer clothing.

As we left the Rookery Pen pulled out ahead on his skidoo, followed by the three skidoo teams – Mark and Bunny, Peter and myself, then Rob and Geoff. Pen rode alone and with his lighter komatik, it enabled him to speed ahead when necessary to search for the best way through the ice, as the heavier convoy of skidoos and komatiks followed his chosen path.

I was first to drive and Peter decided that rather than ride on the pannier behind me he would sit in the komatik, out of the wind, and on an upturned sledge which would be more comfortable. The weather was good, with clear skies giving excellent visibility. Pen stated it was 'a tad under thirty' as we began our journey.

We headed west from Resolute Bay over the moon-like barren landscape, white, featureless and with soft rounded hills in the distance. We soon moved off the ice-covered beach of Cornwallis Island and onto flat sea ice, passing the iceberg from the previous evening. We gave it a wide birth to avoid the soft bits around the edge as warned by Pen the night before. We travelled on the sea ice northwards, moving up the various bays towards our first destination, the Polaris Mine, some seventy five miles away.

Just under two hours later we arrived off the coast near Sheringham Point. Pen drove on ahead on his faster skidoo as we slowly travelled behind him, following the trail left in the thin layer of snow covering the ice. The ice in the distance ahead looked jumbled and not as smooth as the flat sea ice that we were travelling on.

Pen soon returned from his recce, circled us, and waved us to slow down. Shouting above the whine of the engines from behind his frost laden balaclava he bellowed, 'We need to hug the coast because the ice off shore is badly ripped up and we'll never get the komatiks through otherwise.' Offshore? It was difficult to make out the islands from our position, and strange to think we were on frozen sea.

Many of the islands in the area were reasonably large but had been ground down over the millennia by huge ice sheets, so that they had little elevation to distinguish them from the surrounding sea ice. Indeed the shape of Bathurst Island, one of the largest islands and lying out to the west, was only determined by aerial observation in 1947. With few recognisable distinguishing features this could make orientation difficult, so in the past the Inuit used to leave stone cairns of different designs called *Inukshuk* on these low and almost identical islands to help them navigate.

The ice got steadily bumpier, causing us to reduce speed. Peter's once comfortable ride in the back of the komatik had changed as a consequence, and he was now forced to hang onto things so as not to be thrown free as we lurched from one frozen wave to another as we approached the coast. Twenty minutes later we were reliably informed by Pen that we were off the sea ice and back on the beach. It was difficult to tell as they were both covered by ice, and offered no way of reliably telling the difference, unless you had the trained eye and local knowledge that Pen possessed.

We continued travelling further north along the flatter beach. The broken ice out to sea which we were bypassing on the beach, was truly awesome. It had been broken and smashed into a thousand different shapes and sizes as the sea's current forced the ice through the narrowing channel separating Cornwallis Island from Bathurst Island. Many ice blocks rose six, ten, twelve feet into the air, their white edges occasionally streaked with crystal blue harder ice.

It was a truly breathtaking scene, and looked very primeval and unwelcoming. It was impossible to determine a way through the ice carnage off the beach let alone drive through so I was glad we were able to travel along the beach. The ice was much less fractured here and we could proceed, albeit slowly. So, here I was on holiday on a beach! It was a different beach than I had been used to – there wasn't a palm tree in sight, no bathing towels or happy bathers splashing in tropical waters. My! what I would have done to get a postcard of this!

It wasn't long before we encountered the first of many hurdles. Our path on the beach gradually got narrower and narrower because blocks of ice, often like large car-sized ice cubes, spilled onto the flatter parts of the frozen white beach. These blocks had advanced up the beach after being pushed by the ice behind them, no doubt forced on by the changing of the tides.

Our path got narrower still. With ice blocks on the sea side and the rising elevation and bank of the beach on the other, we began to feel hemmed in. Often the path between these two constraints was frozen hard, with bumps or ripples forcing us to slow further. Even Pen on his lighter skidoo, which was pulling a much smaller komatik, had slowed to only twice normal walking pace.

The convoy began to spread out so that each skidoo could rev up to gain some speed and hopefully enough momentum to get over a large, rock hard, ripple in the ice, without them ploughing into the skidoo ahead. Now Peter was sitting behind me on the skidoo seat, because he could no longer take being jolted from side to side in the komatik, as we hit each frozen wave of ice. We both rose from the seat in unison, like jockeys jumping a hedge, as we mounted each new ice ridge.

Mark and Bunny were the first to take a tumble. Hitting a piece of ice at the wrong angle, their skidoo almost toppled over before Mark rescued it with an aggressive but direct change of steering direction – which sent them careering down into a dip and immediately into a wall of ice that stopped their skidoo dead, dying with a plumb of roaring diesel-fuelled smoke. The ice was rock hard, like concrete. They couldn't reverse because they were in a shallow dip and had their komatik tightly behind them. I signalled to Rob driving the skidoo behind me to stop, and Pen pulled back to help them. It was a good point for a rest anyway as we were all saddle-sore and cold by now. Flasks of hot drinks and chocolate emerged from a variety of pouches as we all had a quick chat, a couple of rounds of the ice dance, and then surveyed Mark and Bunny's predicament.

After wildly engaging their skidoo's reverse gear which again drove plumes of exhaust smoke into the air, it was clear there was no way the skidoo could reverse out of the dip. Peter and I unhitched our komatik and eventually dragged Mark and Bunny's komatik back out of the dip, enabling them to then reverse their skidoo.

Fifteen minutes later we found that our path was apparently blocked by a five-foot-high ridge of ice, which was rippled with beautiful deep blue streaks and a light dusting of snow on its upper surface. However, our predicament was more of a driving challenge than a dead-end. Pen was first ahead on his skidoo. After angling his charge he carefully manoeuvred onto the ridge and once on drove over it. He confirmed that the path continued on the other side and that there wasn't much of a drop. Just to prove this on reaching the other side there was a muffled 'Next!' shouted from the other side of the ridge over to us, and shortly afterwards an encouraging hand wave as he climbed back over to us.

The rest of us prepared to go over by giving each skidoo and its heavy komatik enough of a run to get over. Bunny and Mark went first, their engine roaring as they went over. Peter and I were next. After checking that everything was still secured in the komatik we approached as fast as I dared, shot over, felt a big bump and then swerved to miss Mark's komatik on the other side. We had made it. Geoff and Rob were next, we heard them rev, then appear slowly over the top of the ridge. The skidoo went over but it wasn't going fast enough to pull the heavy komatik over with them. Rob jumped off to release some weight – and then their engine stalled.

'What happened Geoffrey?' Pen's voice broke the icy air.

'Don't think I watched enough Evel Knievel as a boy!' replied Geoff, laughing from behind his ice-encrusted balaclava as Bunny took the opportunity of the stop to do a round of the ice dance and warm up a bit. The komatik was stuck about half way up the slope, its rope dangled limply attached to the skidoo on the other side. We all gathered round and without instruction positioned ourselves behind the komatik, ready to give it a push, as Geoff started his engine again. The rope went taut and the engine revs soared, as six cold shoulders pushed themselves against the back of the komatik. 'Heave!' The heavy sledge inched forward as Geoff revved the skidoo engine harder. The komatik slowly got to the top of the slope, stopped for a moment and then quickly ran down the other side straight into the back of Geoff's and Rob's skidoo. 'When do we meet the difficult terrain Pen?' shouted Rob. 'Ha, Ha,' Pen swiftly replied.

Over the next hour, we stopped numerous times as our skidoos hit various bumps in the ice and crashed. The icy path on the beach varied from narrow and straight to meandering and strewn with ice boulders. Sometimes the path was flat and smooth, other times it had ice debris cast over it that moved aside when pushed by the skis of the skidoo. On a few occasions there were hard rocks of ice stuck to the surface that waited for us to hit them with the skidoo ski or komatik, whereupon, like small mines, they would either explode under the weight, or wrestle with us and try and tip a vehicle and its driver over.

Often it was necessary to unload most of a komatik contents to release weight and get over a bump. By now we all knew the intricacies of how to handle our individual skidoos. With the weight of the komatik behind them, the skidoos took time to build up their speed. They did not have the reactions of a sports car, more the slower paced, methodical reactions of a bus. This could make things difficult when the 'road' often had little space between obstacles, and the driver had to judge things right – too slow and you would stall or become stuck, too fast and you could bounce the komatik and unbalance the vehicle as you went over an obstacle.

After a few more hours of driving, our vehicles were showing signs of fatigue. This was not good. We had to look after our transport because we didn't know what the state of the ice would be ahead of us for the next two days, before we hoped to abandon them and begin man-hauling our sledges to the Pole. Mark and Bunny's windshield was cracked. My accelerator wasn't working properly so the engine would not idle, which meant that when I took my hand off the accelerator the engine would stall. After hours of keeping the engine engaged my right thumb ached constantly and I found ingenious, almost contortionist, ways of keeping the engine going, whilst relieving the tired muscles in my hand and fingers.

At times it was difficult to know whether we were still on the beach or not. If anyone thought the going was tough negotiating the obstacles on the beach, we would look out to sea, to remind ourselves of the utter carnage taking place among the ice field there as the current pushed and squeezed the ice between the islands, forming a groaning, pressurised and chaotic scene. There was no way a vehicle could move out there, the only way forward was to continue driving along the beach.

During a tea break, which had now become more of an opportunity for everyone to quickly check that their loads were secured rather than a time to drink and eat, Pen returned to say we were almost through. No one let their skidoo engine stop, in case it didn't start again. I of course couldn't anyway due to the issue with my accelerator, so enjoyed my nuts and chocolate one-handed as Peter checked the load was still secure in the komatik.

By now our method of getting the convoy along the obstacle-strewn ice was tried and tested. Pen would stay ahead of us and then slow down his skidoo when an obstacle presented itself. He would then investigate a way forward. The skidoo behind Pen would hang back. All the other skidoo passengers would dismount. Once Pen had found a way through, and if the terrain remained difficult, all the skidoo passengers would dismount and quickly gather round and remove any heavy items from the komatik following Pen. The driver, with a lightened load, would then proceed forward, around or over the obstacle. This was great teamwork and a joy to watch as we all jumped on and off skidoos, helping each other quickly pack and unpack the contents of komatik, to lighten the load and aid the driver. It was tiring work, and not the easy, comfortable travel I had expected prior to our man-hauling the pulks later in the expedition.

At one point Geoff was due to be first to overcome the latest obstacle, an angled ice cube that rose to almost six feet high. It was steep on one side but, luckily, had a more gentle angle on another. Geoff revved his engine at full speed, Rob dismounted, and then Geoff quickly launched forward and manoeuvred past the ice cube which projected itself onto the path. Unfortunately, Geoff then over-steered and slammed his skidoo into a two-foot-deep hole in the ice. The skidoo engine screamed and Geoff only just managed to avoid somersaulting over the handlebars. Fortunately Geoff was lucky and the only damage incurred was the loss of his hard-won reputation for being the only skidoo driver not to have come a cropper so far.

In order to retrieve Geoff and Rob's skidoo their komatik had to be reversed first. Whilst Rob went to find a rope from another skidoo so it could be dragged out, Pen, with a strength I didn't know it was possible for a man to possess, single-handedly dragged Geoff's komatik backward to get a better rope angle on the skidoo. Geoff then reversed, aided by my skidoo pulling his backwards. He then tried a second time to get past the obstacle, this time succeeding. With the hazard alerted, and the best way to tackle it proven, all the other drivers in the convoy prepared themselves.

Next up were Mark and Bunny. This time Bunny drove their skidoo, and Mark dismounted. Bunny proceeded at full power, following Geoff's demonstration, and bounced off the skidoo seat like a rodeo rider, as he tried to control his mechanical mount as it raced up the frozen incline. The remainder of the convoy proceeded successfully, adopting the aggressive and high risk approach demonstrated by Geoff and Bunny.

Various obstacles, from narrow paths – lined either side by large ice cubes - to bumpy, undulating ice, continued to attempt to eject us from our skidoos, or empty the contents of our komatik. Our speed of travel was severely restricted as a result. All the manual activity of driving the skidoos, jumping on and off to aid colleagues and re-loading heavy items from the komatik caused me to verge on breaking a sweat, in spite of the cold. This was of course to be avoided, as any sweat absorbed into clothing would then freeze as I cooled down. Despite all this activity, and three pairs of gloves, my fingers seemed to freeze every five or six minutes, forcing me to constantly move them around to keep the blood flowing.

Having cleared the worst of the obstacles on the beach, and to our great relief, our path then opened up into a wide vista. The ice at the frozen waters edge remained impenetrable, but we could now see open space to our right as Cornwallis Island stretched out before us, gradually rising to some 800 feet in altitude. The sky had clouded over with a white haze, though visibility was still very good.

The ice became flat and levelled off as we proceeded along the beach. The surrounding area was completely snow and ice-covered, beautiful in its own way but featureless and uninviting. No trees, rivers or even boulders broke the dominance of the white blanket. Whilst the scenery had been outstanding for the past few hours, as we had negotiated nature's work strewn across the beach, I had missed most of it because I was focused intently throughout on the next ten feet of ground ahead of me and the obstacles that awaited.

Given this feeling of apparent immense space that the now open beach presented after being locked in the corridors of ice, we all ran our skidoos abreast of each other and increased our speed to reduce our frustration at our recent slow progress.

As we moved away from the channel we could see that the sea ice was becoming less broken to our left and soon we were roaring off the beach and back onto flat sea ice again. We continued north until we were approximately five miles out into the frozen Intrepid Passage. We drove as quickly as we could and enjoyed the comfort of the ride as we travelled across the flat ice, devoid of any bone-breaking ridges or other obstacles. I glanced behind me and watched as Cornwallis island shrank into the distance, the broken ice that had caused us so much effort and delay, now reduced to a nothing more than a ruffled crispy-looking white edging on the horizon.

After another hour of travel Pen slowed us all down and we decided to set up camp for a night on the sea ice of Intrepid Passage. The ice was flat in every direction, and I could only see the slight rise of Bathurst island in the distance to the west, and the low hills of Sheringham Point from where we had come from earlier on Cornwallis Island to the south east. We stopped the skidoos and komatiks so that they were positioned in a circle, Wild west-caravan-style. With no natural barriers near us, any scent we or our food gave off could travel for tens of miles. I hoped we would not get any large white fur-coated visitors during the night. Pen assured us that we did not need to worry as we were on solid ice five miles out to sea, and the bears tended to look for broken ice that would reveal the sea and therefore seals. The polar bear alarm remained packed in the komatik.

After arranging the skidoos in a circle, we dismounted and carried out a variety of variations of the ice dance. We then all converged around Pen who was getting a signal for his GPS. The ice-cold, and therefore sluggish, LCD display eventually told us that we were ten nautical miles north west of Sheringham Point at 74'47N, 95'42W. Since leaving Resolute Bay we had, as the crow flies, only travelled fourteen nautical miles, which was a bit disappointing, but everyone felt it had been quite an eventful day and I certainly felt tired from the constant activity of packing and unpacking the komatiks to get across each high or awkward icy obstacle.

With the skidoos' engines turned off, and there being little wind, quiet had returned. 'What's happened to your suit Mark?' said Peter looking our leader up and down. Mark's plastic over suit, which seemed such an impressively good idea to deflect the wind, was now in tatters. The plastic had basically lost its flexibility in the cold and much of it had shattered on being exposed to temperatures of down to, with wind chill, minus sixty Celsius. Mark now looked like an Arctic tramp or a Polar Robinson Crusoe as layers of plastic shreds hung from him. 'I suppose I can't really sue them,' answered Mark, 'as I bought this from a car garage in the UK. What do you think Rob?'

'I suppose if they sold it to you to keep oil off your clothes when working on a car and you say it failed you in temperatures of minus 60 on a skidoo in the Arctic – you probably can't claim it's exceeded its 'fit for purpose' guarantee Mark.' The car supplies garage would live for another day.

We were tired, but we set up camp quickly. Now that we were on the ice for real, we knew we had to operate efficiently. Peter and I erected the tent, while the others rushed to do their own jobs. Mark soon had the cooker burning away, and it wasn't long before the temperature rose slightly in the tent. Geoff was taking a good look at the skidoos, as an engineer by trade he naturally gravitated to looking after 'my girls' as he now referred to the skidoos.

I found the evening stillness particularly powerful, especially having had a skidoo engine blaring at me all day. The Arctic sky was beginning to change colour as the sun got lower, the blues in the sky gave way to red and orange. The sun would never sink of course as we had twenty-four hour sunlight at that time of year. The sun sat there competing with the moon as they both gradually circled around us.

The blues and whites of the ice began to take on the yellow and orange hue they reflected from the sky. It was lovely to be out there as I finished putting snow blocks around the tent valance as everyone raced around doing their work. My final job with the spade was to fill a big blue plastic bag with ice for Mark to melt for water in the tent. He was already melting ice on the cooker to make the water needed for tonight's meal as well as the fourteen litres needed for the group's drink flasks for the next day. The first few pieces of ice fizzed in the bottom of the steel pan before filling the tent with steam. As the steam hung in the air we all knew that this would eventually freeze on the tent walls, our clothes and our sleeping bags. No one had brought any other equipment into the tent for this reason.

Rob was opening everyone's komatik and laying their sleeping bags, already prepared in their protective Gore-Tex outers, onto the sea ice, awaiting entry into the tent. Whilst waiting for the first cup of hot tea we all finished our water rations from our flasks; mine was stone cold.

Geoff was pacing up and down past the skidoos, stopping every now and again and, in true garage-mechanic style, tutting as he found each problem, and shaking his head, almost invisibly, under his layers of head gear. This caught Pen's attention and he asked Geoff how the skidoos were.

'All ship-shape in general Pen,' he replied.

'Couple of knocks, Rob's skis are slightly misaligned, Bunny's has a slight dent in the side and Duncan's screen is a bit wobbly.' With that report made, Pen started checking and tightening all the ropes on the komatiks that had worked themselves loose as they had jumped about during the day. Geoff then started the hand-numbing exercise of straightening Rob's skidoo skis, with a spanner and some elbow grease.

'Ready!' shouted Mark from inside the tent. It was a welcome sound as the first small pan of hot water appeared. Bunny started running small cups of tea to the workers. Most of which were almost cold by the time they arrived.

'It has been said that if you throw a cup of boiling water into the air, when the air is minus forty, the water will freeze before it hits the ground,' Peter stated. 'You first then,' I replied, as Bunny delivered Peter's hot brew. Peter thought better of it and responded that he would try another day, needing the warmth of the drink more than the results of the experiment.

Mark, in full control of the tent, then alerted Rob to his next instruction 'Bedding!', to which Rob then started bringing in everyone's sleeping bag systems. As Rob moved the big caterpillar-like items into the tent, Pete and I began to collect everyone's night bag from their komatik. This had everything each person needed for the night – their eating utensils, diary, book and night clothes.

Once inside the tent no one wanted to have to go back out again. It was tempting to go into the tent straight away, but outside there was much to be done and the activity would help to keep us warm for later. Mark wasn't really ready to receive people yet; a string of orders came out of the tent and a line of utensils, food and ice went in, concluded by the odd puff of steam escaping from the tent's entrance. We established a pee spot away from the tent, to ensure that we all knew where the latrine was, and where to avert our eyes.

With all the komatiks checked we began to move inside. Geoff was satisfied that the skidoos were ok. The skidoo keys were then removed from their ignitions – not that we city people expected someone to steal them - but so that the keys wouldn't freeze in the locks overnight.

To the east, the low hills of Sheringham Point on Cornwallis Island looked further away than they actually were. Like all hills in the area, they were low and rounded and with no discernable features such a trees or telegraph poles to judge their distance by. Apparently, the lack of features on hills on the moon had the same effect, making judging distance difficult, and this had been commented on by astronauts from the Lunar Rover. The colour of the sky continued to change as the orange glow of a sun that would refuse to fully set continued to sink in the sky. The white ice become a pink, then orange colour, that tried to conceal the true air temperature with its warm hues.

I took one last look around the empty horizon before going into the tent on my hands and knees, tightly closing the drawstrings behind me. Inside the tent the air was damp and full of steam. The tent walls allowed the daylight outside to stream through them, bathing the contents and polar explorers in a warm orange glow. The tent was crowded, with seven large sleeping bags, night bags and kitchen equipment, all densely packed among our bodies.

Pen sat by the door, with the Argos communications machine switched on. This would signal our position and outside temperature back to Maryland in the United States, whereupon this information could be picked up at Pen's base at the Rookery. We were not scheduled for our first voice radio call until the next day. Pen set the Argos to 'oo' which was code for 'All ok' and informed us that out of the wind it was only minus 22 outside.

Everyone sat on their sleeping bag, with their boots on. It was still about minus 15 in the tent, even with the cooker on, yet it felt remarkably warm. Even after sitting still for ten minutes I felt there was no automatic need to conduct the ice dance. As the temperature began to rise, with the jet-like noise of the cooker burning away in the background, we began to shed clothes, and form little comfort beds in the crowded tent. To add to the steam in the tent some of us also began to steam, as the sweat generated by earlier activities began to vaporise, on exposure to the cool air.

Mark was working like a trooper, filling cups with warm water, and stirring the evening meal of pasta, whilst adding in lumps of calorie-laden cheese. Everyone else was checking their equipment or looking at bruises and scratches. 'Boy my fingers are hard,' said Rob. My own fingertips also seemed to have doubled in thickness after their constant freeze and thaw cycles throughout the day. Everyone else's were the same. It seemed to make sense now why Pen had covered his fingers in plaster tape. 'Stops them from splitting with the cold,' he expertly informed us all.

'A very good day everyone', said Pen cheerfully, 'you all worked well together, everyone feeling ok?' We all responded positively; no aches, no pains, no frostbite. Apart from Bunny. 'I've got a bad pain in my stomach Pen.' Before Pen could answer Bunny bellowed, 'Come on El Porco!' and wiggled his spoon above the pasta temptingly, whilst laughing loudly. Mark threw him a can of Pringles, which was quickly shared and devoured. Quietness returned again as each person's bowl was filled with steaming macaroni-cheese pasta, only broken by the odd crunching or 'umm' noise emanating from the group of hungry explorers. This was supplemented by helpings of nuts, apricots and the obligatory chocolate.

We all drank as much fluid as possible. It was interesting to note that although we were surrounded by water – sitting on three feet of ice floating above hundreds of feet of sea water, the hardest element to obtain was liquid water. Washing up the dishes was simple. Ice has abrasive qualities, so a small soap-sized ice-bar would be used to scrape clean a bowl of any food fragments, though there were few fragments left, as our calorie-demanding bodies devoured every last morsel, to feed the internal furnace warming each of us.

By now the tent was much warmer and people's boots came off. The multiple layers of socks also came off and then the dreaded vapour barrier socks. Given that our feet had basically been inside a plastic carrier bag, which was literally true for Bunny, the resultant moisture was also stuck in there. White feet poked out, all smelling a bit and smoking as the warm trapped moisture met the cold air. Any ice stuck to our clothing had long been brushed off, as no one wanted it to melt inside the tent and drop water on their clothing or bedding which would then freeze later.

With the stove running efficiently we continued making water from ice. It took about three hours to boil all the ice placed in the blue plastic sack to release the drinking water necessary for tomorrow. Each person filled their two-litre flasks. They would put these in their sleeping bags at night so that the water in the flasks would not freeze. The flasks would be re-heated again in the morning.

Making water was so time-consuming, taking over three hours each night, that it was necessary to make the best of any possible efficiency. With the cooker already warmed up, and the air in the tent warm, it was better to keep making water rather than starting again tomorrow and having to warm everything up again, which would take more time and fuel. It would be much faster to re-heat cold water tomorrow morning than start again from ice. The lengthy water-making process determined what time we went to bed.

The talk in the tent was idle, running randomly between women, the next day's travel, and other adventures. 'So tell us about some of your travels Mark,' enquired Peter, to which I was equally eager to listen. A raft of stories covering all manner of things came forth from the lawyers in the group. Rob particularly liked the Pamplona bull run that they had attended and described how they were left in the walled area of the Spanish city overnight with all the other runners.

The annual Pamplona bull run is a dare devil event where several bulls are let loose in enclosed and shut-off streets, with runners locked in with them. 'With little sleep and some drink, everyone is ready for action early in the morning, and you can sense the adrenalin in the air,' Mark said, recounting their story. 'At eight a.m., a rocket goes off and your heart takes off with it,' said Bunny with his usual enthusiasm, 'you then run for your life, wanting to see the bulls chasing you, but at the same time afraid you'll get blocked in with the crowd, and trampled or gored.' 'I was really shitting it', said Mark, loading more ice into the pan. 'Running down the narrow streets with hundreds of others, and pursued by a herd of bulls you eventually got to the bull ring. By which time you were not sure what is happening behind you, everyone is shouting and horns were tooting,' said Rob, 'the noise and chaos were terrific.' It sounded a real buzz.

'Do you remember Mark, as soon as we got into the bull ring we hung a left, expecting to be trampled at any moment?', said Bunny. 'I remember being inside the bull ring, gasping for breath, watching runners entering the bull ring about six feet off the ground, because they were so full of adrenalin and desperate to escape their marauding pursuers.' Other equally interesting and adventurous stories came forth.

'So Pen, tell us about your boat trip,' Peter asked. Pen recounted his record-breaking inflatable boat trip from Tower Bridge in London to the coast of Greenland. He had met an eccentric but very adventurous friend whom he admired greatly. They planned the expedition and got some backing, leaving London surrounded by Page Three models, arranged by their sponsor, before hitting the cold sea. They travelled up the English coast to Scotland and then towards the Faeroes and on to Iceland.

'The seas off Iceland were horrendous,' recalled Pen. 'I don't know how we managed it. I remember taking shelter in an Icelandic harbour and going out again and just hitting a massive wall of water; it was truly madness to the point of irresponsibility. Sense prevailed and we headed back into safety. It was probably, and thankfully, the only time I've turned a boat on a thirty foot wave.' His audience was once again in awe of the young explorer, who at 34, had seen more of the world than most of us ever wanted to.

'Eventually we got to Greenland, my friend had major sea sickness and diarrhoea and was in an awful state. Remember we were in an open boat in the North Atlantic. We were wearing sealed dry suits and I think by the time we got to Greenland his was pretty full to the brim.' We all thought about this momentarily before Pen concluded with, 'It's not a record I would advise anyone to try and break.' He had said this before, but with that description, any potential challengers in the group quickly retreated. Only Rob commented that the trip sounded 'a bit too dinghy for me'.

'Pen, another attempt on the North Pole?' enquired Mark, reflecting on Pen's initial effort to get to the Pole alone and unsupported.

'Yes, a new attempt – and a new method.'

'How intriguing,' replied Mark reflecting the mood of his colleagues, 'Tell us more.'

'Well, expeditions to the North Pole on foot have used the same approach for the last few generations – fill a sledge with all your weighty supplies, and slowly drag it to the Pole. The load is so heavy that travel is slow, meaning you spend longer on the ice and therefore need to carry more weight in terms of food and fuel to sustain you.'

'But materials have got lighter and food more calorific over the years,' countered a slightly confused Geoff.

'You are correct Geoff, but the basic approach still hasn't changed. I'd like to challenge that.' Pen had everyone's attention, and we all listened to the polar master.

'The idea therefore, is to try to get to the Pole very quickly, perhaps in twenty to thirty days rather than the usual sixty to seventy odd. I won't drag a sledge full of heavy equipment and supplies; I'll have a backpack and quickly ski the whole way. I'll be light, quick and highly maneuverable. I'll need less fuel and food. I'm even considering not taking a tent!'

Pen's companions remained silent as we all took in this new idea; it seemed to make sense.

'This is possible Pen?'

'Eminently so my good man. I'm still working on the details you'll understand, and the plan of course; there's lots of work to do yet.' It was new, it was bold, it was Pen; an expert and innovator in his field. We all sat there and took in his aura until Pen concluded without emotion, 'Now you know my secret, you'll understand that I can't let any of you leave the Arctic alive.' 'Well, I won't go peacefully,' replied Bunny, clasping Mark's wooden stirring spatula in defence, as we all sniggered.

The talk continued and we spoke of various personal goals, some sounded impressive but with little hope of ever being achieved, and some just fanciful dreams.

As we quietened down, and in the dim natural light inside the tent I wrote my diary entry for the day. Geoff and Rob were also scribbling with their lead pencils, whose 'ink' was guaranteed not to be affected by any low temperatures.

When the last of the water was released from its icy prison and poured into the remaining flask, Mark switched off the stove. With the considerable roar of the gas jet now extinguished, the tent fell silent. With alarming immediacy the temperature in the tent also dramatically plummeted, as the only heat source for miles around was now switched off. Everyone got quickly into their sleeping bags and put their balaclavas back on, as the ice cold air returned with its normal vengeance.

Getting into the sleeping bag was not without issue. Each person had to get their boots off and store them securely in a bag at the end of their sleeping bag so that no moisture would enter the boot and freeze overnight. The tent was full of moisture from the billowing steam from the stove in the inescapable area of the tent. Additionally, each person would expel approximately half a litre of water through their breath into the dry atmosphere of the tent during the night. Anything that would be affected by moisture or the cold would come into the sleeping bag with its occupant.

The soft inner liners of the boots were taken out and stored inside the sleeping bag at the bottom. Each person would sleep in their vapour barrier bag within the sleeping bag, to ensure that no body moisture would get into the soft lining of the sleeping bag. Lying in the vapour barrier bag was like sleeping in a plastic bin liner. However, body heat would help to keep the equipment kept in the bag warm. As well as boots, body heat would also keep the contents of the water flasks from freezing, so these were also stuffed into the sleeping bag. Batteries, particularly susceptible to low temperatures, were kept in the sleeping bag too.

Cameras had to be kept in plastic bags for fear that their lenses would be affected by the moisture. They also had to come into the tent, as most were powered by batteries which too would need to be kept in their owner's sleeping bag during the night. Peter was particularly proud of his old Olympus OM10 that didn't require a battery and was thus left in his komatik overnight. I didn't like the film to get that cold, as it could snap, so always kept my camera on my person, being careful not to place it next to my moisture-laden skin. Nights were cold and uncomfortable in the sleeping bags that doubled as warm storage areas for equipment.

Pen, still by the door, had the shoulder butt of the gun in the tent, the rest of it outside the tent. He didn't want to get the barrel into the tent as the moisture in the tent once frozen could affect its operation, should we be forced to use it.

With the inner socks of my boots at the bottom of my sleeping bag, camera, batteries, pee bottle and two insulated one-litre water flasks, there wasn't much room left for me. I quickly undressed before sliding into my inner vapour barrier bag, which was like hugging a cold plastic bag, but essential to keep the moisture expelled from my body from getting into the cotton elements of the sleeping bag. I was wearing long johns. Squeezing into the bag was one thing, closing it off was another. There were no zips or strings to the sleeping bag, you got in at the top and a single cord around the head closed it around your face. Whilst I wasn't the biggest man in the group I have quite broad shoulders, and felt particularly restricted within it.

With everyone winding down now, Pen produced a surprise, to much derision from the rest of the group. Brushing aside some ammunition in his overnight bag and, after a little more rummaging, the rugged polar explorer produced a miniature set of books, and then began to read one aloud with gloves and face mask on; 'Winnie the Pooh at the North Pole,' he announced in his stern posh accent. The tent of aspiring Arctic explorers fell about laughing as the Arctic master proceeded, against the protests. Pen retorted that he carried these books on all his expeditions and found them very comforting. He braved on, and eventually his companions enabled him to finish the small book with some dignity intact.

I nestled down into my sleeping bag, full of equipment, between my colleagues in equally large bags. There wasn't room to swing a frozen cat, but I gradually fell to sleep, with dreams of how I would design a more comfortable sleeping bag.

My sleep was deep until some hours later a natural yearning woke me, as my bladder needed emptying. I hoped to be able to hold on and tried once again to get to sleep, but nature was not letting go and soon I had to confront it. Would I leave the tent and go for a quick pee? It would take about ten minutes to get out of the sleeping bag, put my boots on and go outside. Undoubtedly I would trip over someone and, perhaps Pen would shoot me as I re-entered the tent.

Instead I took the easier option and decided to fill my pee bottle, designed for exactly this task. The idea was that I could complete this operation without leaving the warmth of the sleeping bag. But this was more complicated than I had expected. As I wasn't able to turn over, due to my companions being so close to me in the tent, and not wishing to spill any urine in my sleeping bag, I decided to get up and pee whilst kneeling on my sleeping bag. This was the best option and was completed quickly, as all such activities are in the Arctic. Nothing was spilled and I made sure the top was tightly secured on the bottle before returning to my sleeping bag. I brought the half full bottle into the sleeping bag with me, where I embraced it tightly, as the contents offered me some warm comfort, as a hot water bottle would. Leaving the pee bottle outside the sleeping bag would of course condemn it to be frozen solid overnight and most likely the bottle would then split. Relieved, I fell back into a light, cold sleep.

The author pictured at 4 years old, with crew neck on ready to tackle the snow.

A career in the British Army was my early dream, seen here about to go 'on patrol' supported by medical back-up (my sister).

I had a strange affinity with ice and snow ! (Confusing the Seasons 1986)

Climbing Europe's highest mountain taught me a lesson in mental preparation and where to set my boundaries.

Tyre pulling, the perfect way to train for dragging a sledge over the ice. L to R: Mark, Bunny, Rob, Duncan, Peter and Geoff.

Equipment selection was detailed and exhaustive - Pen demonstrates 'wind proof' underwear.

The tiny northern Canadian hamlet of Resolute Bay. "Not the end of the world, but you can see it from here."

Home sweet home. The Arctic sun never sets in spring, seen here at about 8.00 pm. Note skis used to secure the tent guy lines.

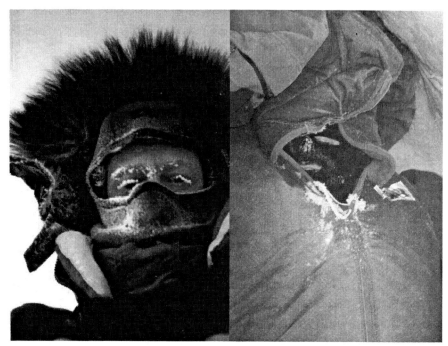

Above left: Any moisture would freeze quickly, whether in one's breath or sweat.
Above right: The nights were always cold. Rob seen in a sleeping bag, fully
protected. *(attributed R Walker)*

Peter on a Komatik sledge, loaded with provisions.

The ice was initially smooth, enabling fast and easy travel by skidoo.

However, this wasn't to last, as the ice ridges got progressively higher, making travelling more difficult.

The view from the beach near Sheringham Point - looking towards the jumbled chaos of ice seawards. The beach offered easier travel.

Bunny takes a tumble. These incidents became more frequent as the ice became rougher - leading to delays and a hammering of equipment.

We weren't alone, evidence of a recent visitor. Each polar bear footprint was the size of a large frying pan.

Remains of a musk-ox, victim of a polar bear attack?

Evidence of a recent polar bear attack - only the backbone of the seal remained. Note the sea ice is very flat, the white line on the horizon highlights a pressure ridge.

The Polaris Mine, the world's highest zinc mine, located in a lonely arctic wilderness. Also a refuelling stop for the expedition.

Bunny and Pen climb to a vantage point offered by a small iceberg to view the surrounding territory, hoping to locate an easier way across the ice.

A cold, but happy, group of adventurers

Five miles off the west coast of Bathurst Island. The sea ice was difficult to travel on so we used the flatter "motorway" pictured above. Unfortunately following this took us further out to sea and away from our goal.

The slight crack in my goggles enabled enough cold air in to freeze an eye shut.

Geoff demonstrates the ice dance -
the only way to try and keep warm.

Pen and Rob light a fire in
Polar Bear Pass.

An abandoned aircraft on Cameron Island is slowly claimed by the ice.

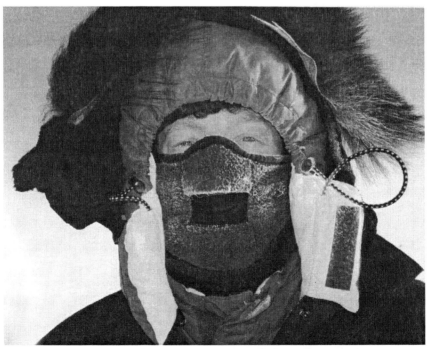

Loving every minute of it!

Erecting the radio aerial from ski poles was slow and finger-numbing work.

Thoroughly dejected on the flight back to Resolute.

An option we hoped we would never have to use to tame the local wildlife.

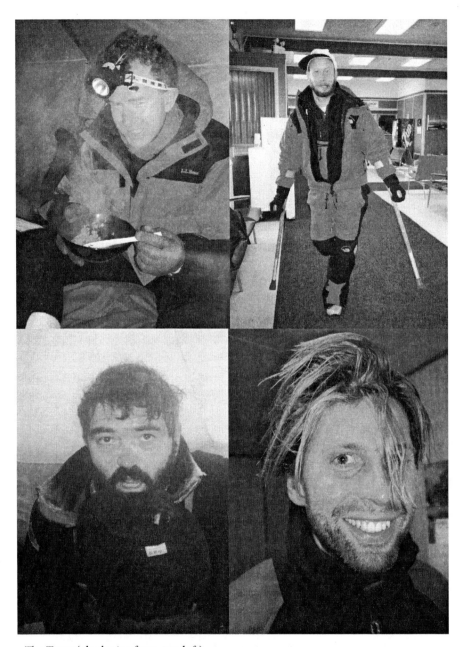

The Team (clockwise from top left):
Geoffrey, happy in the tent enjoying, another sumptuous dosage of calories
Bunny, constantly surprising and humorous, with unofficial kit - walking sticks!
Peter, the youngest of the team, pictured after returning from the ice.
Mark, the expedition leader - struggling with a balaclava frozen to his beard.

Rob - arriving in Canada

Pen - our guide, happy that the radio was working. *(attributed R Walker)*

The result of months of training - standing at the Magnetic North Pole. The ambient air temperature was -42°C that sunny day.

My constant support - my wife Niamh (seen here before I embarked on another expedition).

8

The Last Outpost

*'There is always a risk in being alive, and if you are more
alive, there is more risk.'*

HENRIK IBSEN, PLAYWRIGHT

The following morning I awoke at 6.45 local time. The sunlight was streaming through the orange canvas of the tent as it had done all 'night'. My Gore-Tex-covered sleeping bag was sprinkled with a light layer of ice, dusted like a cake with icing sugar, and glinting in the low orange light of the tent. My balaclava had a crusty feel to it as the moisture in my breath had woven its way into the material and frozen overnight. The other team members' were stirring around me. It was clear Jack Frost had visited us with his icy paintbrush, as the tent was once again decorated inside with a layer of ice. The 'ice wall' had formed on one panel inside the tent again, although this time it had grown during the night to such a size that it made the tent dip down to just a few inches above Bunny's head.

Mark, our restless leader, was, as I expected, first up. As Mark got out of his sleeping bag, Peter also emerged into the cold air. They both stood up in their long johns, their heads hitting the canvas roof and showering the interior with dislodged ice crystals. The tent was too crowded to have two people getting up at the same time, so Mark proceeded and Peter sat back down again

– almost causing as much inconvenience to his fellow tent dwellers - while trying to get back into his sleeping bag.

Mark got fully dressed while standing on his sleeping bag, occasionally grunting, and prodding those nearest to him. 'Would you mind old chap?' he uttered, as he pushed his sleeping companions over a little to enable him to balance as he dressed. His head would merrily touch the roof every now and again and shower his cowering companions with flakes of ice - that somehow always managed to lodge themselves down our necks.

I sunk lower into my bag to gain a few more moments warmth. It wasn't long before Mark was demanding equipment. 'Where are the pans? Ok, could someone please get me their flask,' as the other travellers began to emerge in sequence. My turn soon arrived and I went from being dressed in reasonably warm long johns to full polar gear in approximately one hundred and twenty seconds.

The air temperature in the tent was about minus ten, which tended to hurry your dressing time. The basic operation was to collect your stuff from your bag, jump up, put on salopettes, over jumpers, gloves, and then with your feet up in the air, balancing on your sleeping bag, put your boots on. All this without hopefully kicking anyone else – as fast as possible, with as much grunting and groaning as was polite.

'Where's Pen?' came a startled question. He wasn't in the tent.

'He must have gone out, I didn't see him.'

'I think he's seen sense and buggered orf,' was Bunny's sleepy first words of the day, emanating from the depths of his bag under the ice wall. At that moment the entrance to the tent was unzipped from the outside, and the orange light of the interior dispersed, as the tent was showered in the rays of a bright Arctic day. In came Pen.

'Bring any croissants?' murmured Rob to the new arrival, now unable to continue his sleep with all the activity around him. 'Where have you been Pen?'

'I slept outside last night; it was too crowded in here with all of us.'

'Outside! - where?' questioned Peter.

'In a komatik.'

Sleeping in the wooden confines of a square komatik must have been like sleeping in a coffin. 'Very brave of you to act as polar bear decoy,' stated Mark, before saying that if Pen had come into the tent in the middle of the night he would have probably shot him, considering him to be one of our feared bad boy bears of the white furry coat variety. I must admit I had not heard Pen leave last night, nor had anyone else. So much for us all waking up at the sound of a more serious visitor walking around the tent.

An increasingly smooth operation was kicking in, the sleeping bags and overnight equipment were quickly ejected from the tent as each person got up, providing us all with much-needed room. Mark soon had the stove operational, its jet-like roar confirming its readiness to serve us breakfast. A large vat of 'Hot and Krumbly', which was a sort of sugar-based fruit muesli, was soon brought to life with the aid of water, which turned the accompanying milk powder into an edible sauce. Pen, now in the tent, sliced up a large slab of butter with his penknife and threw large chunks into the pot, to provide the calories needed for the next few hours.

'Right!' shouted Mark at the optimum moment, when the water was heated just enough to melt the butter, as he handed out bowls of the mixture. In the cool of the tent the water soon started to solidify the butter, which created a greasy mulch. I could feel my stomach turn as I swallowed the first few mouthfuls of warm grease, crunchy with ice crystals forming rapidly. I almost vomited as the lumpy, greasy, and icy combination edged its way down my throat towards my awaiting stomach. I then began to pick around the contents of my bowl and decided there and then that tomorrow I'd avoid the butter. I was most disappointed at myself for not being able to force down whatever was given to me. Everyone else eagerly passed their bowl towards Mark, who obligingly refilled them. I looked down at my mixture and, disgusted at myself, continued to pick at it, as the milk quickly iced up, further adding to the crunchiness of the Hot and Krumbly.

Rob was the last up, giving way to Geoff who, being the tallest of the group, found it difficult to stand up fully, with the low ceiling of the tent. The stove was burning merrily away, being fed with ice from the blue bag by the tent door. Water from the flasks kept from freezing overnight in our sleeping bags were re-heated, and given back to each person to add their favourite tipple for the day. Hot tea was the group favourite, although I preferred a blackcurrant drink, formed from powdered flavoured crystals in one bottle, and pure water in my second bottle.

As I stepped outside the tent I could hear Pen announcing that the night had been warm - the temperature only dropped to minus twenty-two. The morning sky was again clear, sharp and blue, with a refreshing chill that awoke me fully, immediately. All manner of items were being ejected from the tent and people were throwing things in any old fashion into the komatiks.

Clearly this could cause confusion which would lead to a slower unpacking operation later, and therefore cold bodies. It was agreed that I should act as Load Manager and determine where everything would go. I gave each komatik a number, and with paper and pencil recorded what went where, as people emerged laden from the tent with cooking equipment, fuel, the rifle, food, hammer and general repair stuff. I directed them to the appropriate komatik where Pete and I loaded the items in. Clearly the weight needed to be distributed evenly and some items needed to be accessed quicker than others. We had of course decided the location of most things the day before at Resolute, when we packed the komatiks outside the Rookery. 'The food needs to go with me,' our cook, El Porco, shouted from inside the tent.

Pen then formally assigned roles to each person, having observed us over the previous two days.

'Bunny. Bunny! You are to start the skidoos.'

'Yesssir,' he muttered, backed up with a gloved salute as he trotted off to the first one. This could be a fairly difficult task, as each machine often spluttered and died on initial firing.

'Geoffrey, you are of course our resident 'oily rag' and should deal with anything mechanical.'

'Ok boss, and hey, chaps – look after my girls please.'

We all ran to our assigned tasks, as much to keep the cold at bay, as any enthusiasm towards the task. It was clear from yesterday's ride on the ice that some komatiks were heavier than others, and the lighter ones were easier to tip over. Eventually after a few hours we were ready to depart. It was 11 o'clock. Today's objective was to reach the Polaris Mine, north of us. This would be the last outpost of mankind before our lonely trip further north. We would travel along the west coast of Cornwallis Island, again out on the sea ice, between the islands and the narrowing gap of McDougal Sound that separated us from Bathurst Island. We all hoped progress would be better than the previous day's miniscule fourteen nautical miles.

The ice was flat and smooth, which was a great start to our day. Peter was driving, and I could tell he and the rest of the group really enjoyed this smooth travel after yesterday's frustrations. I did too, as I wasn't getting bounced around as I sat in the komatik and could take in the view a bit more. With the ice conditions so clear, everyone travelled as fast as our heavy loads and 375cc engines would allow. Wearing ski goggles and face masks, the cold wind whistled past our faces as we travelled at almost thirty miles an hour when at full speed. Our hands still froze every five minutes or so, so to counter this, we constantly moved our fingers inside our gloves to try and force a regular hot injection of blood into each digit.

After an hour Bunny signalled that his skidoo had a problem, so we all stopped. Geoff straightaway started attacking Bunny's machine, to realign its front skis. Fifteen minutes later with the skis fixed, and Peter and I having completed checks to ensure that the loads on all the komatiks were all still secure, we were off again up the coast.

The terrain thankfully remained flat and welcomingly featureless. We needed to make up time after the previous day, so we travelled at almost full throttle and as fast as we dared. Occasionally, a small pressure ridge would appear on the horizon, like a bright white line, until it grew to a foot or two of height, that we would happily travel over. Sometimes a ridge would rise to three or four feet and someone's komatik would get stuck on it, causing us all to get off and push the stranded komatik with a big shove whilst the driver drove it forward with full revs.

After another hour of travel things were going well, now that we had a clear run of the ice. We were however, beginning to see problems with the skidoos. The skidoo that Peter and I were using seemed to be drinking a lot of oil. Whilst we had checked and refilled it at each opportunity, our skidoo was definitely drinking more than the other machines. Also, Mark and Bunny's skidoo was drinking petrol at an alarming rate.

We continued on, until Bunny hit a pressure bump on the ice that caused a wooden strut on his komatik to snap so loudly that it could be heard above the noise of the skidoo engine. The convoy slowed down and we stopped to assess and repair the damage. As soon as we stopped everyone automatically jumped to their respective roles to keep the operation moving as quickly as possible.

It was great to see such a motivated team in action. Only occasionally the odd muffled cry would emanate from behind a thick fur hood or a gloved hand beckon for help, or point in the direction where someone was needed. The komatiks were checked, the skidoos refuelled and oiled. Everyone had a quick bite to eat from their 'nose bag', and a swift pee. These activities were all interspaced with the arm waving, leg kicking and other movements of the obligatory ice dance. Bunny's komatik was quickly re-lashed by Pen using rope to temporarily secure it tightly – he would attend to it further when we stopped for the night.

'Chaps, we've all got to be more careful with the equipment – we depend on it!' said Pen, completing the final knot on Bunny's now repaired, komatik sledge. He continued around the group and did a review of everyone else's equipment. 'Rob', he instructed, 'I want you to act as Fuel Monitor – we need to determine the level of petrol usage.'

On a full tank Pen estimated that each skidoo when pulling a loaded komatik should have a range of sixty nautical miles. At this rate the group should have used 180 litres of fuel, but we had used considerably more. 'Clearly gentlemen some skidoos are performing differently than others. Please monitor your own machine's performance, especially fuel and general handling.'

Geoff piped up and said again, 'I say, look after my girls, chaps.'

We continued on the flat ice with an urgency to catch up on lost time. The difference in performance of the skidoos was illustrated by the fact that Peter and my machine was the slowest to accelerate. It really took time to build up to a canter. After an hour of fast cruising my skidoo came to a slow halt as the engine suddenly died. The convoy stopped once more. On lifting the engine cab Geoff found oil to be splattered all over the cowling. It looked quite gruesome and Geoff tutted and sucked in air in that knowing mechanic's way. It was clear that Pen was growing worried about the skidoos' reliability and not, as Bunny put it, because he 'smelt a large repair bill' on return to Resolute Bay.

After another hour of travelling on the sea ice up the McDougal Sound towards Little Cornwallis Island, where the Polaris Mine was located, we saw another pressure ridge of ice on the horizon. This one stood out at a distance like a shining white line, running from east to west, and was the biggest of the day. As we approached it, it became apparent that we couldn't drive over this one. It appeared to stretch for miles in either direction. Pen waved for us to slow the pace as he looked for a way to get through the large jumbled row of ice cubes that formed the ridge. The pressure ridge was up to six feet high in places with broken ice blocks jumbled all around. Unlike yesterday, the ridge had flat ice on either side which made it easier for us all, especially Peter and I, given our acceleration problem, to be able to manoeuvre the skidoo over.

Pen travelled along the ridge with his skidoo for some way, before beckoning us to come over with a muffled shout and a wave of his hand. We halted our skidoos and all walked over to where he was, gingerly checking our steps to determine how thick the ice was. Within the walls that made up the pressure ridge we gathered around to see what Pen was huddled over. He stood back to reveal polar bear tracks! The footprints were huge – like giant saucepans, as illustrated when Mark stood with both feet together in one print. The footprints trailed the ridge. 'Looking for seals,' Pen explained to his hushed audience. 'I estimate that this ridge is new, perhaps five to six hours old, formed with the change of the tide maybe. He probably passed by hoping to spot a seal surfacing in the sea water exposed by the ridge.'

An overwhelming sense of being in the desolate wilds of nature gripped the group as we surveyed the evidence of the passing monster who had perhaps been here only a few hours previously. Apart from these tracks we had not seen evidence of any life so far. No animal, plant life, bird or fish had revealed itself, such was the desolation of this place. Yet somehow an animal of massive proportions managed to eke out an existence for itself. Clearly every meal would be hard won, and no opportunity could be missed in this barren environment. The bear was of course primarily a carnivore - a meat eater - and the only meat I had seen on the expedition was standing around me in their warm coats nervously surveying evidence of the recent visitor. We decided to move, quickly, onwards.

The skidoos started remarkably easily, and no one wanted to get stuck there. Each skidoo and komatik was wheeled round and backed up, to gain the speed and momentum to drive through the break in the ice ridge found by Pen. Mark and Bunny drove over first following in Pen's tracks. Peter and I followed through, but stalled through lack of power and stopped – right by the polar bear prints. Rob and Geoff caught up, and with Peter all three of them pushed the komatik with all their might as I revved the engine to get through.

We continued onwards as the low white hills of Cornwallis Island dropped away to the east and Truro Island came into focus directly in front of us in the north west. All the lands here bore the names of people and places of my native country. I smiled to myself under the multiple coverings protecting my face and head as we passed Cape Evans, though I couldn't see it, as it was too low and distant to the west.

I wondered whether Mr. Evans of Scott's tragic South Pole party was smiling on the little boy who once dreamt of saving him, and who now saluted him as a grown man, in the Arctic. I felt inspired by his adventure and sacrifice, that had also led to the Cape being given his surname; I was now travelling in the Arctic. The Antarctic storm and unusually cold weather that he and the others had encountered in Scott's 1912 party had defeated them. I felt inspired to overcome whatever was put in my way, to achieve the Magnetic North Pole. Scott's spirit and inspiration to a generation of my countrymen at the turn of the twentieth century, was still as alive as ever.

Helen Thayer had met a lot of fog in the area that we would spend the next day or so travelling through. She had also described being stalked there by a large male bear. Also, whilst travelling on foot she had several encounters in the area of Crozier Strait and the Goodsir Inlet, that formed the narrowest channel between Little Cornwallis Island in the east and Bathurst Island in the west – the channel leading to the dreaded Polar Bear Pass. We expected to be in that area in a few hour's time as our journey continued to follow her path.

Finally, we stopped for lunch, by what appeared from a short distance to be a small brown mark on the ice. On closer inspection it was found to be the remains of a seal. Obviously the victim of a polar bear attack. Just the back bone and a few other bits and pieces were left on the ice. No doubt the seal had had a hole in the ice here, and been attacked by one of our silent and somewhat invisible friends, when it came up for air. The calmness and serenity of the location hid the violence and short struggle that had occurred perhaps a day or so earlier.

We had a macabre lunch at the seal's grave site. Our calorie-rich meal consisted of a Mars Bar, some peanuts, a slice of flap jack, a hot drink, a handful of dried apricots and a frozen salami. Due to the high fat content of the salami it was not frozen, and was more rubbery and kinder to the teeth.

The strong taste flooded out into my mouth as my warm saliva released the salami's flavour. All more fat and sugar to add to those six thousand calories needed for the day. Meanwhile the Mars Bar was almost rock solid.

The ice was still flat around us, continuing our good travel conditions. Pen performed a quick GPS navigation check. 'There it is!' he shouted from behind his frost-laden mask, pointing northwards. There was a wisp of what appeared to be white smoke on the horizon, directly north and in our direction of travel. It was possibly from the Polaris Mine located on Little Cornwallis Island where we were headed, perhaps ten miles away now. After another twenty minutes of travel, what appeared to be a small black dot emerged below the growing, and now confirmed, trail of smoke marching its way across the clear sky in the distance. Evidence of man.

Pen's lighter skidoo, running like a hare compared with our slower camels with their heavy loads, roared off into the distance towards the smoke and the Polaris Mine. Pen had decided to go ahead and try to arrange additional fuel for us. Spurred on by his rapid progress we all rode at full speed, perhaps reaching thirty-five miles an hour, on the flat smooth sea ice, bordered by the low, almost identical hills to our east and west. Geoff and Rob fell behind, so Peter regularly turned his head to check they were still following. It would be easy for the tail group to break down and everyone else to continue for miles in advance, unaware of their plight.

We soon pulled up at the Polaris Mine in convoy, the small black dot having revealed itself to us in all its man-made glory. We slowed down as Pen's tracks led towards what appeared to be a big jetty. As we got closer, we saw a huge building, like a massive shed; all roof and little sides - sat on a promontory above the dock. The dock was inactive at this time of year because the sea was frozen solid and inaccessible by any ship. Behind the 'shed' were the living quarters. On the top of a small hill was a large fuel store.

To find such a large site in such a desolate location was as bizarre as the deep orange colour that the designers had decided to paint the buildings.

As we got closer I could confirm it was the jetty I had seen in a poster at Resolute airport. It looked quite lonely, waiting for the concrete-hard ice to melt, so ships could service the Polaris Mine behind it, when the summer tides came. The jetty was presently quite redundant. We rounded the jetty on our skidoos. I could see Pen's skidoo parked on the ice. We all pulled up alongside it; there was no sign of Pen, only a few footprints leading away up a small hill towards the mine. As the last skidoo stopped, and its engine ground to a halt, an eerie silence settled over us. I sat there listening to the silence and in awe of the two hundred foot warehouse-like structure of the mine bearing down on us. We all must have felt the same for, remarkably, no one spoke.

The Polaris Mine was a marvel of modern engineering, given its location. It is the most northerly-based metal mine in the world. The bottom of the mine was located almost a thousand feet below sea level and there were over fifteen miles of tunnels. Crushed ore is conveyed on a two-mile-long conveyer system through the tunnels back to the surface. The tunnels were located in permafrost, so the icy ground has to be maintained to ensure that the tunnels do not warm up and collapse. A sophisticated cooling system ensured that the permafrost remained frozen, and the mine water-free, during the summer months. The cooling system seemed like an example of selling fridges to the Eskimos! Over a million tonnes of lead and zinc ore have been extracted every year since the mine began operations, over two decades ago in 1982. The ore is shipped out during the brief summer months when the sea, still ice-strewn but passable, allowed ships to get to the mine and arrive at the jetty which we were standing beside.

Suddenly the peace was shattered by a loud roar. It was like a booming stag, except ten times louder. Startled, we all looked round. I was unsure what could be making such a noise; I knew it was too loud for a polar bear, but I found myself jumping out of my skidoo seat as though it were. Up above us on a promontory behind the jetty, perhaps a hundred and fifty feet away, a giant dumper truck had appeared and began to struggle up the hill, the gears groaning under the weight of the truck's load being pulled behind.

Looking through his misted window the driver peered down at us, six people in the wilderness looking back at him, quite startled to see him and such a contraption in such a wild and remote place. It must have looked quite amusing. None of us said a word as we stood with mouths agape behind our frosted face masks, watching his progress. In the clear light we could see the baseball cap of the driver clearly and his face underneath turning towards the road in front of him and back to us again.

You could see written all over his face that he was thinking, 'There's another bunch of madmen!' I looked round at the others still focussing on him. Written in their eyes poking above their neck gaiters were the thoughts: 'That's a mad trucker. What a nutty place to have a job!' 'Bunch of bloody holiday-makers!' the trucker, no doubt saying to himself. The thoughts were transferred without a word being said between us and him. We were surely right. To be a trucker in this part of the world required something; special I suppose. Before the trucker took his eyes off us, he gave a smile followed by a wave, which we all gladly returned. His truck accelerated slightly, causing a plume of white exhaust smoke to dispense into the cold air, before he and his charge rounded the hill and disappeared.

The silence returned again, I felt as though I had just seen some sort of mirage.

'Make sure you look left and right before starting off!' shouted Bunny. We all laughed. I could comprehend looking out for polar bears jumping out at us, but not being run down by a truck in the middle of this Arctic desert! I had a little giggle at our situation. It was quite comforting though to see a slice of civilisation and technology up here in our remote surroundings. It was to be the last lonely outpost of mankind before we moved into the unknown.

As we all waited for Pen, our minds started to drift.

'I wonder what the bar is like in there Bunny?' pondered Mark softly, not wishing to disturb the silence.

'Dying for a glass of rouge, eh Markey?' replied Bunny, synchronising his words with jumping up and down to keep his blood circulating.

'To be honest, I'd just settle for a sit down in a warm bar.'

'Why don't we just go in?' interjected Rob, slapping his arms together. 'By the time Pen arrives with the fuel we'll all be plastered.'

'You never know, a stupefying amount of alcohol might –,' he paused in mid sentence abruptly.

'What?' said Mark, awaiting his first taker to challenge the temperature taboo.

'Well, stop one from, err, overheating.'

'Hey, we could even end up with a job up here Mark.'

'What in construction Bunny?' queried Mark.

'Yes, I sued my builder once, so I suppose that gives me some legal experience in the construction field, and probably makes me the local expert for about a thousand miles or more.'

'But this is a mine,' said Mark confused.

'True. I have some of that experience too – if defending against a gold-digger qualifies?!'

We all chuckled in the cold air and hoped Pen wouldn't be too long. Rob checked the oil levels in the skidoo engines while Geoff was busy looking at the engines. I took a couple of photos of the mine and just tried to adjust to our bizarre situation.

Pen appeared at the top of the jetty and made his way down to us, empty-handed. 'Can't get any fuel here, so I've made a phone call to Mike back at the Rookery to arrange a fuel drop by air. Not sure how long that will take but the weather is good there for a flight.'

'However, I think we should call it a day and get the tent ready.' I suppose we were all a bit surprised by this, and hoped we'd be able to continue whilst the ice and weather were good. Pen knew best though.

We set up camp a little way from the mine, not far from the rubbish dump – a favourite ground of scavenging polar bears, apparently. And an iceberg locked in the sea ice about two hundred yards away seemed exactly like Pen had described off the Resolute coast, as 'perfect bear ambush country'.

Following our well-rehearsed tent-erection routine, we soon had set up our orange canvas-walled home. Just then, and about an hour after Pen's call, a twin Otter plane from Bradley First Air flew over and circled before conducting a perfect landing nearby. The plane had two propeller-driven engines and was fitted with short skis over its three wheels so it could land on the sea ice, which was probably about two or three feet thick there, providing a safe a flat landing strip for the pilot.

Once the plane had come to rest the side doors opened to reveal Gary. He stood there with six large fuel drums, a wide smile and a red nose. The jerry cans from our komatiks were soon filled up. We thanked Gary and the pilot, and soon the engines were roaring and throwing up all sorts of ice fragments, as we stood back to watch the Otter gracefully take off, with a very impressive climb rate.

'We've just lost the expedition's unsupported status chaps,' shouted Pen, as the plane became a dot in the distance, after our re-supply. As we'd never promoted this as part of the expedition criteria and, the situation necessitated this, no one was too worried.

So with the events of the day behind us and the tent now up, there was nothing to do but get an early night. The evening was noticeably colder, if that seemed possible, and the gyrations of the ice dance got faster and more dramatic, so we were all pleased when Mark invited us into the tent with a large bellow, 'Tea's up!'

Around the hissing stove Mark announced, on behalf of all of us all, 'Pen we invite you to join us in the tent tonight.' With tongue firmly in cheek he then jested, 'We feel you have proven yourself in a manner that warrants you to join our company this evening, my good man.'

'Hear, hear!' came a voice from the back.

'Thank ye Sir, thank ye most kindly,' Pen replied in his best, but not very good, English west country yokel accent, gently touching his head as if to raise an imaginary cap.

One of the highlights each evening was the GPS position reading which Pen conducted. 'Seventy-five point twenty-five degrees north,' he paused, as everyone scribbled in their diaries, and then continued, ninety-six point fifty-eight degrees west.' We'd travelled forty nautical miles which was ok, but I think we hoped we would have got further. We needed to.

'We are going to get to the Pole aren't we Pen?' asked Mark, disappointed after the efforts of the day were rubbed out by the lower than expected mileage.

'Well let's hope so,' Pen replied as he switched off the GPS.

The Argos communication device registered the temperature as minus thirty-five and Pen set the transmit code to 'oo' – all ok. Mike would pick this message up at the Rookery. With our individual tasks completed there was nothing more to do, except conserve our fuel, so the stove was switched off. The tent was much colder than last night, and as the stove was switched off the temperature inside the tent plunged so dramatically you could almost see the steam crystallise in front of you and drop to the ground as ice.

The victim to sleep under the ice wall tonight was to be Peter. I managed to get in closer to the middle of the tent, which I hoped would be marginally warmer than the outer edge where I had been the night before. The tent was noticeably more crowded with Pen's presence but, whilst there was little room to move at all, it was only fair to have him inside. Pen began reading aloud another 'Winnie the Poo' story, but I only managed to hear two chapters before falling to sleep, exhausted.

The morning of Wednesday 26th March, 1997 brought the same, by now well-honed routine. Mark was up and had started the stove. The rest of us rose individually and quickly dressed. I had found the night, again, particularly uncomfortable – cramped and somewhat cold. I welcomed rising, to stretch my legs and warm up. Today I had my first toilet experience; I was beginning to wonder whether I was constipated, which would not have been a good thing. Armed with a spade, I surveyed the iceberg near the tent and found my spot, being careful to ensure that I wouldn't become something's meal when at man's weakest. For the uninitiated, toilet paper was not used for two reasons: the first being its bulk on the sledge and secondly an ice wedge being equally practical and more environmental. A zip that ran from my belly button down between my legs and up the base of my spine made the activity easier. Despite my scenic surroundings, the operation was completed quickly, to limit my butt from exposure to the minus thirty-five degree temperature.

We left camp just after ten o'clock. I ensured everything was in the correct komatiks. Bunny had all the engines started on time, supported by Geoff, though one of the machines took a little persuading to start. Rob had all the fuel levels gauged and checked. The weather was again perfect with no breeze, clear and calm. The ice was also good and we followed the same configuration as yesterday, with Peter and I sharing turns driving. We all knew we needed to make up some big miles today as we had covered just over a third of our 250 mile journey by skidoo.

After two hours we approached Black Point, just visible on the horizon. Black Point was a rounded hill on Bathurst Island of some 500 feet high. Black Point would lead us to the Goodsir Inlet at the mouth of Polar Bear Pass. How different our weather was to Helen Thayer's at this point. We had visibility for miles and for all intents and purposes we were alone. Recalling her story, she was not so lucky at this point, encountering dense fog and numerous polar bears, that her dog Charlie alerted her to, as she was followed and stalked in the mist.

It wasn't long before we met our first pressure ridge of the day. These ridges were expected because the narrow passage between the islands on the Crozier Strait squeezed the currents between them, disturbing the ice. These pressure ridges were thankfully not very high, unlike near Sheringham Point two days earlier, and rose to a maximum height of, perhaps, five feet. The flatter ice 'gulley' between the pressure ridges led in the direction of our course, so travelling on the flatter ice between the ridges was not only more comfortable but also productive. As we continued further, the ridges became more frequent, one perhaps every fifty feet, the ice more scattered and ruffled, until an hour later, we were seemingly in a maze. Our speed slowed accordingly and I feared another day of low mileage.

The first set of polar bear prints of the day was pointed out by Pen riding on his lead skidoo. Within thirty minutes there seemed to be bear prints everywhere, criss-crossing the flatter paths between pressure ridges leading through the now jumbled walled maze of ridges. Because the ice was now littered with small stones of ice, we were travelling at walking pace and driving over the bumpy frozen ground. We couldn't see over the higher ridges, so as each one approached I gingerly looked around, half expecting to be rushed by a polar bear disturbed from his sleep. Hopefully they had long gone or our engine noises had frightened them off, but they were inquisitive beasts and as masters of this region, had little fear. The ice didn't seem that new, with no evidence of thin or open water, so opportunities for bear prey – seals – were also, I hoped, very low.

By now the skidoos were again getting quite a bashing, as we manoeuvred between the growing crowded confines of the ridges, over small bumps, avoiding gullies, and occasionally going wrong and crashing. The maze was getting more difficult to drive through and Pen was constantly looking for the best way ahead, often climbing a ridge on foot, hoping the extra elevation would enable him to pick a good path through. After another hour Pen called a halt and our convoy, which now stretched over a distance of about three hundred feet, came to rest. We automatically started our duties, interspersed with breaks for helpings of nuts and hot drinks from our day bags. The oil leak from my engine seemed to have cleared up, thanks to Geoff's mechanical skill. Peter and I checked our load and made sure everything was tied tightly down in the komatik.

Geoff, who was riding at the rear of the group, walked up the line towards Pen. 'All ok Geoff?' I asked, as he passed me.

'Bloody fingers like dead sausages, oh and we seem to have lost three jerry cans of fuel.' Sure enough there was a gaping hole at the back of Rob and Geoff's komatik.

'Any idea Geoff?' enquired Pen, who would have looked alarmed if his balaclava wasn't hiding his emotions.

'Nope, seriously, they could have come off anywhere from here all the way back to the Polaris Mine, but I expect they came off as we bumped through this maze.'

There was no choice – we would have to go back for them. Peter and I volunteered to do this, as our skidoo happened to be in a slightly wider part between the ridges, where we could just about turn our machine round and travel back. We unhitched our komatik and began to drive back. As we passed by the last skidoo Rob shouted out encouragingly, 'Now lads, if you pass an off licence on the way – you know what to get.'

'Two crates of wine?' Peter replied.

'Yes, that's right,' shouted Rob, 'oh, and better get something for the others too.' Rob waved us off and wished us luck.

We travelled back through the maze, over the bumpy ridges and past polar bear prints, following our previous tracks, in search of the three valuable fuel cans. The group soon disappeared into the maze behind us.

'Typical!' Peter shouted in my ear from the saddle behind me above the noise of the engine. 'Mark is now left with not only the food but the rifle as well!'

'Not to worry mate, we'll soon be sledging, which is what we came here for.'

I had my hood down to ensure maximum visibility. We had travelled only a couple of minutes when we were joined unexpectedly, but welcomingly, by Pen at the rear, armed with the rifle. We continued for only another ten minutes when we came upon the three orange-coloured cans scattered across the ice. I was quite relieved and so was Peter. One jerry can was almost empty, but we hauled all the cans onboard the back of the skidoo and managed to find a space between ridges to reverse the skidoo and travel back to the main group. On catching up with the group I picked up our komatik and parked the skidoo at the front of the queue, so as not to be last when we started up again. This was Peter's and my reward for driving back for the cans.

The group moved off again and continued into the frozen maze, with no let-up from our unforgiving surroundings for the next two hours. Peter took his turn and did the driving as I rested on the seat behind. The sun was high and very bright. Even behind my darkened ski goggles I found myself squinting as the light bounced off the white walls and floor of the ridges of the maze. I had given up on sunglasses almost immediately when the expedition began. Not only did they expose my skin but my breath seemed to freeze on the lenses within seconds, ruining visibility and making them useless. Whilst I had two pairs of sunglasses, I only had one pair of ski goggles. Unfortunately these now had a crack in them, caused I suspect, by being crushed in the crowded tent or komatik.

With Peter concentrating on the path ahead, every now and again I would look round to check that our komatik and the following skidoo, driven by Mark, were ok. At one of those moments, Mark took a ridge badly and his komatik swung round violently. I jumped up and waved to him to slow down before he had a bigger accident. Again the group stopped, and with engines running we all managed to manually nudge Mark's heavy komatik over a bit so that he could drag it onwards correctly again.

Later on, a jerry can jumped off the back of our komatik, as we landed with a big bang, after tackling a seemingly small, but as it turned out, dangerous ridge. This event was signalled by Mark's shouts and pointing hand as he bellowed, 'I say, I say!' Given that we were still only moving at a fast walking pace, Bunny quickly jumped off Mark's skidoo, picked up the can and delivered it alongside on foot, securing it in the komatik 'Tighter than a ten pound note in a miser's wallet!'

Finally Pen signalled the way ahead was clear, as the ridges gradually got smaller and our speed rose as we cleared the Strait. Eventually the ice became as flat as it had been some hours before. After the recent confines of the pressure-ridged maze we all ran our skidoos at full speed abreast, enjoying our re-found freedom. Peter and I shouted at the tops of our voices, 'Yee-hah!' as we raced Mark and Bunny towards Black Point.

We swung round Black Point. In front of me I was presented with my nightmare of the last few months – Polar Bear Pass. In the sunlight the entrance to the pass didn't look that sinister. I had imagined a narrow gorge where all the bears would have to pass through, making it impossible to avoid any of these menacing travellers. Instead I saw a wide pass, maybe two miles across, and bordered with the familiar flat rounded hills common to the area. Polar Bear pass ran across the middle of Bathurst Island, at its narrowest point from east to west, and was naturally the place for all bear traffic to go through. The pass was low lying and not far from the sea. North and south of the pass the island rose up, (according to the map), with hills rising to a thousand feet to the north and about the same to the south.

It was now almost three o'clock in the afternoon and we continued to travel at racing speed, now moving directly westwards towards the entrance to Polar Bear Pass. Seeing Rob and Pen falling behind, we slowed down to let them catch up so, we could continue travelling abreast together again.

'This is just fantastic Mark!' Pete and I shouted over, as we raced alongside each other. Mark returned a thumbs up, with Bunny, arms spread out and flapping, as if flying along.

'Polar Bear Pass,' I pointed out to them – 'Polar Bear Pass!' I could see Mark turning to Bunny and passing on the message above the roar of his engine. Bunny responded with a glove slicing ominously across his neck. Chatting whilst we drove along slowly, waiting for the others to catch up, we noticed that Pen and Rob had now overtaken us, now we were the ones falling behind. We soon caught up with the group, then Pen stopped us all so he could take a navigation reading on his GPS.

We had entered Polar Bear Pass. After an hour travelling in the pass, with not a polar bear track in sight, we gained an idea of just how long it would take to get to the other side of the island. The pass was about a mile wide now with white, rounded hills bordering it. There was a great feeling of space as the channel between the north and south sides of the pass was flat ice. I wasn't sure whether this was sea ice or tundra, but the main thing was it was flat. We were in the pass to avoid the broken ice at the top of Bathurst Island alerted to us by a satellite photograph at the Rookery. During a short break and equipment check we got into discussion about the pass.

'We will be another day clearing the pass,' Pen said, with the map out, as the other six travellers looked on with interest.

'That's a lot of time and fuel,' Rob, the Petrol Monitor, replied.

'We need to go north west as that is the most direct route, but we are travelling due west,' I stated, while looking at the map.

'If we could cut across here, excuse me,' pointed Bunny as he put a gloved hand on the map and drew it upwards in a north westerly direction. 'We could probably knock off two days travel by a more direct route.' What he was suggesting was true. Our current plan was to drive west across the island via Polar Bear Pass. However, this wouldn't take us any further north towards our goal. We needed to go north, the reason for not doing that was the hilly terrain bordering the pass that would stop us. Bunny was challenging that notion, and asking us to consider taking the skidoos through the hills.

As we stood in the middle of the pass the options for best travel were being weighed up. Everyone was keenly aware that we had limited fuel, that we had made a detour that would drink more fuel and would lead us back out to sea, where it was unclear what the conditions were – all we knew was that our current route along the pass would be a long one.

'Going over the hills is not an option,' Mark forcefully replied. 'Look, there's no way the skidoos with the weight in the komatiks can tackle any sort of an incline.' The map at this stage was of less use than it had been, as the contour lines were not detailed enough to make any sort of accurate decision as to whether a path could be found through the hills or not.

'One should remember the trouble we just had on those minor pressure ridges,' cut in Geoff. Bunny raised his voice a little to make his point. 'We are driving in the wrong direction chaps, and we don't have the time to do that. I don't know if my skidoo will hold up for another day.'

'Get someone else to drive it then,' Rob interrupted, sensing an opportunity to start winding everyone up.

'What's your view Peter?' Pen enquired, ignoring Rob's comment.

'I want to get sledge hauling.'

'And Duncan?'

'Well, I don't think we can make a decision here, we certainly can't cross the island right here anyway.' I was looking at Pen's GPS and had taken a reading to see exactly where in the pass we were. The crossing point Bunny was suggesting was further along the pass.

'Ok, what I suggest we do is continue along the pass until we reach the vicinity of where Bunny thought that we make the crossing through the hills, and take a further view there,' instructed our guide Pen. Everyone was freezing up again. I noticed Rob banging his feet with some vigour on the ground to get his circulation pumped back into his extremities. I too had cold feet, yet my hands were warm. We all agreed with Pen's suggestion and the expedition moved off again, with Pen at the lead using his GPS to estimate where to stop for the next reading.

About an hour later, Pen slowed down at the approximate best point, near a small inlet. I could now see why it had taken until 1947 to get an accurate map of Bathurst Island. According to the map, we were travelling on 'Tundra' yet it was as flat as good sea ice. The map also showed rivers coming down from the hills bordering the pass by us, but clearly these were still frozen over and I found it difficult to believe they ever would be anything but that.

With the map out again, Mark and Bunny unhitched their komatik. 'You've got to be joking!' said Mark as he surveyed the hills. They were low lying hills, but even here it was difficult to see what we would be up against if we were to carry out Bunny's suggestion and try and go the more direct route and cross the island through the hills. The map indicated a height of 1140 feet. 'But we're not going over the hill Mark, we're going to go around it,' Bunny stated enthusiastically, as he pointed to another contour line that showed a more reassuring 50 feet of elevation.

'Pen has this been done before, I mean crossing this section on a skidoo?' I asked.

'I'm not sure,' came his reply, 'probably.'

'What about with a laden komatik?' enquired Geoff, more specifically to our situation.

'I don't know,' said Pen, 'probably not.'

There was no point everyone going, so Pen took his skidoo and Mark and Bunny took theirs with Bunny driving, and headed off to investigative a possible route. They soon disappeared behind a hill, whose apparent flour-covered surface immediately muffled their engine sounds, and returned us once again to the Arctic's overwhelming silence.

Geoff, Rob, Pete and I, whilst waiting for the others to return, decided to stretch our legs and walk up the nearest hill. It wasn't conceivable to just wait for the others coming back as, without moving, we would have got too cold. As we walked up a small hill we hoped that the increased height might help us to see a way across country, or if not, at least have a good eye view of the others making fools of themselves on their overland skidoo mission. It was bitingly cold now, and my feet felt like ice blocks, so we all pretty much ran up the hill to keep the blood flowing. There was no wind to rob us of heat, just pure unadulterated freezing air.

At the top, perhaps two hundred feet up, we found a great view of the pass, which we all took the opportunity to scan for any wildlife of a particular fearful kind. Polar Bear Pass was spread before us, it was beautiful, but so desolate. Apart from our skidoos at the foot of the hill there was no sign of man. We were utterly alone with nature. The hills on the southern side of the pass, low and rounded, looked back at us, as they had done for millennia and would continue to do so for long after we had gone.

Looking north, towards the hills where our investigative party had disappeared, it wasn't possible to see much of a way through. We couldn't see or hear the others, and hoped that they would have better luck on the ground.

'Hey, chaps,' said Rob, breaking into our individual thoughts, as we surveyed the scene before us in silence.

'What Rob?'

'You know Mark isn't here right now.'

'What of it?'

'Well I just thought I'd say, I'm cold, fucking cold, and I've been cold ever since I got off that bloody plane.'

Spoken like a true paratrooper, to which we all had a good chuckle, before Geoff, looking at Rob through his frost-lined ski goggles, shook his head in recognition that the taboo about the cold had just been broken and responded with, 'Clap that man in irons, Sir!'

About half an hour later, and back down by the skidoos in the pass, we heard the approaching sound of the returning party.

'Well?'

'We can't see any clear way through the hills,' said Mark, disappointed.

'I still say we make a go of it,' insisted Bunny again.

'On what basis?' Rob asked.

'Well, the reason we took this course of action – to save time.'

'Yes, I know – but your exploration didn't reveal a clear way through the hills.'

'No, but that's not to say we can't get through,' insisted Bunny.

'Ok, chaps,' cut in Peter, 'it's too cold,' looking at Mark as he said the forbidden word, 'to have a legal argument right now. Did your recce reveal to you some hope of getting through or not?'

'Yes,' replied Bunny confidently.

'No,' replied Mark confidently.

We had to take a vote. We all agreed, except Bunny, that it was too risky to take a detour through the hills, on the basis that the terrain was not suitable for skidoos and we'd probably have to turn back at some stage anyway. We decided to stay with our current plan, which was to cross Bathurst Island by travelling westwards across Polar Bear Pass. Bunny reluctantly accepted the decision.

Before we moved off Geoff had a look at the skidoo Peter and I were driving, in an attempt to fix its growing acceleration problem. He decided to change the drive wheel. It was hand-chilling work for him, and more delay for the team. As I found my hands didn't seem to get as cold as Geoff's I did as much as I could to help under his instruction, while Peter re-checked the komatik.

Before long we were running through the pass again. The wind had risen, dropping the temperature further through wind-chill. With our approximate speed of twenty-five miles an hour we were being exposed to wind-chill of some minus sixty degrees Celsius.

As I sat on the skidoo behind Peter, who was now driving, I hugged him closely, to stay out of the wind. The wind was however, coming through a crack in my ski goggles. It was really, really cold. The skin around my face felt like it was burning, so I put my hood over my face and closed my eyes as I buried my head in Peter's back to stay out of the wind. Every now and again we had a sudden jolt as Peter hit a bit of hard ground. By five o'clock and heading due west the sun was directly in front of us, low and shining straight into our eyes. It was a low, bright sun making visibility ahead quite difficult.

We all changed drivers more regularly, to reduce the time the driver spent in the direct wind. With hands and fingers freezing more quickly now, especially the accelerator hand on my skidoo, which still remained difficult to work. Every now and again my hood blew back, but Peter thankfully put it back up, leaving me to concentrate on the ice ahead.

We were making good progress due to the flat ice. Pen wanted us to get as far as possible while the daylight was good. By now one of my eyes was frozen shut as the wind rushed though the small crack in the lens of my broken goggle. Driving with one eye was nevertheless easy on flat ice. After another twenty minutes Pen slowed down to stop, to initiate another drivers change, when Geoff, following – and only able to see a washed out grey object in front of him due to the powerful sun - failed to see Pen stop. At the last moment he veered off, but his komatik ploughed straight into the back of Pen's motionless komatik, puncturing a jerry can. Another twenty litres of precious fuel was lost as it flooded onto the ice.

Having stopped to repair the damage we initiated an advisory hand signal routine to indicate when we were slowing down. Pen would raise one arm, the passenger on the following skidoo would then raise two arms indicating to the driver behind of the slowdown; this signal was to be repeated down the convoy.

We conducted another inspection of the equipment. Mark and Bunny's komatik seemed to be falling to pieces, with some of the komatik's securing rope having become loose, allowing the wooden structure of the komatik to work its way out of shape. The komatik's wooden frame was beginning to come apart. Though we were all very cold, it was to our disappointment that Pen decided to camp, stating Bunny's komatik was 'An accident waiting to happen'. Major repairs would now take place as the light began to fade.

We found a good area on the shore of Polar Bear Pass to camp for the night; we were almost directly half way along the pass. It was particularly beautiful in the evening light. We moved our skidoos in and formed our customary wagon wheel defensive circle. Pen and Geoff started work on Bunny's komatik immediately after we had stopped. Peter and I started the tent erection routine, with Mark starting the water-making. We were now all working together like a well oiled machine. The tent was set up on the ice, secured with ice screws, in defence against any wind getting up during the night.

About forty feet behind the tent was solid ground. Small grey flat stones littered the ground. I attempted to pick one up as a small souvenir, but found it to be glued to the ground. Even kicking it hard failed to move it. Further behind the ground rose to form the hills of the pass. These were mainly white and snow-covered, with the occasional rocky outcrop breaking through.

9

Polar Bear Pass

'Adventure is just bad planning.'

ROALD AMUNDSEN, POLAR EXPLORER.

As we set-up camp the temperature remained very low, hovering just under minus forty. The evening was again beautiful but, as ever, there was much work to be done to get the camp organised and the skidoos prepared for the next day. We also had a scheduled radio call to make to Resolute, so Pen had a keen eye on the time.

Pen and Geoff left their work to get the radio. 'Komatik Two!' I shouted, as they headed towards the wrong sledge.

Peter retrieved two small bundles for them, the Spillsbury radio – a box about the size of a shoe box - and a length of wire tied round a stick. I grabbed four ski poles and followed them over, leaving Peter to feed Mark's demands; 'Cooking pans Peter!' We would now set-up the radio.

The antenna for the radio had to face Resolute Bay, where the signal would be received. As Pen unpacked the radio I erected the antenna. The antenna wire was about fifty feet long. During transmission this wire would get hot. It was necessary to raise the wire off the ground and to do so four ski poles were used. These special ski poles, from the Norwegian Army, enabled the ski basket and handle to be unscrewed leaving just the pole. All the poles were then screwed together forming a single twelve-foot-high pole to which the mid point of the antenna wire was attached to the top. Thus the antenna was fifty feet long, secured at each end and raised to some twelve feet in the middle.

The radio was switched on and it immediately generated a crackling sound. Pen hunched down on the cold ground with the microphone in his gloved hand, checked his watch, then said our expedition call sign clearly into the radio, 'Victor Oscar Oscar Two-Six-Four calling Resolute Two-Six-Three.' Mike, back at the Rookery at Resolute Bay, was known as 'Resolute 263'. The radio crackled a bit more before Pen said again, 'Victor Oscar Oscar Two-Six-Four calling Resolute Two-Six-Three.' Again nothing was heard but the lonely sound of static noise.

Pen adjusted some dials on the Spillsbury radio and tried again, this time ending in 'Nothing heard,' in case Mike could hear us but we not him. After a few more unsuccessful tries he tried calling Resolute Airport, who knew of our expedition and acted as communications backup for us, and many other expeditions. 'Victor Oscar Oscar Two-Six-Four calling Resolute Two-Six-Nine,' he said, using the call sign of Resolute airport. Again nothing was heard.

He scanned the airwaves and occasionally picked up some garbled communications between what sounded like two Daleks, or perhaps very drunk men, neither understandable. Pen continued to try for the next fifteen minutes, until the cold forced him aside as the sun sank to its lowest point. The light faded but couldn't be classed as dark, our white surroundings quickly changed from bluey-white to orangey-white and then a silvery-white with strong hints of blue. It was really quite beautiful.

We dug a hole in the ice and placed all the expedition's rubbish into it before it was set on fire, encouraged by soaking it in a little fuel. Whilst the heat generated from this was negligible, it gave comfort to the team, who momentarily stopped all their jobs and gathered round the dancing orange flames in the minus forty temperature.

'Well chaps another good day,' said Pen, as we all watched the flames jump from one box of rubbish to another.

'Truly beautiful here Pen, I love it,' I stated, without taking my eyes off the fire.

'Where's the polar bear alarm Duncan?'

'That'll be in komatik Three Pen, hang on I'll get it for you.'

'Thanks, might be best to get that out tonight, given that we are in Polar Bear Pass,' said Pen.

The others went about their jobs as Pen and I put up the polar bear alarm. This consisted of a thin wire that would encircle the tent about a foot off the ground. If it were broken for any reason, like a bear passing through, it would sound an alarm. It was set about ten feet out from the tent. The wire had to be carefully passed through the ski poles that held the tent up, to keep the wire off the ground. Putting up the alarm was fiddly, finger-freezing work as the wire was so thin you couldn't put it up with thick gloves on.

On more than one occasion, and just as Pen and I had managed to get it all set-up, someone would forget it was there, not see it, and walk across, breaking the line and setting off the alarm, forcing me to start again. Eventually I drew a line in the ice under the wire with my boot to show people where the hair-thin wire was. Pen disappeared off into the tent as I completed the work.

Given the wagon wheel circle of the komatiks we hoped that any bear would investigate the contents of those before heading to us in the tent. Whilst I finished setting up the alarm, something caught my eye in the distance. I stopped and looked up, taking off my goggles to ensure I had a clear view. I thought I saw something move. I couldn't quite make it out. It was perhaps quarter of a mile away coming from the back of the bay against the side of a hill.

'Rob, check this out,' I cautiously said, as he worked on the tent behind me.

'What's that?' he said taking his hood down.

'Over there – movement?'

He confirmed what I could see, an object that appeared to be moving on all fours, coming towards us. He looked at me, and I at him. I swallowed then said out loud to those in the tent, 'I think we have our first visitor of the evening.'

All the noise from within the tent stopped immediately. Pen shouted out, 'Could you say again please?'

'Something is coming towards us from the back of the bay, from the hills.' Inside the tent I could hear a muffled 'Where's the gun?'

'It's over by you.'

'No, I moved it outside because it was in the way.' I then heard the opening of the gun case's plastic covering. Just before Pen emerged from the tent armed, the moving mass had been recognised – it was Bunny! His shape had been disfigured by a small, but almost invisible, mound in the foreground hiding his legs, making his arms look as though they were legs. Legs from shoulders that would have been a polar bear.

'Bunny! we were about to shoot you!' yelled Mark, now outside the tent with everyone else.

'Pen do it anyway, go on, we'll all say we thought he was a polar bear and you acted correctly,' came the instruction from Rob, the English solicitor. A small argument ensued about Bunny's fate. As Bunny got back to the camp Pen reminded him, quite forcefully, not to take any further unescorted walks without telling anyone. Bunny took it in his stride, no jokes this time.

Once we had all retired into the relative comfort of the tent – it was only about minus fifteen inside with the stove on – it was clear we were all a bit edgy. We were in Polar Bear Pass after all, no longer in the bears' backyard, but in their front room. As if to signify this, Pen placed the rifle next to him by the tent door. We waited around the stove writing our diary entries for the day and chatted.

As the meal of pasta and dried beef began to bubble in the pan, our leader announced, 'Tonight we will open the first group present.' An excellent idea, and one I suspect most of us had forgotten about, due to our daily activities. Bunny insisted that it was his present to be opened first, and given his enthusiasm, his deep blue eyes were sparkling and almost rolling out of his head, no one could possibly refuse him. Out of his night bag he enthusiastically brought out with great anticipation his 'Love Ewe' – a plastic blow-up sheep, at which everyone had a great laugh as it bounced around the tent after being quickly inflated. Everyone apart from me of course, as I had also brought a 'Love Ewe' thousands of miles over the Atlantic, through North America and Canada, dragged it over the ice - only to find the beginnings of a flock. What were the chances of two plastic blow up 'Love Ewes' being in the same tent a hundred miles from the North Magnetic Pole? Sick minds think alike.

Spurred on by the reception of his first present, Bunny quickly decided to get out his second present, this time some edible stockings! With great excitement he immediately jumped up in the confines of the tent to try them on, knocking down all the damp socks on the drying line above his head. Ignoring our shouts as the socks come down, and realising the jelly stockings would not fit over his boots, he started to eat the stockings, before handing bits of them around. Bunny then got his third present out, to laughing screams of 'But you're only allowed to open one present.' His final present was a book entitled 'The Book of Bowels.' He began reading it out aloud to roars of laughter. It found Pen's sense of humour. Pen had a great laugh at the book which relegated "Winnie the Pooh" to tomorrow evening. This frivolity was needed after a long, cold and hard day on the ice, and Bunny was the best person to deliver it.

Finally, attention turned to the more pressing, serious discussion. 'Thank you Bunny, one never expected to have such an, err, well I'm not really sure,' Mark struggled, 'evening in Polar Bear Pass.' Twisting his thick beard in one hand and gently stirring our dinner in the other, Mark waited for the group to calm down before beginning what he termed an 'Alderney discussion.' Something which Peter and I didn't know the meaning of, and never did find out.

Mark stated, 'We are clearly behind schedule, our fuel is low and our skidoos knackered. Gentlemen, your views.'

I chipped in first and got straight to the point.

'We can get back on schedule, and I suggest the only way is to get a plane to pick us up and fly us to the Findlay group of islands and start man- hauling from there. This is after all where we are trying to get to with the skidoos.'

'I'm not sure I agree Duncan,' said Mark, still stirring tonight's dish.

'The expedition is to be an overland expedition,' stated Mark, as the contents of the pan began to bubble and froth indicating boiling point.

'Well, I thought the overall objective was to get to the Pole and right now, as I see it, that's the only way we are going to get there. We are going to have to fly sooner or later, given our slow progress.'

'I agree with Duncan,' said a supportive Peter.

'Well I appreciate what you are saying, but we are an overland expedition, so should continue our present course,' Mark restated. 'In fact, to be honest, I'm really enjoying the skidoos, and the thought of man-hauling at this stage doesn't seem much fun.'

'By jove! you're right Markey,' exclaimed Bunny, with shredded pieces of edible jelly stocking scattered over his lap. 'I've had such a hoot with the skidoos. I came off today, ended up in some hole and just sat there and laughed my head off.' We all smiled.

'Well you might only have a couple of days left to laugh with your skidoo, look at the state of it,' I pointed out. 'If it fails, then what?' We all reflected on the damage done to the skidoos, and how this was likely to continue.

There was clearly beginning to be a division in the group, centred around how we were going to get to the Pole.

'Geoffrey come on, what's your view?' enquired Mark.

'Well, my body is getting knackered I can tell you. My hands are solid most of the day and I must admit the thought of pulling a sledge at two miles an hour is less attractive now than a month ago.'

'But Geoff, one of the reasons your hands are so cold is that we are all suffering massive wind chill caused by the speed of the skidoos. We must be facing a wind chill of minus sixty or something. If you walk your body will be much warmer,' Peter correctly stated.

'But you can't walk to the Pole from here, at least I couldn't,' said Rob.

'Look chaps, let's get a plane. The weather is still good so we have that option; it might change in a day or two,' I said again.

The bowls of warm, steaming beef and pasta were now circulating in the tent and the discussion was briefly replaced by the immediate matter of food.

'Pen, your views please,' asked our leader Mark.

'Well, as the group's guide I will take you on the best way you decide, but that decision is up to you. I think you have stated the current situation and the options for going forward, correctly.' Pen wasn't taking sides.

The discussion raged on for another twenty minutes, until Mark terminated it by telling everyone that he was the leader and would make the decision on the way ahead. Whilst this was annoying for Peter and I, we had all agreed that Mark would lead the expedition; it was, after all, due to his determination that had turned an idea formed in a pub a year ago to the present reality of us all sitting there on the sea ice. We respected his position and fell in line accordingly.

With no real conclusion we all agreed that the next day we would have a good long crack on the skidoos and see how far we got.

Pen got out his GPS unit, and concluded the first part of the evening. We were positioned at 75.51 degrees north, which showed how little northern progress we had made, and finished at 98.3 degrees west, which showed how we had been moving westwards most of the day.

'So we have done twenty-nine nautical miles today,' Pen stated. It wasn't far enough, and I could feel the disappointment of the group matched my own. The only bright light was when Pen said, 'The temperature is way up to minus twenty-eight,' he made it sound as though it was a heat wave, but at least we might get a better night's sleep.

'Ok, here's a question' announced Geoff as we digested the evenings meal.

'If it's zero degrees today, and it's going to be twice as cold tomorrow…. how cold will it be ?'

Before anyone could answer correctly, Rob replied. 'Well, if it was going to be twice as cold as zero degrees tomorrow, it wouldn't be cold at all. It would be a bloody heat wave compared to what we have here !'

'Yes,' said Peter, 'and if your forecast is not forthcoming Geoff I'll be holding you personally responsible'.

'Sorry', said Geoff sheepishly.

'Sure you didn't get that forecast wrong, they didn't say minus four-zero degrees today and twice as cold tomorrow by any chance?' asked Bunny.

'Scattered sun with light rain, improving later' concluded Geoff. Mark then returned the conversation to a more pressing issue.

'Will you be retiring with us this evening Pen?'

'No, I think the komatik will suit me better tonight.'

'Oh come on Pen, there's no class system here – we all want to be equally uncomfortable, can't have you out with the polar bears in a comfy komatik,' Geoff explained.

'What? Come on chaps,' shouted Bunny with his usual grin, 'with that polar bear alarm being as flaky as I think it is, I would rather have Pen roaring his head off as the bad-boys-in-the-white-coats gnaw his leg off. Can't think of a better alarm than that.'

'I'll keep my mouth shut if they do,' replied Pen, 'just to spite you.' Pen decided to stay with everyone in the tent however, in order to keep up morale and keep the group together, after the Alderney discussion tensions of earlier.

Once again we all welcomed a good sleep in our cotton-like cocoons, to rest our weary muscles. Again it was cold in the bags, despite them being rated down to -45C 'comfortable' and -55C 'survival'.

———

The next day brought renewed vigour from everyone. We had to clear Polar Bear Pass, and much more. We weren't actually getting any nearer the Pole, just going westwards to get across the island. It was therefore wasted time and must be got through as fast as possible.

We had started a breakfast of Hot and Krumbly as per usual. The first of the six thousand calories that would be consumed today. As I ate through the sugary crust I found today's breakfast was more crumbly than usual. On investigation I discovered that I was eating a tooth filling. I spat out a mouthful of sugar and mercury, and used my tongue to feel around my mouth, to examine what the damage was. Not too bad, but it felt as though I had a crater-sized hole in my jaw.

As I stepped outside the tent for the first time that day, I was again blasted by the Arctic light. It was like falling into a mountain river as the cold air sucked at my skin and completely enveloped me, whilst my eyes were overcome by the sun's brilliance. Within moments my nasal hairs froze and the skin on my face immediately felt strangely hot, before losing its feeling and going numb. It was however, such an intensely positive feeling, almost like entering the world from the warmth of a womb every morning, as one's senses were sharply and freshly awoken.

Before we got into our routine jobs, Pen announced that he wanted to attempt another radio call. As we had made the previous radio call from the bottom of the pass, Pen felt that some increase in elevation might get us a better signal. He therefore grabbed the ski poles, radio and aerial wire and trudged off up the nearest hill, with Geoff, Bunny and Mark in tow.

With the tent still up it seemed particularly cold today. My feet really were freezing, since the moment I put my foot into my boot this morning they just seemed particularly cold.

The biggest temperature impact in nature is obviously when the temperature falls to freezing and liquid water turns to ice. After that my own observations noted that from zero to minus twenty or thirty, whilst progressively colder, was quite manageable. Once the temperature reached minus thirty this seemed like another milestone, and even our modern equipment began to struggle against the temperature. Any exposed skin seemed to freeze almost immediately, hands and feet were constantly cold, and it seemed that all man-made materials struggled, along with their human counterparts.

Pen had said that he had been in the polar regions for so long now that he could estimate the air temperature with an accuracy of about two degrees. According to Pen, the temperature was 'hovering just under minus forty' this morning. It felt like it. And yet, the sun remained bright and the skies clear and blue, which helped to keep our spirits high.

Rob complained of exceptionally cold feet too. After some serious movements, which I think even the 'ice dance' would not now reflect the violence required in our movements to push the blood into our extremities, Rob and I retired briefly to the tent. We switched the stove on and together Rob and I re-heated our socks and inner boot liners, just to ensure that no moisture had got into the boot overnight which may have now frozen, possibly affecting the temperature properties of the boot. Rob and I took it in turns to massage each other's feet over the stove, in two minute bursts, to try and warm them up. Satisfied that the boots were free of any frozen materials we got back on with the work in progress.

With the camp now remarkably quiet due to the majority of the team being up the hill with Pen and his radio, I decided to set up a few posed photos and arranged the pulks accordingly for a 'heroic set shot'. With the weather and the lighting so good Rob and I took a few shots of each other,

Rob with his sponsor's materials as props. We might not get the chance again if the weather closed in.

The others soon returned from the hill looking glum – 'Nothing heard,' said Bunny disappointed. On seeing our little posed set Mark, with immediate assumption of control declared, 'Duncan, you're team photographer, can you take a few shots of me?' By this stage my camera had iced up, so another was sought. Mark erected the Oyez flag and the group gathered round. Additional shots of Mark with the flag and holding the gun were taken. If we got to the Pole in white-out conditions the photos would simply be dreadful.

'Geoff what's that?' I pointed to a hairy football-like object he was carrying under his arm, as he arrived back at the camp slightly behind everyone else.

'Last night's meal.' The ball was actually the head of a dead musk ox, a sort of hairy bull crossed with a deer.

'Polar bear victim?'

'Not sure, probably not,' replied Pen. It wasn't long before this featured as a macabre prop, alongside the gun in some shots of this most manly team. Bunny was using his sunglasses as mirrors to check his vanity. By blowing breath on his hands he then pushed this moisture onto his beard, where it froze almost immediately, to give him that 'Arctic-worn' appearance of a frosty face. As newly promoted team photographer I was soon setting up the shots, ignoring Mark's pleas for his best angles to be taken into account. Seeing that he was not getting his way with me, when Pen appeared Mark announced, 'Pen, you must have experience taking pictures.' It was my shortest photo assignment ever, as Pen took charge of the camera.

'Say polar bear please,' he chirped, as we smiled behind our balaclavas.

'Come on Pen we're not on some lovey-dovey trip to the Caribbean, polar explorers don't smile – think of Scott.'

'Dear God this is an awful place,' quoted Jeff.

'Now, Pen you must join the next shot,' requested Mark, but Bunny protested. This was over-ridden by Mark with the caveat from the protesting Bunny, 'Ok, but Pen isn't to look heroic.'

With the photos eventually done to everyone's satisfaction – local sponsors and personal vanity requirements all met, we took the tent down and resumed our individual jobs. Everyone began to get things moving. We needed to get on and cover some major mileage today. Once Mark, as cook, had completed his tasks, he began to order others about. Peter began to grumble. This was not good. The strains were beginning to show. We needed a few more laughs.

At this stage of the departure the environment was remarkably quiet.

'Problems Bunny?' enquired Pen as normally by that time the air would be full with the sound of coughing motors, resisting being woken from their frozen idleness by Bunny's encouragement. Not this morning, not a sound apart from the odd grunt from Geoff.

'The start wires seem to have frozen on all of them,' stated Bunny slightly frustrated. We were losing time. This attracted Pen and Geoff. With the toolkit and his gloves off, Geoff meant business. It was cold, finger-numbing work as he coaxed each skidoo out of its hibernation. As each skidoo awoke a rider would jump on to keep it alive, by driving the skidoo around to prevent the engine from stalling. Every now and again, confident that all was well, the driver would come back and stop the machine, but then, with a slight whine of defiance, the skidoo didn't start again. Serious problem!

Whilst waiting between jobs each member of the team gyrated like a madman, flailing arms and waving hands, as well as spinning legs round to keep the blood moving. It was desperately cold. Almost as soon as we stopped our appendages froze, a grim numbness attacked the limbs with an perseverance only experienced in the polar regions.

I utilised my vigorous movements to try and dislodge a small pebble from the pass. The small grey stone, looking like a grey slate, as all the rock seems to be up here, eventually gave in to me and released itself after a number of kicks. This was to be my geological present to my dad. I still carried the stone he gave me from his garden, ready to be left at the Pole – it was an Eadie thing!

Eventually we were ready to leave and all the skidoos roared in approval and filled the air once more with the sweet smell of diesel. Geoff could be rightly proud of his skills. With all of today's problems and delays the convoy didn't leave until three p.m., our latest ever. The convoy left, more desperate than ever to make up distance and time.

We continued to drive due west along the pass, as fast as we dare towards its exit some several miles away. At this time of the day the sun was again directly ahead of us, low on the horizon and it cast its brilliance right in our faces, making vision forward extremely difficult.

Sporadically we would speed over some polar bear prints. We didn't have time to stop and investigate, and given our anxiousness to make up ground, I didn't even follow them with my eye into the distance. It reminded me of my expedition to the Antarctic, the first time we had met a whale, or group of penguins, everyone would rush on deck to look at them. A couple of days and many, many encounters later it raised little interest as such marvellous beasts swam by the boat without causing any excitement.

As the hours wore on the pass became slightly wider as we approached the sea. The low, rounded hills had remained largely unchanged since we had first entered the pass. The sea ice continued to remain very smooth enabling us to progress quickly. Eventually Pen raised his arms to indicate he was slowing down, to which each skidoo driver in turn then followed to warn those behind them against the intensity of the western sun still blindingly low in the sky.

We found a good area on the north shore of Polar Bear Pass to camp for the night. It was particularly beautiful, with a low hill running out into a small bay that had some broken ice ridges at its entrance. According to the map we were in Bracebridge Inlet, not far from Bradford island. The Bracebridge River was nearby. It was difficult to imagine that the river might emerge briefly during the summer months from its current icy coma.

Our skidoos moved into the small, but beautiful, bay and we formed our customary wagon wheel defensive circle. Pen and Geoff started work on Bunny's komatik which was giving continued signs of distress as another rope had worked its way loose. Peter and I started to put the tent up with

Mark soon starting the water-making. The evening routines began without a word being said.

Geoff's hands were again freezing – he seemed to be particularly affected by the cold. Together, Geoff and Pen completed the repairs on Bunny's skidoo. Pen decided to make another attempt at radio communication and went off up the hill at the end of the small bay to erect the aerial. With most of the jobs done and the evening perfect in this setting, the remainder of the team followed Pen to take a look around. I remained at the tent and took some more photos.

The others arrived back after twenty minutes, Pen was again disappointed with 'Nothing heard' on the radio. We all retired to the tent, and given that it was Easter I insisted on opening one of my group presents. Despite the high consumption levels of chocolate, my surprise group present of small Easter eggs went down particularly well. I read an Easter note from my wife as others completed their own quiet contemplation of the day and wrote in their diaries. As Mark had some hot water remaining from that night's ice melting, I made everyone a hot Glayva whisky with cloves as my second treat, which was appreciated by all. My third present, my own 'Love Ewe', remained hidden at the bottom of my komatik.

Whilst we had the polar bear alarm set for the night Pen brought the evening into focus when he stated, 'I think we should be prepared for a visit tonight,' which immediately sent a chill down my spine, and I expect everyone else's. 'It's prime polar bear country here, there is newly broken ice at the end of this valley, and the aroma of our cooking has probably already drifted five miles downwind by now.'

'But we haven't seen any bear footprints in this bay Pen, and there wasn't that many in the Pass,' countered Geoff.

'It's a wide pass,' was Pen's reply, 'and clearly there has been a lot of ice activity at the eastern end where we came through early yesterday morning.' Pen paused. 'You have to remember these animals can travel a hundred miles in a day.' I thought back to the size of the first massive bear print we had discovered, and the complete lack of anything edible seen on our journey thus far to support even a mouse, let alone a quarter of a tonne, top of the food chain, predator.

'Seriously Pen,' questioned Mark, echoing what we were all thinking, 'What are we going to do if we get a visit ? It takes me a good ten minutes just to get out of this sleeping bag – by which time there won't be much of me left.'

'You look, sort of like a sausage roll, in that big sleeping bag Mark,' said Rob quietly. 'All round and crispy on the outside and warm and chewy on the inside; you don't even need to be warmed up for eating.'

Pen broke the stare that Mark was giving Rob. 'You'll hear any visitor,' said Pen, before changing his mind, on seeing everyone's disbelieving faces, '*I'll* hear any visitor,' he quickly re-stated.

'If you don't Pen, and I get eaten, can I rely on you Mark to sue his arse off?' said Rob, starting howls of laughter from the lawyers.

'*You* won't hear anything Pen, I know I won't,' said Geoff reflecting everyone else's thoughts.

This argument raged on for about five minutes before Pen decided to go out and walk round the tent to make his point. Everyone was quiet. The wind had picked up a little and the tent flapped slightly in the light breeze. We all sat in silence, ears pricked for the slightest sound as Pen walked round the tent.

'Can you hear him?' whispered Geoff.

'Nope, can't hear a thing.'

'He's over here by me,' said Peter. Then from the other side of the tent came the posh voice of the old Harovian.

'I'm actually over here.' Pen's test had failed…

On re-entry to the tent, with us all now depending on Pen's sense of good hearing, Pen sat on his sleeping bag and got out his trusty novel, and another reading of "Winnie the Pooh" by our polar guide completed the evening. Today we had covered quite a few miles, but we had not been in the saddle long enough. Additionally we were still going west, not the required north, and thus were not really moving nearer our goal. And all the time the skidoos were getting more bashed and the fuel was getting lower.

The stove was switched off as the last of the water bottles were filled before they sheltered in people's packed sleeping bags. With the hush of the stove, the temperature dropped like a stone, within moments of the last flame dying. Lying in my sleeping bag with my balaclava on, I stared at the orange tent wall as it occasionally flapped.

It was at that moment in the silence of Polar Bear Pass that I decided to share with the group some old Inuit hunting advice, given the current subject of everyone's thoughts. I pulled my balaclava down from around my mouth as I lay in the tent and narrated the tale.

'An old Inuit hunter told me the best way to catch a polar bear. Let me explain. Firstly, you need to dig a hole in the ice and surround it with a circle of peas before hiding.' The tent remained silent as everyone listened in.

'Yes, that's right peas. When the bear comes along to investigate the food,' I continued, 'when it bends down to have a pea – you jump out and kick it in the ice hole.'

The tent remained silent. People were either asleep, or the joke did not hold its humour given our specific location and it's relevance. I pulled my balaclava up again and sank into my sleeping bag.

'It wasn't that bad a joke,' was my last conscious thought as I drifted off to sleep.

Later that night I was woken by Peter sitting bolt upright in the cramped space.

'Shh! Do you hear that?!' You could just make out his freezing breath drifting across the tent powered by his alarming words. The only thing I could hear was my heart banging like a loud drum, as my rib cage struggled to contain it. I held my breath and listened intently, but there was nothing.

'Over there,' Peter pointed in the gloominess of the tent. The tent flapped slightly and a bit of snow brushed against the outside. By now others are also intently listening, including Pen. I couldn't make out anything but Peter was clearly convinced. Pen, with loaded rifle, quickly struggled out of his sleeping bag and stepped outside to investigate. The crunching sound of his footsteps disappeared and the tent went quiet again. Everyone listened intently in the still near-darkness. After a few moments which seemed like ages, Pen returned, proceeded by his crunching footsteps, with no evidence of anything sinister, so we all drifted back to sleep again. I was so tired that I think any bear could have probably feasted on all of us without waking me.

10

The Meeting

'As far as polar bears were concerned, I was food. They don't care about the refinements of technique and reaction time.'

HELEN THAYER, OLYMPIAD AND POLAR
EXPLORER.

My eyes opened slowly, not just because I was still tired, but because one eye was stubbornly refusing to open - due to a small strand of ice that had welded it shut overnight. I awoke to find that there had been no polar bear attack. While we were still ok I think that everyone just wanted to get away from the place – I know I did. It was unknown what the ice conditions ahead would be like, as we still had had no radio contact with the Rookery base, and therefore no chance of a satellite update to inform us what the conditions ahead would be like. We were going to turn north once we had cleared the farthest western end of the island, so the earlier we got going the better.

We started out reasonably early at 9 a.m. as the skidoos thankfully woke up with little trouble, much to Geoff's relief. There was a slight wind, perhaps ten miles an hour, that occasionally found some loose ice and brushed it across the ground at our feet. After about an hour in the saddle we cleared Polar Bear Pass. With no bears seen, indeed very few tracks encountered, I must admit that the Pass was different than I had feared and very much a non-event – thankfully, however, somewhere I was happy to leave behind. Even the sound of the skidoo engines seemed to change, to show their sigh of relief at leaving Polar Bear Pass. Directly ahead of us now was the sea, still frozen as far as could be seen, up to the horizon.

Pen's skidoo, up ahead and leading the convoy, made a slow right turn, to bring us around ninety degrees – we had cleared Bathurst Island! We were once again heading north towards the Pole. We aimed to hug the coast of the western side of Bathurst Island and go north on the sea ice to the Findlay Islands. Here we would leave the skidoos and komatiks and walk the rest of the way to the Magnetic Pole, pulling our provisions in sledges. It's what we'd been training months for and I couldn't wait to get at it. At least that's what the plan was. Right now things weren't going to plan. The general attitude in the Arctic was either 'plan for the worst and hope for the best' or 'the only certainty in the Arctic is the uncertainty'. We had to keep moving and reduce the distance to the Pole before we ran out of fuel, or the skidoos failed.

We hadn't been travelling long before we met pressure ridges again. They were very small initially, with large flat tracts between each one that enabled us to travel fairly unhindered. It wasn't long though, before the ridges grew to some three feet in height. The ground between them was very hard and fairly bumpy, which forced us to slow down to avoid damaging the skidoos and komatiks.

Luckily the ridges were running parallel to us so we didn't need to cross them very often. The pressure ridges fascinated me. They had been formed as the sea's current forced the plates of ice covering its surface together. Where these ice plates met they would rise up as if in a battle, and would fight each other, to build a chaotic pyramid of smashed and broken ice fragments. Yet after this violent birth they were still and frozen. I knew that all around me new ridges were being formed but I had not seen this as yet, making their apparent inactivity all the more fascinating. The resulting pressure ridge forced by these opposing plates of ice could rise up many feet. As the currents were not too strong here they would reach a maximum of about five feet in height – still more than enough to provide an almost impenetrable barrier to a skidoo pulling a heavy komatik. These same currents could also pull two plates of ice apart leaving an open expanse of water, called a lead.

A similar activity was also played out far below the ocean's surface with results somewhat more dramatic, as tectonic plates came together over the millennia, and the meeting point, like the ice pressure ridges far above them on the surface, formed elevations that resulted in continents and mountain ranges.

As the hours passed, Bathurst Island almost disappeared from view behind us. We were about four miles off the coast, and the pressure ridges and our path between them whilst remaining straight and undulating, seemed to be taking us in a steady direction further out to sea, away from heading due north and our direct route.

With little or no elevation it was difficult to see how to get back to our intended route without having to cross the pressure ridges. The ridges sometimes glinted back at us as the sun, still low in the sky, reflected off the brutally hard ice hidden under this magical scene. On a number of occasions Pen would shoot off ahead on his light skidoo, and then dismount and climb up on a ridge to see if there was a way ahead.

By now the ridges were getting higher, the flatter surface between them was closing up and, to make things worse, our path was still taking us further out, seawards.

As luck would have it, when we were about seven miles off the coast we came across a small iceberg. It was about thirty feet high and almost round, in fact it looked more like a white hill than an iceberg. It wasn't long before Pen and Bunny were scrambling to the top.

'Anyone catch what they are saying?' I said to the terrestrial group now waiting around me, their skidoos spluttering in the background.

'No, I can't make it out. They seem to be doing some pointing which is encouraging,' said Rob, with his ice-covered balaclava pulled down so as not to muffle his voice.

We watched their arms extend and point at things which we couldn't see from the ground. Their frozen breath cast a small cloud in front of their faces momentarily.

'They seem to be pointing in different directions,' Mark observed, meaning that there were either many ways ahead, or none at all. Whilst we couldn't see or hear what they were discussing it was clear that there wasn't an obvious way forward. Eventually after further pointing in all manner of directions they came back down, Pen almost descending on his face as he stumbled slightly on the steep, slippery surface of the 'berg.

'Well?' we all waited in anticipation. It was an extremely cold day, with the temperature hovering just below -40°C. The ice dance was not too successful at this temperature, and as our bodies were tired we all used the opportunity to have a quick tea break.

'The motorway, (as Pen called the straight narrow path that gave us a reasonable travelling speed), 'is set to take us further out to sea. I can't see anywhere where the ice is better, further out or further in.'

'What do you recommend Pen?' enquired Peter, finishing his tea.

'Well, given these conditions, and I could see for a few miles from up there, at some stage we are going to have to bite hard and tackle these ridges and get back towards the coast.' This was bad news and we all knew it. The pressure ridges were too high and too numerous for us to try and cross them with the skidoos. The skidoos and komatiks would hardly be able to take the battering and whilst we wouldn't get lost it would be almost impossible to take a route without some guessing as to whether it would offer a better path.

'What about going back?' Peter suggested

'The way we came?!' scowled Mark, obviously rejecting the suggestion. And having escaped Polar Bear Pass intact, I tended to agree with him.

We finished our tea and then checked the equipment, which was by now a task so routine that we looked on our skidoos like babies or pets, needing constant attention or monitoring. Pen unhitched his komatik and headed off on his skidoo on his own.

I could see Geoff hunched over Mark's komatik, so I wandered over to see if I could give him a hand.

'What's up?' I said, looking for evidence of damage to the equipment.

'Geoffrey's got frost bite,' replied Mark alarmingly, but not convincingly. Geoff looked up and pulled his ice-laden balaclava slowly down.

'Well I hope not, but they are so cold,' referring to the two numb clubs at the end of his arms. He really meant it. Mark and I both grabbed a hand each and gave it a short massage. I'm not sure this made any difference but it showed our concern. Geoff didn't have frostbite, just numb hands, as we all had had between ice dances. Whilst we were protected from the wind when we were at the bottom of the pressure ridges, when we got up to speed on the skidoos we were at times subjected to wind chill temperatures of -60°C, especially when we had cleared the Pass earlier in the morning and were travelling at full speed. We all stocked up on chocolate, hoping that this fuel would get burning quickly in our bodies' furnaces.

Above the low growl of the engines ticking over, we could occasionally hear Pen's engine rev hard in the distance as he crossed over some ice obstacle, only to be silenced as he went behind another sound-limiting wall of ice. Bunny was half way up the iceberg again looking to spot Pen. Peter was using the opportunity to get more warm tea inside him.

I had an altogether smaller, but most annoying, issue. My toe seemed to have poked its way through what must have been a hole in my sock. It annoyed me intensely as I constantly tried to draw the cold toe back into the sock. It was too minor to risk giving my feet further exposure to the cold by taking the boot off and replacing the sock so, I'd have to wait until tonight in the tent, and tried to put it to the back of my mind until then. Compared with what Geoff was complaining about I felt almost stupid.

Rob was jumping up and down to get the blood back into his feet. I joined him, and we bounced in synchronised cooperation. 'Lovely day for a dance.'

'Yeah, if you tread on my feet don't worry,' he exclaimed, 'I won't be able to feel it, just try not to do it too often, there's a good chap.' 'Fred Astaire eat your heart out.' We both had a laugh at our situation: miles out to sea in a maze of ice, trying to escape to a destination that was as featureless as the moon.

Pen soon returned, turned the skidoo around and hooked up his komatik.

'I found what I hope is a point where we can make our way back towards the coast. It's a bit of a maze so we'll all have to be careful.' He stopped abruptly and motioned to Peter to come nearer to him, which Peter did as I took over our skidoo's throttle to keep the engine from stalling. As Peter, who had his hood down, got nearer, Pen again motioned for him to come closer still. He looked Peter straight in the face then shouted, 'I want you all to see this.' We quickly walked round to Peter and Pen. Peter had taken his hood down for only a few minutes and he had his balaclava pulled down around his chin as he ate. At the end of his nose, a small white pimple had appeared...

'This is frost nip,' Pen pointed out from a big-gloved hand. The skin had frozen, and against an already cold face, was unnoticeable to Peter. 'You won't feel it creep up on you – so don't expose yourself.'

Mark looked at Bunny. 'Might have to get some of that, can't go home looking like I've been on a beach; can't have you going back looking more heroic than me either Peter.'

'Let's have a look,' said Bunny, approaching Peter. Peter rubbed his nose quickly and put the balaclava up, not wanting to be seen as a bad example.

'It's particularly cold again today, so make sure you look after each other; remember we're in an unforgiving place and we are all a team, take care of each other,' instructed Pen. Point made; the cold lurked all the time and would take advantage of even the slightest weakness.

Pen led the way and we all followed in single file behind him. After about two hundred yards he took a right over a small gap in the pressure ridge, avoiding the smaller rock-like ice fragments strewn across the opening. We drove over to the next pressure ridge some twelve feet away. The ridge was only three feet high but was too high for our heavier loads to cross. We travelled on for another hundred yards and another opportunity presented itself. Again we turned right, and we crossed a gap in the ridge of only about half a foot high. The skidoo bumped as it went over. The challenge was always to get the speed right in these tight spaces. There wasn't enough room to build up much speed so the group was quite dispersed to get a run up. We carried on in this fashion for another thirty minutes – it was clearly going to be a very long day.

I felt lost as I couldn't see any way ahead further than the next few ridges. The only reference I had was the thirty-foot iceberg behind, but that had now gone from sight. Pen was navigating using his compass and the sun. Knowing the magnetic variation at this point from his charts, very strong of course due to our proximity to the Magnetic Pole, he could work out our direction more quickly than powering up the GPS.

Following the correct direction was of course very difficult, as we had to take the opportunities to cross the pressure ridges, regardless of whether they were precisely on the course to the Magnetic Pole or not. The ridges remained remarkably parallel to each other, so it was tempting to just drive along the ground between them, but this would take us further west, out to sea and away from our now northerly required direction.

Two hours later, and crossing another of the countless gaps, Geoff and Rob's komatik hit a bump and turned over, falling as if in slow motion and landing on its side. It was inevitable this would happen as our frustration grew and we tackled bigger and bigger ridges. The convoy stopped and we all ran back to help Geoff, who was already surveying the situation. As I ran back to help, my foot disappeared through the ice into a hole and into sea water. Fortunately, my boot wasn't wet – just the rubber toe cap had gone in.

'Careful boys, we seem to be on thin ice!' I shouted. That's all we needed. I continued walking, not running, towards the toppled komatik.

With the komatik lying on its side we again took the opportunity for a break. We didn't have lunch just a series of quick snacks of Pepperoni, cheese, nuts, chocolate and a drink, whenever the opportunity presented itself. 'Bugger!' expressed Geoff out aloud, 'Just broken a tooth I think,' as he spat out a mixture of peanut, chocolate and enamel on the ground, 'not my day today.'

Before the others began to pack the sledge I felt nature call again. This time it wasn't a biological calling. As I looked over the Arctic wasteland I was once again transfixed by its beauty. To the strains and grunts of people working behind me trying to keep warm, and the coughing of engines ticking over, I walked off, just to spend a few moments alone. It was strange that in such a desolate place none of us were ever really alone for more than a few minutes. We had come so far to experience this great lonely wilderness and yet spent all our time in close proximity. There was hardly a moment of privacy during the entire trip – even going to the loo seemed like a public occasion!

My boots made the slight but familiar crunch, as I walked away from the komatiks towards the sun. I looked down at my tracks – likely to be the first ever in that spot. The ice crunched and squeaked with each new step. As I looked back at my tracks, I felt the same excitement that I had experienced as a child emerging from my parents' house in England on a cold winter's day, to find that it had snowed overnight and transformed my world. My first urge had always been to run out into the garden and leave my trail in the virgin snow. But I would wait a few moments to take in the quiet stillness of the new white ground before running roughshod over nature's beautiful creation. I carried on walking, soon reaching a small pressure ridge, perhaps three feet high and stretching out as far as I could see.

Leaving the 'motorway' behind me, I found that the ground became littered with lumps of various shapes and sizes. I was soon at the next ridge which was perhaps five feet tall. I crossed it and found another broken ridge of about the same height with a sort of gully between the two ridges. It was covered in what appeared to be a thin layer of snow, giving it a soft rounded complexion. When I touched the snow I found it was as hard as rock.

Bits of blue-stripped ice occasionally broke through the snow, revealing a concrete-hard slab that was waiting for the spring thaw underneath. It was clear that this would have taken ages to get through on the skidoo. Sticking to the 'motorway' was our only choice. The voices of the others were by now only murmurs, not so much because of the distance as I was only a few hundred yards away, but simply due to the sound-absorbing effect of my seemingly soft white flour-dusted surroundings.

Climbing over the other side of the third rise I decided that I would plonk myself down for a few moments. I knew by now that this might be the only privacy I would get on the expedition. The air was still. I thought for a moment I could hear a slight burble or hiss coming from under the ice. But no, it was my imagination. There was no noise. I looked across the long plain out across the frozen sea. The sun was bright and cast a thousand small shadows from the various lumps that spread in all directions into the distance.

I could see castles, small cars, cats and all sorts of strange contorted faces that nature had etched into the infinitely different lumps of ice before me. Some of the lumps were small and squat, others tall and thin with edges that looked sharp as a razor. I sat and absorbed the scene, completely content with myself and the world. This was indeed beautiful. I said 'beautiful,' to myself over and over again in slight whispers, not wishing to disturb the serene scene in front of me, but glad to become part of it, if only for a moment.

After a few minutes I began to feel that something was missing from this lonely scene. It was birds. How I missed those small fluffy friends. To me they represented life and friendliness. But however hard I listened I knew there would not be a chirp or tweet, this was indeed a lifeless place. Soon my hands were beginning to get cold, despite the futile efforts of the sun. I gave them a slight rub and put them back into my large outer gloves, feeling the warmth come back immediately. I could sit here for hours I thought, perhaps until the ice itself broke up in a couple of months' time. I took my camera out from my pocket to take a photo but then decided to put it back again. No photograph could ever do justice to this scene. I knew the memory of this moment would be more powerful than any photograph.

I was completely relaxed and wished I could have painted what I saw before me. The different shades of white, cream and blue would stretch the talent of any artist. The glorious blues of the sky stretching from the deep shades on high to the lighter blues touching the ice on the horizon. Every now and again the sun would catch some drifting ice crystals in the air, which would twinkle as though someone had thrown thousands of diamonds into the atmosphere, or the stars had forgotten to retreat with the night. This scene had been repeated here for millions of years, I was merely an observer, for the slightest instant in the passage of time.

Such strange shapes around me – I could never get over them. I felt as relaxed as I would lying on top of a grassy hill in summer with all my cares in the world gone with the wind. With my back pressed against the ice ridge, I looked up and stared at the thin, stretched, clouds dancing high above me. Each one offered a different shape, playing with my mind's eye as the wind paraded a constant stream of shapes for me to judge.

Then something caught my eye from the right. I listened for someone to shout – they were probably preparing to leave. I ought to get back I thought, as I made the redundant action, driven by habit, to look at my watch. Just before I could get up, something moved again. I looked round to the right, my neck turned to full extent. And there it was, standing behind a small block of ice perhaps six hundred feet away – a bear?! A Polar Bear! I remained where I was, motionless...

The bear looked quite small. It stood still, looking in my direction, its head raised as if sniffing the air. Its coat was a pale cream colour against the blazing blue and white of the ice around it. The seemingly fluffy coat contrasting with the sharp hard edges of the surrounding ice. The bear didn't look threatening and was probably wondering what sort of a creature I was. I wasn't even sure he could see me. His black eyes and nose moved to and fro in the air. It seemed motionless as if in a dream. Time had stopped. I was amazed, not so much at seeing such an animal, though it was an incredible sight, but at myself as I didn't feel at all worried.

At that moment I felt in perfect harmony with my surroundings. I looked on the bear in an inquisitive manner, and calmly believed that he felt the same way. I was probably the first person he had ever seen. Two strangers, each intrigued by the other. I stared at him for what could have been at eternity before he ducked down, turned and went on his way. He may already have forgotten me but I knew in that brief moment he would leave an impression for the rest of my life.

'Wow!' I said out loud, as I watched him trot off and disappear back into the ice maze. The ice remained unchanged, the sun shone high in the sky, the wind was motionless. I drew a breath. What an incredible day. This was probably the single best moment of my life I said to myself. I could now feel the adrenaline rise, much the same as when I had stood in the church on my wedding day as my wife-to-be walked towards me down the aisle. 'This is just incredible,' I said, again and again, as I stood up without a care in the world. Even the cold seemed to have left me.

Turning to cross the ridge I could see the others still packing the toppled sledge. Some working, a couple of others huddled around what must have been a hot drink. They were further away than I had thought. I couldn't wait to get back to them and tell them of my find. A photo, I must take a photo I thought to myself. I fumbled for my camera and took a picture. It looked just like anywhere else of course, with no evidence of our meeting. The bear may be gone but our brief meeting place would always be special to me.

Taking one last look around I began to make my way back. I decided to travel along the bottom of the pressure ridge, not wishing to re-trace my original track but instead head back on a more direct route. I had lost track of time and the others might be waiting for me. At what I thought was probably the right spot I decided to climb to the top of the ridge, which rose to almost five foot high, of broken ice. As I stepped up I could see the others packing up, with one red coat standing in the distance, probably having a pee. My period alone was now over. From my position of height I looked in the direction of where my friend the bear had disappeared. No sign of him.

Boy would this be a story to tell the others! I knew from their casual activity that they hadn't seen him. I put my mitts back on and quickly zipped up the front of my jacket. I began to slide down the other side of the ridge, eager to get back to them and tell them my story. Before I reached the bottom something again caught the corner of my eye. This time it was on my left side as I turned my head quickly. A polar bear! I landed in a heap at the bottom of the ridge, my concentration no longer on a safe landing.

I didn't move. The bear was about three hundred feet away along the gully. I was sure it was the one I had seen earlier. It seemed much bigger now, probably not a cub after all. Its head was down, apparently smelling the ground. It no longer looked cuddly as I saw its huge front paws scraping at the ground, and making a sound like chalk being drawn over a blackboard.

Pure panic began to set in, as I realised that this predator had moved along the gully behind me from where I had seen him last. He *had* seen me earlier. He hadn't gone away. He must have picked up my earlier trail. There were fresh bear prints the size of sauce pans where I sat. No longer did it look so charming – this was a wild animal that was hunting me. I was nothing more than another animal in the food chain to this monster.

Fear shuddered right through my body as though a sharp spear had been plunged into me. I felt totally alone as a gladiator in an arena and shivered with terror from my head to the pit of my stomach. I was completely unarmed and had no way of defending myself against this monster. This savage beast could outrun me and easily crush my skull with one swift sweep of its giant paws. What a fool I was – 'my friend the bear' indeed! In my mind death was supposed to occur somewhere dark and ugly, not in this bright dream-like scene surrounding me.

I felt the cold around me, hugging me like grim death. My heart began to frantically pound as if it was desperately trying to get out of my chest. I could feel I was beginning to take short frantic breaths as adrenaline raced around my body. Shit, I might be in real trouble. I wasn't sure he had seen me yet. But he must have done, surely.

My eyes were now fixed intently on him, my body racked with tension. Should I stay still or run ? I wasn't sure what to do, but realised that there wasn't going to be much time. I looked over at him, my breathing increasingly frantically, his head now raised. His big cold bottomless black eyes slowly rose about to look upon me. I thought I could hear him pant, or in my now raging fear and panic – perhaps growl. Moments before his gaze came upon me I began to run. I ran faster than I had ever run before in my entire life.

I couldn't remember whether or not it was a conscious decision, but my legs were carrying me towards the five foot high ridge in front of me at full speed, as I was desperate to escape the danger, desperate to save my life. I hurtled over the broken ice of the ridge, tripping on the other side. As I got up I thought I saw some more tracks, but I couldn't be sure as I raced ahead. It was just then in my blind panic that I had another awful thought. Maybe there were two bears! I picked myself up, looked left and right not knowing what to do if I saw another bear.

There was now just the small three foot ridge and then the plain, between myself and the party. Safety was in sight, but I ran even faster. Not looking over my shoulder as I ran I threw out the contents of my pockets, hoping that any pursuer might stop to investigate them rather than me. The sledges looked further away than ever. I felt the soft ground of the plain beneath my feet like quick sand slowing my pace.

My muscles began to scream in agony for a rest as I drove them on. I may have stumbled a couple of times – I can't remember. As I got nearer I saw some red hoods look up at me. I couldn't shout, as my mouth was doing it's best to take in huge lungfuls of air. I slammed into the first sledge, almost delirious. I still hadn't looked behind me. Where was Pen's sledge? Where was the rifle? As I attempted to get off the ground I caught sight of the rifle. Pen's hand was attached to it.

The others' attention moved from me, to behind me. I looked round, still crumpled on the ground. This time I couldn't even get up. Not even if the bear was right behind me. I panted and panted. But there was no rifle shot, the others voices came into focus above the pounding of my heart. I finally got up. A voice said, 'You alright Duncan?' I don't know who it was. All eyes were on the ridges. Everyone had stopped what they were doing and were looking with me towards the ridge. But none so intently as I.

'Get a fright Duncan?' It was Pen. I raised a finger and pointed in the direction from where I had run.

'A bear! A bear!' I said in a muffled voice, barely audible even to myself as I gulped in spadefuls of cold air. There was no 'Shoot the fucker' joke or any other giggles. Everyone could see the panic on my face, and from the speed I had run, knew something had definitely scared me, and that it wasn't far away.

Pen moved forward towards the ridge with the rifle, now loaded, and without turning shouted, 'Geoff you might like to hurry on the repairs, the rest of you start the engines,' – a new sternness in his voice conveying a direct order. The others all jumped into action. I was just getting my breath back and thankful for my return to safety. As my heart began to calm down I could feel wetness in my trousers. An uncomfortable feeling, more embarrassment than anything else began to come over me. I hoped I hadn't peed myself – that really would be too much. I would tell them later about my idiotic inactivity when I saw the bear first or the first bear, I still wasn't convinced there was only one, but not at peeing my pants. Shuffling my hands I realised it was actually cold sweat. My back was soaked as well and now getting cold as it began to freeze.

I had been lucky enough to have never known true fear before in my life. Sure, I had been frightened before, but this was different. Now as I sat, a collapsed wreck in the cold of the Arctic, but safe, I felt truly frightened. The delayed fear and rush of adrenalin still racing around my body almost made me physically sick, as I shook uncontrollably.

'Where was the bear Duncan?' It was Bunny. Rob had given up asking me anything, as I wasn't responding to him. I hadn't heard him even though he was standing right next to me. I was watching Pen intently, as he stood still about thirty feet from the first small ridge, his hood down and the rifle in his hand. After pausing for a while he stooped down and picked up my camera and a small bag of sweets, the random items I had hastily ejected from my pockets. Everyone was standing now, the thin red line, all quietly scanning the horizon.

'Over there,' shouted Rob. Pen held his rifle tighter and looked in the direction that Rob was pointing in.

'Are you sure Rob?'

Rob paused, staring intently, before muttering that maybe he was mistaken. We were all quiet, scanning the ice. Nothing moved. You could have heard a pin drop. Then I thought I saw something move, a little way from where I had run from. But no, there was nothing. The jumbled shapes carved into the ice playing tricks with my eyes again, laughing at me. I looked round to see Mark and Geoff nervously looking in the other direction, covering our flank.

'Well done.' A hand squeezed my shoulder, causing me to jump a little – it was Pete. 'The first to see a polar bear! Did you get a photo?'

'Blimey! Pete I tell you the thing virtually trampled me. It was so close. The bastard tried to sneak up on me. There might even have been two of them.' It was all flooding out now. 'I was sitting there admiring the view and minding my own business when I saw him dart behind the ice. I think he was hunting me. He's still out there somewhere.'

Geoff started an engine. There was a pleasant, safe feeling emanating from the sound of the man-made mechanical growl of the skidoo. I felt I was back in civilisation again, and away from the coarse savagery of nature. Geoff was now alone as everyone was gathered around me wanting to hear more. Pen's order to get ready to leave had been forgotten in the excitement. 'Did it chase you?' 'How big was it?'

'What did you do?' came the flurry of questions.

'Where is he now?'

Pen came back to the group and handed me my possessions, that I had discarded during my run.

'You Ok Duncan?'

'Yeah, no problem Pen,' my voice quivering a little, 'sorry about the smell,' as my hand motioned to jokingly indicate I had filled my underwear. There was a laugh in the background.

'You're not the only one Duncan,' someone said in a supportive manner.

'Did you see anything Pen?' enquired Mark. Pen didn't respond. With rifle in hand he walked directly over to Geoff and with a sterner more concerned voice asked, 'How's that engine Geoff?' as it began to splutter furiously. Before Geoff could reply Pen turned and bellowed, 'Bunny!, Bunny come back here!' Bunny was walking over to the ridge. He turned and with arms raised let out a muffled cry – protesting that he wanted to see what all the fuss was about.

Pen looked round towards me and with a big grin said, 'Looks like you scrambled the whole way!' pointing to the skid marks that I had made across the ice. He was probably right. I could begin to feel bruises forming on my elbows and knees. I had probably tripped on every damn piece of raised hard ice between the ridge and where the group were, in my desperation to put distance between me and the bear.

Mark was now buzzing. 'Pen, was it a bear Pen, did you see it?' He had given up on getting answers from me in my semi-shocked state.

'There's definitely a bear out there,' Pen said to the group, who were by now standing closer than normal to him and his rifle, their heads moving nervously to and fro, trying to make out any movement from the jumbled ice forming the ridge.

'Can we go and have a look Pen?' Pete piped up. Before Pen could answer, Mark countermanded with, 'Let's get the fuck out of here,' quickly seconded by Rob giving a 'Smarter than the average bear' impression. Mark wasn't waiting for an answer as he turned towards his machine before waving at Bunny and shouting, 'Bunny! Run!' causing him to look over his shoulder as he moved back to the group. Then Pen politely shouted, 'Can you come back quickly now Bunny,' a sense of urgency communicated through the frozen air.

'I think it was probably a cub. There's a line of small footprints over there,' Pen pointed towards where my tracks emanated from. The group all started nervously laughing at my fright over a cub.

'Where there's a cub there's a mother, which may be a bit confused or angry by now, so we should really be on our way,' Pen spoke in my defence. The group's laughter died down and their gaze went back to the ridge.

The noise of the engines starting grew louder, as Geoff got the last skidoo going before immediately doing the ice dance to get the circulation back into his hands. We all mounted up with a speed I had not seen before. Peter was doing the driving for our skidoo. Pen shouted, telling us to keep an eye out and, as if to re-enforce the point, slung the rifle over his shoulder in readiness. We all moved off. Bunny and Mark took up the rear as they swung wide to pass near the ridge to look for any further evidence of bears, before overtaking us to catch up with Pen and shouting back to us, 'Its behind you!' before their giggles were drowned out by their speeding engine.

I just kept thinking what would have happened if I had sat with my back against the ridge enjoying the apparent tranquil scene for a few minutes more, blissfully ignorant of the approaching danger. What would have happened if I had gone back the way I had come and directly into the path of the bear following my track? It may have been a cub, but even a cub would be twice the weight of an Alsatian dog, as well as twice as hungry, and perhaps angry. I quickly put the thought out of my mind before a grim vision of struggle and carnage enveloped it. There was no need to take a photo of this place – this memory was indeed going to be a permanent one.

That day, I had found true fear in its most basic, primeval and dark form. I also felt unbelievably stupid, ashamed even. After the months of preparation and being so near to Polar Bear Pass I had stupidly put myself into a bad situation. There was no excuse for it, especially as Pen had warned us not to go off alone. I felt completely humiliated. How could I have been so stupid, to wander about on my own. Another lesson learnt, and almost learnt to my cost.

I glanced over my shoulder one last time, returning a thumbs up to Geoff as he sped by. I then zipped up my hood and looked forward, as Pete moved off with greater acceleration than normal. At that moment, in my fear and embarrassment and with my confidence on the floor, I decided that I would keep this incident to myself.

11

Duncan Point

'My right foot has gone, nearly all the toes - two days ago
I was proud possessor of best feet!'

CAPTAIN ROBERT FALCON SCOTT, ROYAL NAVY,

POLAR EXPLORER.

After the polar bear incident we drove on without stopping for at least an hour and a half. I don't know whether this was because we wanted to get on, or whether it was because we wanted to get as far away from the scene as possible. I knew why I wanted to stay in the saddle.

It was still very cold when we eventually stopped for a tea break and equipment check. Pen decided that now was the time to go back aggressively towards the coast, and get off the motorway completely, and hit the big ridges if we had to. With the clear travel offered by the motorway it was tempting to keep following it. It was, however, taking us westwards. We needed to be going north if we were going to get to the Pole. Pen was right, at some stage we needed to cross the ridges that were forcing us westwards.

We hadn't seen any more bears, or tracks – but we understood now that that didn't mean they weren't there. We were under orders not to take any excursions away from the skidoos into the jumbled ice maze. I don't think anyone needed to be told that now. Pen still had the rifle slung over his shoulder.

The motorway was beginning to disintegrate; the wide clear open ice that we started the day with was now quite bumpy and also had narrowed to a width of about three skidoos wide. At the appropriate time we turned north off the motorway. Big chunks of ice littered the ground between the ridges. It was tempting to push them out of the way with the skidoo as we travelled along, but more often than not they were stuck hard to the floor, meaning the skidoo banged over the top, sometimes resulting in it toppling over or misaligning the front skis.

Some bumps you had to power over, which meant once you got over them you almost crashed into the slower moving skidoo in front. Often we could drive no faster than walking pace, with the passenger ready to jump off to steady the load if necessary. On many occasions a skidoo would get stuck so we all had to go back and help. It was clear that with little elevation to find a way through, it would be very easy to get lost here, and it was very slow going with no end in sight.

Looking ahead the ice seemed to get worse, so Pen decided that we would have to turn round and get back to the motorway and go on a bit further in the hope of finding a better route. Picking a route would be very much a guessing game. I climbed to the top of one of the ridges, but with such low elevation I could see nothing but jumbled ice all round.

We didn't have room to turn the skidoos and komatiks so we had to go further forward until we found a small break in the ice that would have enough space for us to turn. We all stopped and had a scout around. No one strayed too far. It was too easy to be jumped. Anyone seeing any bear prints was to alert the others. Eventually, Pen found a space not far from the main run where the skidoos could be turned and the path rejoined back to the motorway.

One by one the skidoos turned around on our makeshift roundabout. It was almost a traffic jam as the space was so tight, bordered by ridges and lumps of ice. As each skidoo came round we stood ready to jump off as the skidoo went by and help push it over various bumps. Many traverses required a lot of speed and then a sharp turn once over the bump to avoid another ice wall or waiting skidoo.

Bunny didn't turn in time and ended up in a two-foot deep hole, which dislodged his windshield. All he could do was sit there and laugh! Luckily, just a small fix was enough to steady his windshield, but it all added time. Pen managed with lots of revving, to back the skidoo out of the hole once we had unhitched the komatik.

Eventually we got back to the motorway. By now the light was receding and it was time to look for a camp. The ice had improved somewhat and the ridges got a bit smaller but we were still not clear of the bumps. It was a hard day, and frustrating. I wondered how long we could continue until we ran out of fuel or the skidoos broke. There was no way back or clear way forward. We could only continue and hope we found better ground.

Miraculously, we came across a large flat clearing, bordered by an ice ridge. We set about organising ourselves in our well practiced way of setting up camp. The polar bear alarm was set with extra due diligence and Pen took a good look around for any tracks, or cracks in the ice, before we settled into performing our usual duties.

As usual I was one of the last to enter the tent, relishing the final moments outside – the only period of the day when I felt I wasn't busy or in a hurry, and had a few moments to really enjoy the surroundings. Occasionally, I would be disturbed with a 'More Ice!' order from Mark as his pan bubbled and fizzed with the water-making for the night's brew and the next day's drinks. My last job of the day was to place ice around the tent, to weigh it down in case the wind got up. The snow and ice was so dry I could cut large square 'polystyrene' blocks with my spade. On other days it had been just too brittle and would disintegrate in my hands, forcing me to search for a better supply.

I scanned the horizon even more intently than usual that night, ignoring the beauty of another dying Arctic day. With my early experience still fresh in my mind I concentrated on locating any movement on the ice, any at all that could suggest we were not alone.

We had seen some difficult ice today. This was of course nothing compared to that seen much further north, off the most northern coast of Canada. There, with the Arctic Ocean currents pushing ice against the top of the continent, pressure ridges of twenty feet high were not uncommon. It was usual for polar travellers on foot to cover no more than one or two miles a day there due to the conditions. As ever I was thankful for my lot, and the rest of the team were as bubbly as ever. Nothing would let our spirits get down, despite being half frozen and tired, having been wrenched all over the place today on our uneasy charges.

As I entered the tent for the evening, having been careful to empty my bladder before doing so and thus saving inconvenience during the night, I met the familiar and by now most welcome scene. The mini stove burner was on and with a jet like roar turning the fizzing ice in the pan into hot water. The air was steamy inside the tent and whilst cold, felt like a furnace after being outside. Everyone was attending to repairs; to clothing, small bruises and cuts, writing in diaries in the dim light, or trying to dry their sweat-filled socks. Pen shared out the Pringle crisps and the necessary salt content was quickly absorbed. It was as crowded as ever, but that was ok. I squeezed myself in and found my spot on top of my mammoth sleeping bag.

Mark was busy filling water bottles and giving out very welcome hot drinks. He still had his balaclava on as it was frozen to his beard. Eventually with his head over the stove, trying to get rid of all the ice, he tugged gently at the balaclava to release it. 'Argh' he protested as a bit of his beard came away.

'Come on Mark, just pull it off.'

'It's all right for you,' he grumbled with half of his balaclava hanging from his face.

'Just don't get any of that in my broth,' ordered Peter, as Mark hovered dangerously above his cooking equipment.

This was the life. Jokes were bandied around about the day's activities – the acrobat-like displays of jumping off sledges, avoiding ice obstacles and the resulting crashes, and the general seemingly mad situation that we found ourselves in.

Pen had the map out, and with GPS in hand determined that we were a couple of miles off Herbert Point, on the western end of Bathurst Island. That didn't sound too bad, I thought, we might be as far as ten miles off the coast. Pen checked the responsibilities of everyone in the group, as each reported the latest developments.

'The skidoos are taking a hammering Pen,' said Geoff. 'On each one of them I've had to re-align the skis; on two of them the engine cowling is cracked, and Bunny's windshield wont take much more of a beating. I've also got concerns about Peter and Duncan's engine and my own.' He then looked up, 'Come on chaps, you wouldn't treat your own daughters like this.'

'I can smell a big bill arriving,' joked Bunny, looking at Pen.

Rob gave his assessment of the fuel situation, which wasn't too good. We weren't travelling many miles but were drinking lots pf fuel, due to all the inefficient use of our engines pulling heavy loads at low speed.

Mark quickly started giving out some gorgeous broth liberally sprinkled with cheese, freeze-dried chicken and salami, that steamed and hissed as it struggled to remain warm in the sub-freezing air temperature of the tent.

No doubt to any outsider the haggard-looking group of men would have smelt awful, making it a challenge for anyone to eat among us. No one had changed their underwear or had a wash since we left. In the cold, the sense of smell was deadened, and we were all the same, so no one cared. I loved my luxury 'Wet ones', the fragrant wipes that due to their alcohol-saturated content meant they didn't freeze. I used them sparingly to give myself a brief wash when in the sleeping bag at night. There was nothing to get dirty from in our ultra-clean environment where not even dust existed – the only contaminants coming from our own bodies.

Having settled in, with my jacket off and balaclava drying in the overhead section of the tent, I decided to take my boots off and deal with the minor annoying problem of the day – the hole in my sock. The big boots came off easily with a tug. The difficulty was trying to do this without knocking into anyone else. Various techniques were employed, the best generally being to lie on my back with my legs in the air, and pull them off.

As the boot inner was removed I could see the sock of my right foot and immediately noticed there was no hole in it, as I had imagined all day. I put my hand on my toes to warm them up and found that they were really cold. I mean really cold, frozen in fact. Something was wrong. I swallowed hard and carefully took all the layers of socks off to reveal my foot. Three toes were white and hard at the top. Two of which were completely white from the middle joint up. I touched them and they felt as hard as rock, or wood, and were completely unfeeling, as though they were not really attached to me.

I had got frostbite. It was a funny sensation, the realisation that I would lose some toes. A real feeling of 'ah well' came over me in resignation of this fact. As there was no panic caused by rampant pain it was easier to be much more calm and balanced about the situation. This slightly surprised me but I suppose I had never really expected to be caught out like this, or again, as this was my second surprise of the day after the bear. The sensation I had felt all day of my toe, I believed, poking through a hole in the sock was clearly where the toe was being frozen, past which there was no sensation. There was no hole in the sock after all.

Pen could see me fiddling and caught sight of them. 'I don't like the look of them.' He came over immediately, but carefully, avoiding pots and pans being upset by his movements. Taking them in his hands he blew on them and rubbed them.

'How long have they been like that?' he enquired, as the occupants of the tent followed his interest.

'Only today, but they have been very cold over the last three days.' He rubbed them carefully but furiously with his bandaged fingers, trying to get warmth back into my toes. This carried on for five minutes or so, until I heard him sigh. He then sat at the end of my sleeping bag where my feet were and unzipped his trousers around the crotch. Carefully grabbing my foot, he then slid my toes inside his trousers. He pulled my foot in further until my toes reached deep inside, coming to rest on his testicles. The others gave him the room he needed.

'We're not too late,' Pen explained. I was quite comfortable, lying down on my sleeping bag. It was the best rest I'd had all day as I hated sitting up in the tent as it gave me a tired back. It was Pen I was sorry for.

'Bunny, this is what heroic explorers do,' Pen said with a certain satisfaction, and making the best of a bad situation. There was no response from Bunny, who was probably more happy to risk a moment of frost nip on his face to boast about when he got home, rather than placing his balls against a block of frozen flesh. Pen had placed my toes against the warmest part of his body. Placing my feet under his armpits would have drained the blood further from my toes.

My mind wandered. I knew I would soon be asked to make the choice; stay or go. I felt I could go on, I could still walk and wanted to get to the Pole. However, if there was any chance I knew I should request a medical evacuation, so as not to break my rule to avoid losing any part of my body – if the opportunity was there. I said nothing, but decided to see how things were the next day. I wondered where any plane would land, it wasn't clear that the large pan of ice that we were camped on would be big enough.

Robert Peary an American Arctic explorer who became (arguably) the first man to stand at the North Geographic Pole once stated that 'A few toes aren't much to give to achieve the Pole' – now that I was in a position to make that decision myself, I wasn't so sure. My cold feat had not included me getting cold feet, not this cold at least.

It was an eventful day – too eventful. We talked about the polar bear and the rough travel, breaking off every now and again to see how my toes were. The stove was kept on longer than normal to try and keep the air temperature up. I wasn't sure whether this was for my benefit or Pen's gonads – it didn't matter really. Every now and again Pen would move a little to get more comfortable. Inevitably, talk turned to how the day's events would affect the expedition.

'We simply can't get to the Pole without a flight Mark,' was how Peter brought the conversation directly into focus.

'Yes, progress was slow today,' admitted Mark, 'too slow.'

'And it could be the same tomorrow,' interjected Pen, moving a little as he spoke with a slightly uncomfortable look on his face. A flight was of course inevitable now, if we wanted to get to the Pole at least. We simply didn't have enough time or fuel, and the skidoos couldn't take much more of the battering that we were giving them without them breaking down. No decisions were made as yet. Pen wanted to see what the condition of my toes were the next day. After three hours he finally released me. My sticks of wood, remained just that. Hopefully Pen had no ill effects.

'After the nurse, you should see a good lawyer,' added Bunny looking at Pen and trying to keep a straight face. 'Did I introduce myself?' said Rob, holding out his hand, 'no lost body part too small to claim for.'

With everyone tired and less hungry after Mark's delicious servings of dinner, we all prepared for a night's sleep. Pen read us a "Winnie the Pooh" story before bed – *Heffalumps*; it was surprisingly comforting. After making a final radio check from inside the tent, again with no luck, Pen set the Argos code to 'oo' – which would be interpreted at the Rookery as 'all ok', which was a very good sign to me.

As we all once again packed the tent and huddled into our cramped and cold sleeping positions, a grumble emanated from one of the sleeping bags.

'Had you been eaten today Duncan, we would not only have had more room in the tent tonight, but I might even have had a second portion of food.' Rob's last words to the stunned group were, 'Yes, one must try harder to be eaten for all our sakes.' I drifted off to sleep, hoping tomorrow would bring better luck for me and the expedition.

The next day I awoke and reached down into my sleeping bag hoping that my toes were ok. Hoping in fact that yesterday was a dream, or nightmare. But no, I still had three seemingly dead appendages. My frozen toes were no longer part of me, they were lifelessly stuck to my foot, cold and unfeeling.

The new day started with some tough decisions. My toes hadn't improved overnight so Pen described the choices that I had. He was still sticking to his guide role and I appreciated his advice.

'The options are simple Duncan. You could continue, and if the temperature improves you might be ok. If it's as cold as yesterday, or if it gets colder, for any time during the rest of the expedition you could be in trouble.'

'Lose the toes?' I asked.

'Quite possibly. Once they have been frozen they are very susceptible to the cold and could easily get worse.'

Umm, I thought, not good, probably not much chance of a heat wave today either.

'I should add that the weather is currently borderline for a plane evacuation, and the weather may get worse in the days to come, therefore cancelling that option for you. The pan of ice we are on is flat, looks stable and is probably at the minimum landing length. If you were looking to be lucky, and get a flight out, this is probably as good as it will get.'

The decision was mine. It wasn't a difficult decision. I didn't want to leave, but I also didn't want to lose the toes and I certainly didn't want to hinder the expedition further. The rest of the gang all kept remarkably quiet, there was no one trying to egg me on one way or the other. Of course I had actually made the decision in England a few months ago. I wouldn't be carried on by personal feelings of failure or fear of letting the group down. I also would not be buoyed along by the high spirits of the group.

I thought about whether I was being soft, whether I should carry on. I was after all still fit and could continue. But was this another Elbrus moment where I would make the wrong choice at a critical moment? The decision was made before I entered the Arctic based on what I had learnt from my experiences on Mount Elbrus. On those facts and my predetermined strategy I had to go. I wouldn't make a second mistake, the facts spoke for themselves. I informed Pen and the group quickly and confidently, but hiding my bitter, bitter disappointment.

'Pen, it's a choice of leaving you all or leaving my toes. It's not a choice I make easily. Sorry, but the toes win this time. I'm afraid I've no other choice but to request an evacuation flight out of here.'

I paused for a moment as the occupants of the tent remained unnaturally silent. Each giving the time to listen to me, uninterrupted and, perhaps, consider their own situation and options.

'Sorry chaps, you have my best for the remainder of the trip. I don't want to hold you up any longer. I'll see you at the Pole.'

With that decision made Pen needed to discover whether anyone else wanted to go, given the opportunity that the evacuation plane would offer. He asked each person in turn, and each made their decision. This was very good on Pen's part as it was important to get each individual's opinion and not that of the group as a whole, given the dynamics of the team. No one else wanted to go. I was very glad to hear that.

I thought Rob was close to leaving, especially as he would probably be next in line if the weather remained the same. He had been displaying the same tendencies as me in regard to his feet. Rob was tough – and he actually had a harder decision to make than I did. My choice was clear. His condition, however, could get worse. Indeed my feeling was that if we had another day like yesterday then Rob would be in exactly the same position as me. Geoff thought about it – his hands were being badly affected by the cold. He wrote in his diary later that day that he would 'get the next frostbite special out of here should anyone else drop out'.

I had made my choice, no one commented and everyone looked at the ground as I stared around the tent. Each was quietly contemplating his own position now that the expedition had taken a slightly unexpected and more serious turn.

Pen checked the weather outside, which was still good enough for a plane. He then made a radio call, but there was still no response so he set the Argos code to code 221. This would be picked up at the Rookery and translated as 'need to evacuate four or less people, not urgent'. At least we assumed this message would be picked up – as clearly without the radio we were not within direct communication with the Rookery and actually had no way of knowing whether they had received any messages from us at all. The Argos would also send our current position of 75.37N, 100.49W.

Leaving the radio on and calling occasionally Pen continued to receive background noise punctuated occasionally by a distorted smattering of a human voice. These voices could have emanated from anywhere over the northern Arctic as the radio waves bounced around the atmosphere at the top of the world. We had no way of knowing whether the Argos code was being received either, though the chances are it was. Every hour Pen would change the code to 136 – 'Conditions good for collection'.

Pen kept the radio on inside the tent, occasionally calling Resolute or trying to break into other radio messages that he had picked up. He finished each call with 'Resolute 264, Nothing Heard, Nothing Heard'.

Luckily the area of ice we had camped on was reasonably clear of debris and Pen said it met the minimum length required for a runway for a Twin Otter. We moved the pulks along the length of the border of our newly found runway, which was short even for a Twin Otter with its legendary minimum landing capability. We hoped that the red canvas tops of the pulks would help highlight the borders of the runway, and the surrounding pressure ridge, for the pilot. We also filled some black plastic sacks with ice and left them along the edge of the runway.

The 'runway' looked to us like a very a long space, having been used to the cramped spaces of the motorway and its surrounding maze. However, I knew from the air it would be like landing on a postage stamp. Hopefully the pilot could land as the next suitable spot could have been days of travel away for us to get to.

We then just waited and hoped. The weather was still good where we were, but we had no idea what it was like in Resolute. It was nine o'clock in the morning. The stove was kept on in the tent. We talked a bit and played various games. No one had brought any cards, which was good as I hated card games. Spirits were still very high. Boy would I miss this.

Most of our chat revolved around food – women had been long forgotten about as a subject matter. 'It's great here with you lot, great scenery, great food, away from the office and no one annoying me,' said Mark in a self satisfactorily way that was shared by all of us.

'That's most disappointing to me, Mark, given my great efforts over the last few days to annoy one,' said Rob disappointedly, in response to Mark's statement.

'Seriously, where would you rather be?' Bunny egged on, about to get another game going. 'If you had to choose your ideal location – and partner, where and whom would they be?'.

Mark cut in, 'And what meal would you have?'

We all chewed our thoughts over a list of idyllic locations. The group was beginning to look quite weathered now with varying degrees of stubble, sunburnt faces and worn-looking noses that had varying degrees of flaking skin peeling from the end.

Mark started. 'I think I would meet General Haig, you know the general from the First World War'. The tent grew quiet, I suspect as we were slightly surprised at his most serious choice of dinner companion. 'I'd like to see what sort of a man he was, clearly troubled and with a terrible weight on his shoulders.'

Rob, the other military man in the group, joined in. 'I think he worked out that as we had more men than the Hun, and given the stalemate and rate of attrition in the trenches, they would run out of men first. A terrible strategy in human terms.'

'And what about food Mark?' Bunny asked, before visions of terrible slaughter engulfed us all.

'Ah! Something exquisite washed down with bottles of good red Bordeaux,' he sizzled as we all began to dream about what we might order.

We didn't get as far as where this bizarre meal would be held before Geoff jumped in and took the conversation to its earlier, and much lighter, expected destination.

'Well for me the meal would be fairly ordinary farmyard food, a range of good cheese, Brie, Cheddar. Umm!' he paused. 'One of Mark's pigs, and then Julie Christie.'

'A good choice for mains – and afters Geoffrey,' said Rob, never one to miss a chance.

'When she was young – in the sixties, I mean,' explained Geoff.

'I'll have her for my afters too,' roared Mark running his hand over his beard.

'Come on Pen what about you?'

Pen considered. 'I'm not sure of the location,' he mused, at which point Bunny shouted out, 'Probably here!' 'But it would be with the company of my wife and a good bottle of red. Must be more than ten pounds a bottle mind you – never buy red wine less than ten pounds a bottle,' Pen advised. I was getting hungry again at this stage as we sat in the tent.

'I'd share this event with my wife,' I said, 'on the Indonesian island of Lombok. The sweet smell of Indonesian wood littering the warm atmosphere and the quiet and gentle sounds of bamboo drums drifting through the night.'

'Aw , you old romantic,' said someone.

'Oh, and fish and chips would be the food.' I imagined all that thick hot batter, packed with energy-giving calories.

'And for you Peter?' we enquired enthusiastically to the youngest, unwed, member of the team. Peter ran his fingers through his long blond hair, which was beginning to look slightly matted, as he paused in thought.

'As I don't have a girlfriend at the moment I think I'd join the queue for Julie Christie.' He paused for a reaction which didn't come. 'As for wine, I think I'd nick a bottle of Mark's, if that's ok?'

'You are welcome to my best wine anytime, Sir,' said Mark obligingly.

'As for me,' said Bunny, 'I would have lots of rouge – all *under* ten pounds a bottle – so I could have more,' he grinned.

'And as for whom I would share this with, well,' he paused suggestively, 'it would have to be one of your wives,' he said looking around with a glint in his eye.

'You can have mine,' someone said quickly, 'but not my wine.'

'Yes, I'd have to find out why on earth they let us on this misadventure, then instruct them not to be so obliging again!' We all had a giggle and licked our cracked lips, for all manner of reasons.

The morning continued with talking, writing in diaries and listening for the sound of a plane. Sleep was taken where it could be. Pen would occasionally try the radio again or look outside to keep an eye on the weather. We kept the stove burning, knowing that a plane would bring more fuel. I was aware that the expedition was on hold because of me, and not making any northerly progress.

Suddenly, at one p.m. we heard the distant but steady drone of an aircraft. Faint at first, but the mechanical sound being so alien in our natural surroundings it quickly distinguished itself. We all pulled our jackets on, jumped out of the tent and started waving. The twin engine Otter aircraft, fitted with skis and painted in the white and red livery of First Air of Resolute Bay, circled low around us against a light white sky. We could clearly see the pilot returning our greeting. The plane then banked away, turned, and slowed down to a point where it almost seemed to hover. It slowly descended, just missing the top of the pressure ridge that defined and surrounded our ice pan and quickly came towards us on the marked out temporary runway. It was a magnificent landing.

The plane quickly came up to us, kicking up ice into the air from the wind generated by its propellers. We were all in awe of the pilot and his machine, for being able to land in such a tight spot.

Pen shouted above the din to make sure I had got everything out of the tent. I returned a thumbs up as I stood there with my tent bag, skis and poles, which would now be of no more use to anyone. I quickly retrieved my pulk from its marking position on the edge of the runway. Peter asked if he could have my hat, which I gladly donated. No one else took up my offer of surplus kit. I was now displaying a slight limp as I put all my weight onto the non frozen foot – not because I was in any pain but simply because it seemed the sensible thing to do.

The plane pulled up next to the tent, which strained against its guy ropes in the man-made gale. The side doors of the Otter opened with a swoosh and Gary, Pen's aid in Resolute, poked his head out and shouted in his Canadian accent, 'Who's the lucky one with the one way ticket to Resolute?' 'Not me, mate,' I shouted back, 'mine's a return ticket – I'll be coming back.'

With a broad smile he began to empty two hundred litres of fuel from a big drum, which the team quickly transferred into the empty jerry cans strapped to the komatiks, carefully watched by Fuel Monitor Rob. The pilot kept the aircraft's engine running, he wasn't hanging around for a chat.

I shook hands with everyone and we wished each other good luck from behind our face masks. The roar of the aircraft's engine making it almost impossible to hear anything. I felt absolutely terrible getting on the plane alone and leaving my friends behind. We had all started as a team and I wanted us all to finish as a team.

Soon I was on board the plane. It was empty inside apart from my pulk, skis, the tied down and now empty replenishment fuel drum and a few basket seats. The ribs of the plane were clearly visible from the inside – we were on a freighter after all where there was no need for any luxuries.

The pilot, after checking the load was secure, closed the door and turned to me and, with eyes bulging, shouted above the engine noise, 'The survival gear and emergency beacon are stored in the tail should we crash,' before he turned quickly and went up to the cockpit to join the navigator. His was the Arctic translation of more comfortable airline's 'In the unlikely event of landing on water passengers should take advice from airline staff'. I shouted back to him, 'What did you say the in flight movie was?' as he took his seat and strapped himself tightly in. Gary and I, the only passengers, prepared for takeoff.

The plane turned around to face the 'runway'. The engines revved up, causing a rear gust that blew snow towards the tent and the six remaining polar travellers. They were lined up to wave me off, and quickly became grey figures in the swirling snowstorm. With brakes applied the pilot continued revving until I felt the plane was about to explode as it tugged at the brakes eager to race forward. Everything that wasn't tied down tightly in the plane rattled under the strain. The brakes were let off and we sped forward at great speed towards the pressure ridge marking the end of the short, very short runway. We cleared it with inches to spare, such was the skill of the pilot. The aircraft rose quickly, giving me that almost weightless, feeling until my stomach descended back into position.

The pilot circled once and I waved from the window. 'Goodbye chaps, goodbye beautiful ice, goodbye wilderness,' I said to myself, unable to withdraw myself from the glorious view. Gary asked me if I was ok – I nodded, too cut up to speak. He must have sensed this as he chose not to say any more but turned in his seat in front of me to face the cockpit and left me alone. The noise of the engine was too much for conversation anyway unless you shouted, but I wasn't up to that.

I looked at the white, wild terrain below that I had left behind. The expedition team were now just a shrinking blob of colour in a harsh, primal white world. Already we were separated, not just by distance but because I was heading back to the 'civilisation' of radios, colour TV's, hot food and water on demand. I didn't relish that and it didn't take long before tears welled up in my eyes and I had a good cry.

I don't mind admitting that. I felt awful leaving everyone, I felt I was letting everyone down – the expedition, my wife and myself. I felt cheated, guilty and terribly unlucky. I was still strong physically, my spirit wasn't broken – I was just unlucky. If push came to shove I could have still carried on, I knew I could. However, I stood by my decision to leave given the opportunity and the circumstances, my only comfort being that I had learnt something from my experience on Mount Elbrus – make a decision at the right time, taking account of your circumstances, and stand by it.

As I looked at the beautiful ice-covered crust below I knew I must come back one day. I made another promise to myself – I would return to the Arctic. Just as generations of Britons before me I felt strangely attracted to this place, I too now had ice in my blood and the 'polar fever' that had gripped many before me.

What had caused my circumstance I'll probably never know. It was easy to blame the equipment. Perhaps the boots had failed in some way, I also had doubts about whether I had used them correctly – maybe I didn't store them properly at night, perhaps allowing a small drop of condensation into them, which later froze compromising their ability to insulate my feet from the cold. Perhaps it was just my build – Pen had said that we would all feel the cold in different ways. Geoff and his hands, Rob and I with our feet. It was all such a damn shame, all the training, all the preparation and dreams. I felt completely gutted.

As I flew off, the others returned to the tent, and the silence of the Arctic reclaimed its territory once again with the disappearance of the plane, and me with it. As they warmed themselves up Pen decided it was time to take stock of this event, and instructed everyone that they must look after each other more and not to forget that we were in the polar regions where things can get out of hand quickly. In essence to take more care of yourself and each other.

'Check regularly for frost nip on each other's faces. Anyone must say if they are getting very cold to avoid this situation again,' he instructed them with great gravitas.

Taking him literally, Bunny and Rob looked at each other and then immediately piped up in unison – 'I'm bloody freezing!' to which everyone immediately roared with laughter destroying, yet again, Pen's attempt to have a serious conversation. The taboo subject – don't mention the cold – was now broken, officially.

However, the expedition couldn't afford to lose anyone else. Bunny started laughing, 'Pen smells a court case coming on. Miles from nowhere, with a tent full of lawyers, one of whose members gets frostbite.'

'Look everyone,' Pen reminded them all of the seriousness of the situation, 'If the weather had been worse in Resolute or here, then the plane could not have taken off, or landed, and that could have been the end of the expedition.' No one spoke. Pen had put his foot down. He was of course right and everyone respected his views, despite the leg-pulling.

It was always challenging with the group. We were very serious, professional, reasonably tough and willing. The group all knew what it would be like in the Arctic and they weren't silly about it. The thing was to make light of serious situations and to keep everyone laughing. It had proved to be the best medicine, as found by adventurers for millennia caught in much, much worse circumstances than ours. It made me wonder at what point on the Franklin expedition one hundred and fifty years ago in this very part of the world, that morale broke down completely once the crew faced their inevitable deaths.

'Mark, let's have a brew,' Pen said, to break the silence. Mark began fiddling slowly with the cooker and Pen, a bit annoyed, got the fuel out and started adding it to the burner to speed the process up. All of a sudden he dropped the fuel bottle which began spilling fuel all over the ground sheet. Within seconds it burst into flames ignited by the cooker flame. Everyone jumped up and Peter's automatic reaction was to throw water on it, to the cries of 'No!' The water didn't quench the flames – it just made them worse as the burning fuel, now floating on the water, spread even faster across the ground sheet of the tent. Snow for the cooker was quickly thrown on the burning liquid and the fire was put out. However, not before it had burnt a hole in the tent floor.

In the dense smoke-filled tent Bunny began to snigger then said, in a voice clearly trying to imitate Pen's accent, 'You've all got to be more careful and look after each other.' Pen joined in the laughter – more out of relief at still having a tent than anything else!

———

Looking through the aircraft window, I saw that the ground hadn't changed since we had taken off – lots of white flat ice with the occasional wrinkle, which I knew at ground level meant pressure ridges and lots of hard work. The land looked from the air as flat and featureless as when I had travelled past it some days ago. I tried to recognise something, any indication that we might have travelled through it, but found nothing. It was as though we had never been there, as though our journey didn't count. As I flew in minutes what had taken us days of travel, it all seemed so futile. The Arctic has the funny habit of squeezing human efforts into insignificance.

The flight lasted under an hour before we came upon Resolute Bay. It was quite cold in the aircraft and I still wore my full outdoor polar clothing. My ears told me that we were descending as the plane began its approach. Through the windows I could see the familiar empty road that connected the airport to the hamlet of Resolute Bay.

We landed easily this time, with what must have seemed like miles of open runway to the pilot, not a pressure ridge in sight. After off-loading my kit into Gary's van we drove the short distance back to the Rookery. Nobby and Mike were there and both offered their sympathies at my early return. They also informed me that I could stay at the Rookery for a few days if I wished until the next Penguin North Pole team came around, whereupon I would have to go back to the Arctic hotel in Resolute to await the return flight of the expedition.

After a quick cup of tea, Gary drove me into town to the Resolute Medical Centre. This building had the most modern-looking interior I had seen in Resolute. It had clean white floors, florescent lights and that disinfectant smell that always accompanies medical environments. It also had lots of alcohol abuse posters inside. An Irish lady doctor, who undoubtedly had seen much worse cases than my own, confirmed that I had frostbitten toes. 'You'll keep the toes,' she said reassuringly, in her strong Kerry accent. 'Just keep your weight off them as best as you can.' She handed me a packet of anti-inflammatory tablets that were labelled in English and Inuit, and instructed me to take one tablet three times a day. I thanked her, and as I waved from the door she reminded me, 'Remember, no football now.'

I dropped in to see Terry at the Arctic Hotel and arranged for her to put me up for a couple of days in a few days' time. As I entered the hotel I was greeted again by the warm, welcoming, deep pile carpet. Terry also invited me to have a hot shower. I suspect that this early invitation was because I probably smelled a tad. It was a lovely feeling, with the warm water running over me, being clean again. I massaged my wooded toes, but they remained stubbornly numb.

Back in the Rookery a brew was put on and Mike and Nobby started to de-brief me. I told them of the bad radio, skidoos basically falling to bits, but how spirits were still very high and that the group was absolutely determined to carry on. Mike needed to hear this, as without voice radio communication he was only able to get a picture of things from the Argos codes. Mike and Nobby had been tracking our progress on a map and assumed, correctly, that bad ice had caused our slow progress. I told them of the fuel situation and how we considered trying to go across Bathurst Island as well as the expedition group's discussions regarding how to get to the Pole.

'Will they get to the Pole?' asked Mike.

'Yes,' I replied, 'And I'll be there with them.' I wasn't out of this trip yet by a long way, and had every intention of standing at the Pole, not by the means expected but nonetheless I wasn't going back home until I'd been there.

Back out on the ice Pen decided that it was too late to start travelling – by the time the tent was packed the light would be fading. A second night was spent camped at the newly named 'Duncan Point'. The conversation was subdued, but not too much so.

12

The Pole, but under different circumstances than expected

'The Pole yes, but – under very different circumstances from those expected.'

CAPTAIN ROBERT FALCON SCOTT, ROYAL NAVY,
POLAR EXPLORER.

I woke to a strange sound. It was the sound of a telephone ringing. I dreamt I was at home. I opened my eyes and then realised where I was: in the Rookery. The unexpected sound was merely part of Pen's office up there. Mike had also woken up and was scrambling about in the dark for the phone. Nobby remained fast asleep. I then heard Mike talking to someone – a journalist – and giving details of the women's polar relay team. He also politely scolded the caller, reminding them that 10 a.m. in London was 4 a.m. here in Canada. I drifted off back to sleep again, taking advantage of having a warm comfortable bed, one in which I could turn over as often as I liked without finding a boot, another head, or a knee competing for the same space.

I was awoken again later from a particularly deep sleep by something. It wasn't the sound of a phone ringing, or some of the other less recognisable noises in the garage-like mild chaotic atmosphere of the Rookery, but the sweet smell of bacon. I don't know where they had got it, or how long it had remained frozen, but I wasn't interested in those details. I was soon sitting on a pile of sleeping bags tucking into bacon sandwiches with Mike and Nobby. This was the life. We discussed the plan for the day and I of course volunteered my services for any task that they felt would be suitable for me.

I was charged with packing the day food bags for the next team of the Penguin Polar Relay expedition's attempt on the North Pole. This expedition was the first all-women team aiming to get to the North Geographic Pole in stages. Each team in the group would be flown onto the ice and have to walk one degree of latitude, which is sixty nautical miles.

This was very difficult for the first few teams, who started on the Canadian coast, where they had to overcome massive pressure ridges of ice. Gradually these ridges would occur less frequently as the team got nearer the Pole. The only person going from start to end was the guide, Matty McNaire, an outdoor expert. The next, and final team would be flying in tomorrow night from the UK, to prepare for going on the ice. Their goal was to get to the Pole itself. I was looking forward to meeting some female travellers.

Mike was outside, making sure everything was ready for the new team. I weighed and bagged each food pack. Like our rations they consisted of nuts, chocolate, salami, apricots for day travel and cheese, smash potatoes and various freeze-dried rice dishes for evening meals.

I took every opportunity I could to leave the confines of the Rookery and get outside. Each time I went outside I still found the intense cold and sunlight breathtaking, physically and spiritually. There was still little movement in Resolute. Sometimes the odd dog would bark, and occasionally a hunter would come across the horizon with his dogs pulling his komatik. The airport would leap into life once or twice a day as a plane arrived. Either a local Twin Otter, or, less frequently, a larger jet carrying passengers and cargo in equal amounts.

Resolute Bay's power station, with its chimney that dominated the village, would sit slowly passing steam into the air, like an old man quietly smoking a pipe.

I used the Rookery's satellite phone to call my wife. She was with her family in Ireland and I wanted to report in to let her know my situation. Mike and Nobby were very reluctant to give out information when an expedition was in progress, as often part information could lead to unnecessary worry to a family. They didn't seem to mind too much in my case, which I was pleased about.

'Hi Colm, it's me,' was the way I introduced myself to my father-in-law as he picked up the phone in Ireland.

'Err, Is that Duncan?' he asked. 'I wasn't expecting a call from you yet, is everything ok?' he seemed a little taken aback, as he was not expecting to be hearing from me so early, and was clearly wondering what had happened.

'I've been taken off the ice,' I replied. 'I got a frostbitten foot, nothing serious but I didn't want it to get any worse.' I was trying to imagine what he must have been thinking as he took the call in an Ireland just entering spring.

'It's nothing to worry about, honest, and I'm really ok. The rest of the team are still on the ice. Is Niamh there?'

My wife wasn't there so I relayed the rest of the details for him to pass on, informing him that I would be back at the arranged time and still hoped to get to the Pole – but emphasising that I was ok. As I put the phone down I realised I would be repeating this story many, many times over when I got back and didn't particularly relish the fact. In fact I was already wishing that I hadn't mentioned my frostbite.

As the day wore on, both Mike and I had our eyes on the time, and we convened in the communications room in the Rookery. A few minutes before 9.00 p.m., when the expedition team was due to make a scheduled call, Mike switched on the radio, and we both listened for any communication from them. The room filled with a crackling sound from the radio and a low light from the radio's dials engulfed the small room with an eerie glow. Mike adjusted the radio's dial to and fro, hoping to pick up a better signal, should the team be able to communicate.

I didn't expect to hear from the expedition, after so many days of trying without success I had concluded that there must have been a problem with the team's radio. We sat huddled around the radio. A faint glow shone from its dials, and the air cracked and hissed as the atmospheric interference played its ghostly music. Occasionally a Dalek-like voice drifted in and out as voices from other expeditions bounced around the atmosphere. Still we heard nothing, as the communication window came and passed.

Mike kept the radio on for another five minutes, hoping to make contact. I could imagine that a few hundred miles away Pen was crouching over the radio in the cold saying, 'Nothing heard, nothing heard.' Mike looked up at me and switched the unit off after muttering a disappointed 'Two-Six-Three, Nothing heard'.

Mike then turned to the Rookery computer to dial into the communications system in Maryland to look at the status of the expedition's Argos communications device, the alternative to the radio. Sure enough it reliably reported the position of the group. Mike read the codes and stated 'Zero, zero – all ok,' that was good to know.

The Argos read a temperature of -25°C which was very cold, given that Pen usually set up the Argos in the tent. Their position read 75.57N, 103.59W which meant that they had travelled some 19 nautical miles, a good day. Mike was happy and so was I, but I wished desperately that I was out there in the silent wilderness with the expedition.

After a long, but very enjoyable day, we had dinner. This was interrupted by the drone of a large plane landing. Mike, looked at his watch, jumped up and shot off to get the truck and collect our mystery guest arriving on the flight. Nobby and I kept eating and drinking, a small stereo playing in the background and the Hell Hole toilet steadily humming away on its own behind the modesty curtain.

It wasn't long before our guest arrived, ushered in by a cold draft as the door sprang open. She was a tall lady in her late thirties, with her head wrapped up in a white shawl which probably looked very elegant and trendy in London, but slightly out of place here in the back of beyond, where fashion had not so much been forgotten exactly, it had just never arrived.

I was introduced to Caroline, the Penguin expedition relay founder. She would be travelling up with the final team, due in tomorrow, to walk the remaining sixty nautical miles to the North Pole. She was very bubbly and excited to be there and it was clear that the men enjoyed her company too. It was even better when she produced three bottles of wine. We all immediately became best friends, alcohol being rarer than a heat wave in dry Resolute Bay. With great restraint we only finished the one bottle of wine before retiring. The effect of this one bottle was enough and I had a very good, warm, night's sleep for the second night in a row.

The next day was another busy one. Caroline was checking ice conditions from satellite images faxed to her, and I was fully engaged with Nobby in the preparation for Caroline's team arriving later in the day. I was doing as much as I could to help out – checking all the skis and the pulks, weighing and bagging more food, but there was only so much I could do until the team was on hand. I spent the afternoon down at Terry's as I would be sleeping there for the rest of the duration until my group arrived back.

Word soon got round the hotel of my arrival, and I was now quizzed by a variety of polar travellers eager to know of the ice conditions, any polar bear sightings and why I was back so early. Most of them somehow knew the news about my frostbitten foot, probably gained from the air pilots or ground staff. Word travelled far and quickly in a small town, and none was smaller than Resolute Bay. No one knew of my polar bear experience and I stuck to my promise to myself to remain silent.

Two Japanese gentlemen bowed on my arrival, and followed me round to hear my story. They were supporting an expedition of a Japanese man who was on the ice travelling to the North Pole on a motorbike! They nodded as I spoke to them but they didn't really ask anything. I later found out that they had been in Resolute almost two months and were bored out of their heads, 'As any normal person would be after five minutes here,' added Dave the photographer, still there and not missing an opportunity to moan about his plight. They still had a month to go before their Suzuki man would return from the ice.

Amongst all the onlookers two men particularly stood out. They were very tanned – not the sort of outdoor wind tan that stops at the neck, but the all over golden tan sported by people from hot climes. These two Englishmen lived and worked in Saudi Arabia, a place that couldn't have seemed further away from where we all were.

'Can't stand the heat,' said one, which made sense as to why they might be in the Arctic, but not in the other sense as to why they lived and worked where they did. 'We've been looking to be the first people to raise the Saudi flag at the North Magnetic Pole.' I wished them luck. They had also crossed the Greenland icecap, so were seasoned in Arctic travel.

Dave the photographer was even slightly more fed up, if that was possible, than when I had left him when my expedition left for the ice. He slept as much as he could and seemed to be trying to remove himself from the glorious surroundings of the ice that he found himself in. Being a man of the city he required bars and night life, and there wasn't any of that sort of thing for thousands of miles around. In fact, the nearest place with any nightlife was probably Vladivostok in Russian Asia. 'A few weirdoes living in plastic houses in the dark,' was his parting comment to me, reflecting his views on life in Resolute Bay, as he went back to bed now the day's excitement seemed to be over.

I spent the rest of the afternoon shaking people's hands and being asked to remove my sock numerous times to show my 'wooden companions' off, as I began to call them. My new found celebrity status was an interesting way to break the ice, as it were, but soon became tiresome, as the seemingly continuous stream of travellers would ask to touch and prod them.

My toes remained defiantly numb despite my fairly regular, and increasingly Lady Macbeth-like, rubbing of them. I was now more of a museum exhibit, illustrating the dangers that perhaps awaited the other travellers and providing an example of what to avoid. Now I was in warmer climes the dead whiteness seemed to have gone from them and a pinker colour seemed to emerge, which made me more hopeful despite them still having no feeling.

There were many interesting and varied people at the small hostel. Given the limited time window in which polar travel was possible, and how far north we were, these people represented a large proportion of the Arctic's polar travellers for the year. I lapped up what they were all trying to do and dearly wished I was out with my expedition, not sitting there drinking fruit juice and relaxing in deep pile carpeted comfort.

Whilst sitting in a comfortable arm chair, I struck up a conversation with a middle-aged Englishman, who was also attempting to walk to the North Magnetic Pole. His expedition, like those of most of the other people in the hotel, was not publicised and was basically a personal trip. This was why Pen had been unaware of their existence, and mentioned earlier that our expedition might be the first to the Magnetic Pole this year. The man's story was that he had been made redundant, with a good pay-off. He had a keen interest in the outdoors, and had planned for the last two years for this trip.

A young and very slight woman joined us. The man introduced her as Debbie. He explained that they intended to walk together to the Magnetic North Pole, having met on a camping trip some years ago. This was quite surprising to me, as the woman didn't look physically strong enough. 'We are going to take a dog with us, one of the Inuit ones,' she said confidently. I couldn't even imagine her being able to hold on to such an animal, let alone walk to the Magnetic Pole whilst dragging a sledge.

We spent most of the next hour chatting, with them both grilling me about what I had seen and the conditions I had encountered.

'I can't believe you went through Polar Bear Pass!' she exclaimed. 'How did you get permission?'

'Well err, Pen got it,' I hesitated, not knowing that permission was needed, and informed her that Pen had definitely got such permission, so as not to embarrass anyone. Debbie was very fearful of the polar bears and, like me, had read Helen Thayer's account of her journey, many times. I didn't mention my own experience with a bear, and hoped that they would both be ok when they went out onto the ice as planned, in a couple of days, weather permitting.

Another Englishman introduced himself as Sergeant Chapple, a Royal Marine, and described how he hoped to become the first from his regiment to reach the North Geographic Pole. He hoped to get himself a name as their 'cold man' and planned an attempt next year. He was in Resolute for acclimatisation training and equipment check. The Royal Marines had an affinity with this area, having accompanied the 1845 Franklin North West Passage search, and many subsequent Victorian naval expeditions.

It was great to be lazing about. I hadn't realised how tired my body was until I had begun to rest. My muscles and joints all seemed very weary after days of moving heavy supplies on and off komatiks, and being bounced around on the skidoos. My appetite had not yet subsided to its normal rate and I found myself hovering around the kitchen with other members of various expeditions, constantly on the look out for some grub, and annoying the cook who, whilst extremely friendly and chatty to her new visitors, no doubt felt slightly stalked as we watched every move she made. We did of course have nothing to worry about, as we were all well fed at the hostel.

This was different to the situation that I found myself in when climbing Mount Elbrus in southern Russia, where all the meals had consisted of a calorie-less watery soup, cabbage and lettuce with biscuits. It left me and the climbing expedition members constantly hungry. At the time though I had appreciated the food because the climbing expedition was close to the Chechen border and so food was scarce.

The people sharing their food with us had all been women or children, with mouths full of gold teeth, (as was customary in the region), fleeing the Chechen war. At the time I had not dared ask where the men were.

Whilst these women had been very interested in us westerners, the one question I knew they would ask, which I had managed to avoid for a while, had eventually been spluttered out by a young female translator; 'How much do you earn?' I couldn't avoid it any longer so told them, 'About three thousand US dollars a year,' to which they had all expressed surprise at someone earning such a vast sum. Apart from sparing their feelings, I knew that kidnapping was not unknown locally, in fact we had been warned about it, so I was keen to avoid telling them my real salary.

The day carried on in Resolute and I found myself working back at the Rookery, doing all manner of odd jobs, which I was very happy to do. Caroline's final Penguin relay team was flying in tonight and she was busy preparing for them. It wasn't long before I heard the sound of an aircraft rushing overhead, its engines going into reverse mode and shattering the peace of the hamlet. Mike was soon in the truck, unplugging it from the wall and its engine heater, and went off to pick up the next group of girls, after dropping me off at Terry's once more.

The evening was livened up with the arrival of these women at Terry's. They looked so fresh, and didn't carry the weather-worn faces of the other guests, who seemed to have now disappeared. The women arrived with Mike and a mountain of bags. There was much noise and excitement and Mike introduced each of them to me. They had all replied to an advert on the radio placed by Pen and Caroline: "Walk to the North Pole, no experience necessary." A selection weekend had been held at Pen's house on Dartmoor and from this the candidates were chosen. All had no previous Arctic experience – just an eager desire to succeed.

The group included a mother and daughter team. The mother had had breast cancer, resulting in a mammary being removed. She joyfully told me that during the selection weekend when Pen got everyone to swim across a lake with their backpacks on, her false breast had detached itself and floated away! These new people seemed like lots of fun, and I looked forward to spending as much time as possible with them, as their guide, Geoff Somers, took them through their final preparation tasks.

By now I was beginning to get into a routine at Resolute. Waking early, getting a good breakfast into me and then helping out at the Rookery. Then taking a short walk if I could before lunch and helping out at the Polar Travel Company's base at the Rookery again in the afternoon.

The activity at the Rookery had gone up a level now that the new Penguin team had arrived. They would train and acclimatise for a week before going up to the Pole and swapping with the team coming off the ice. A large aeronautical map of the North Pole region was on the wall, and I could see the progress of the various relay teams scrawled on it in various colours.

The earliest team, starting from Ward Hunt Island, on the Canadian shore, had the hardest job and made the slowest progress. They were faced with mountainous-like pressure ridges of up to twenty feet in height that made the ridges I had to negotiate on the skidoo look like small feed. Progress for this team was accordingly slow, and covering two miles of travel a day in these conditions was considered good.

The team at Resolute now should have the easiest journey. The pressure ridges they would meet should be small, if any, although the ice plates were likely to be moving, and negotiating large expanses of sea were likely to be their main issue.

My role that day was to pack more food bags for the final leg of the women's Penguin team, giving each team member a specific amount of nuts, chocolate and cereals. Each bag would be labelled, by colour, for the relevant member of the team. I headed straight towards a mountain of chocolate bars, armed with bags and weighing scales. I thought I would secretly add some fun for the girls. I had found an old *Viz* comic in the Rookery and carefully cut it up, and packed into each food bag a small cartoon or joke that I hoped would warm their spirits when they were on the ice, (I later read in a book that one of them published, *Frigid Women*, that they did indeed enjoy my daily joke).

A couple of hours later, having finished the food packing, I took my daily walk. Rather than walk around the hamlet as usual, I decided to be more adventurous. After zipping up my multiple layers of clothing I left the Rookery and headed out to the frozen sea. In front of me was a large hill on an island, and before that was a watery channel, which was of course frozen. The ice underfoot was flat and I had soon walked a mile or so from shore, the hill strangely seeming just as distant as when I started walking. I took a few photos, and enjoyed the sun-bathed scene. Resolute Bay was behind me and looked even smaller and insignificant than it felt from within the hamlet. As I continued walking over to the hill, my feet made polystyrene-like crunching sounds as each footstep touched the dry ice.

It was then that fear grabbed me. I was alone, unarmed, and no one knew I was here. If a bear appeared I would be in trouble. I looked around intently and could see nothing moving, but decided I was ill equipped to travel further and would be pushing my luck to do so. I returned back to shore and skirted the outskirts of the hamlet.

Back at the Rookery, the new Penguin team were trying on their new suits and boots. Inevitably equipment was strewn everywhere, with the women helping each other to try on different size boots, ensuring that they fitted as they performed funny walks across the room. Ski poles were tried for size, and there was much laughter at how silly everyone looked with their face masks on. I'd seen it all before and the chaos, colour and excitement of a kit frenzy was just as good the second time round. If he had been here, Pen's dog Baskers would have hated the chaos and left the room.

Time pushed on, even in a place where for many people it seemed to stand still. Mike and I were back in the radio room with its equipment humming, and were turning dials, hoping for some contact with Pen. Again, there was nothing heard so we checked the Argos communications device. The Argos stated the team had set it with a code of oo indicating all was well, which was particularly comforting.

They had moved twelve nautical miles since yesterday and reached a position of 76.2oN, 104.02W. Checking the large map on the wall above the radio we determined that they must be camping near the abandoned air station at the south of Cameron Island. The temperature was reported by the Argos to be +1.5°C, indicating that Pen must have set the Argos from inside the tent after the meal when the tent was at its warmest.

The following day passed much like the others. I was waiting to get my chance to get to the Magnetic North Pole. It was still clear to me that the expedition was not progressing quickly enough to do anything other than fly there. Peter and I would be proven right: lack of progress sledging or skidooing meant that the team would have to fly there eventually – or not get there at all – given that the expedition was running out of time.

I just wanted to make sure I got to the Pole, so I packed everything that I needed for an additional stay on the ice, ready to be used at a moment's notice. I still intended to fulfil my dream, and knowing that the expedition team members would have to be picked up by plane, I intended to fly up with them to the Pole.

At the scheduled radio call time with the expedition, I again had little hope of communication with Pen, and eagerly awaited the Argos report, rather than placing any expectation on radio communications. Mike, Nobby and I sat down in the radio room in the Rookery and checked the Argos. To our surprise we found it was not exhibiting its usual 'oo – all ok' but was set to the code '08'. This meant 'Pickup group, not urgent'. At last they had decided to be airlifted out. I couldn't imagine what the discussion in the tent had been like to come to this decision.

Mike scanned the airwaves, then suddenly, at the scheduled time, we heard what appeared not only to be a garbled human voice, but that of Pen's. Whilst we couldn't quite understand what he was saying exactly, given today's

Argos message to pick up the team, we addressed what we thought he would be asking.

'This is Resolute Two-Six-Three, most unlikely to get a plane to you today. Do you copy? Over' said Mike.

The air hissed and hummed again. Mike now had his ear right up against the radio. I could just about determine the Dalek squawking 'Why? Why? Over.'

'There is no plane available. Over,' conveyed Mike into the radio's microphone. The air hissed again and the part-man, part-Dalek voice re-entered the muffled airwaves.

Mike pushed the microphone button again on his handset, 'Believe you said one skidoo and one komatik are with you. Please confirm.' A rush of electronic bleeps and whizzes filled the room. 'Say again. Over.'

'No fuel,' Pen said, this time quite clearly. Mike looked at both Nobby and I, wondering if he had missed something.

Mike asked, 'Which day did you leave the skidoos behind? Over. Was it Sunday? Over.'

Nobby, at this stage, believing his hearing and translation skills were slightly better than Mike's or mine, took control of the microphone.

'Two-six-three, trying to ascertain what your situation is. Three skidoos, I say again, three skidoos at seventy-five degrees, one hundred and three. Are these skidoos working? Over?' He paused again, then said 'Please reply with 'Roger' or 'Negative'. Nobby shook his head at the faint 'Negative,' reply.

'Please confirm that two skidoos work and one doesn't work. Over.'

A garbled squawking sound emanated from the radio.

'Say again. Over,' requested Mike, hoping that Pen could hear us better than we could him.

'Please confirm that one skidoo works and three don't work. Over.' 'Roger,' said Pen, 'Skidoos left at seventy-five degrees fifty-seven north, one hundred and three degrees, fifty-nine.' Nobby looked up and nodded to Mike and I. Mike needed to know what the state of the skidoos were, so he could prepare for their rescue trip, as the plane would not be able to carry both the skidoos and the expedition team.

We didn't know what the radio reception was like out on the ice. It could have been just as bad there as it was for us. I tried to imagine what they were doing. Were the team members in their sleeping bags? or were they sitting around the stove listening to Pen chatting as each member checked his equipment or wrote his diary? Or perhaps Pen was alone at the top of a hill, where reception was possibly better. They were either as frustrated as us with the bad signal, or receiving us well and wondering why we seemed so confused. We spoke for another ten minutes. Communication was difficult, but we were able to determine the status of the team and their abandoned skidoos.

'Next radio schedule seven a.m. tomorrow morning, Resolute time,' stated Nobby.

'Two-Six-Four, be back for dinner,' said Pen, this time clearly.

The inevitable was now happening. The expedition team needed collection from the ice and would have to fly the remaining distance to the Magnetic Pole.

Nobby sprang into action and made a call on the phone. Half an hour later two burly men knocked at the Rookery door. One was Inuit and the other was Caucasian. They were introduced as Rick and Randy, respectively. These were the two men who, though it had always been planned this way, had the unfortunate task of picking up the abandoned skidoos and driving them back to Resolute. There simply would not be enough room in the aircraft for the expedition team and the heavy skidoos. The expedition team, including me, would then fly on to the Pole.

Nobby got a map out and pin-pointed where the skidoos were left. Rick and Randy were given a GPS each and shown how to use them; something that made me slightly uncomfortable, as I hoped that they would be familiar with such a device already, in the unforgiving world that they were going into. I found out from them that they had been resident in Resolute Bay for some years and worked at the power station, so I guessed they were seasoned Arctic travellers. We all retired for the evening, with me a little more excited than the previous night.

Friday, 4th April came around, and I awoke, early and excited. Today, weather permitting, would be the day that I would reach the Pole. Not long after waking I was picked up by Nobby from Terry's, and I was soon at the Rookery. Mike greeted me at the door. Today I was a customer again of the Polar Travel Company, and Mike was helping me reach my goal, as opposed to previous days when I was helping him in any way possible.

After a hot cup of tea and a Penguin chocolate biscuit he eagerly informed me that, having been in contact with the airport, he had learnt that First Air would be ready to fly us up to the Pole that afternoon. Mike had spoken with Pen at seven and all was still ok. He expected a flight out of Resolute at one p.m. Rick and Randy would also be flying with us and were on hand, armed with a rifle, some food, survival equipment, and a bag of tools to mend any broken skidoos. They would drive two skidoos that we would drop them with to pull the derelict skidoos all the way back to the Resolute.

Pen was updating the Argos communication every hour and Mike was constantly checking it. The code Pen set all those hundreds of miles away still read 'Awaiting pickup' which also indicated that the local weather conditions were favourable. Generally pilots on any expedition flight in the Arctic need to have good weather conditions at three sites: where they are taking off from; where they are landing; and a third site - in case an alternative emergency diversion is needed.

We all went next door to Gary's house to have a wash. Nobby and Mike lived in the Rookery, which did not have any washing facilities so they often took advantage of Gary's facilities and his kind offer to use them. Gary wasn't in, but he had left the keys in the Rookery. We helped ourselves to a brew, and I nervously kept an eye on the weather and the time.

The First Air pilots that were going to fly us to the Pole were all remarkable men. They offered one of the main communication services to communities all over the high Canadian Arctic. As there were no roads or railways connecting people in these communities, travel was either by skidoo, air or ship. Ship movements are very limited of course and very slow, given that the waterways are frozen solid most of the year, and in the early summer an icebreaker is needed to clear a path.

The First Air pilots mainly fly the small and now obsolete Twin Otter aircraft. This is a twin engine propeller aircraft that is perfect for polar expedition flights. It's small and so is easy to store when not flying, simple to maintain, light enough to land on ice, and has the benefit of only needing a very short take-off and landing, which means it is perfect for polar activity where airstrip facilities are mainly non-existent. The Twin Otter is used as a workhorse all over the polar regions, and many modern polar explorers owe their lives to this aircraft, and the skill and bravery of the pilots who fly them.

One o'clock came and went. There was no sign of our flight. Mike was in communication with the airport, but they had delayed the flight until two p.m. pending more information on a weather front. Two p.m. came and went. Mike was checking the Argos and the expedition were still transmitting 'ok for collection' status code, indicating that the weather around Cameron Island, where they were located, remained ok for aircraft.

Just as we got stuck into the tea at Gary's house there was a firm knock at the door. It was the pilots! They both introduced themselves. This was surely a service even first class passengers didn't get on major airlines – the pilot calling at your house to pick you up when it was time to fly! We hurried out with them in their truck and drove the empty mile up to the airport. We quickly got to the runway where the aircraft was waiting, painted in the white, red and black colours of Bradley First Air.

Rick and Randy began to put their two skidoos onto the plane. They were both incredibly strong, and lifted the skidoos into the hold through the open door at the side of the plane. Though I was helping them it was very apparent that they didn't need me. The plan was that they would use the two skidoos that they had loaded into the aircraft to tow the abandoned and broken skidoos and komatiks behind them back to Resolute. They also loaded a komatik into the plane. They would use the komatik to carry any unserviceable skidoos. They also loaded a large barrel of fuel. Everything was tied down in the aircraft, because none of us wanted any of the heavy equipment rolling around once we were airborne, or when we landed, on what might be a bumpy landing strip.

The weather was still clear. Nobby gave us a farewell wave as we set off, and he was soon lost in a blizzard of snow kicked up by the plane. The noise of the Twin Otter's propeller engines drowned out Nobby's cheers of good luck. We were soon into the air and Resolute Bay was quickly swallowed up by the flour-white of the sea and the land encased in ice. Aboard there was little point in talking, because the engines were so loud. After an hour's flying we approached our first target, the abandoned skidoos. The skidoos initially appeared as pinpricks on the ice, and were picked up by their GPS position, rather than any eagle-eyed pilot. The pilot circled a couple of times to check the position. Pen had chosen the landing strip well and the pilot soon dropped in low, decreasing the engine revs, and virtually gliding in. I only felt a slight bump as we landed. Rick, Randy and I jumped up from our seats and threw our seat belts off as we exited the plane. The pilot kept the engine running.

Rick and Randy surveyed the wasted skidoos in the snow. It felt great to be back on the ice again, miles from anywhere. The icy landscape welcomed me back by immediately numbing my face. We soon took Rick and Randy's equipment and skidoos off the plane. I wished them both well and hoped that they would have an uneventful journey back to Resolute. It seemed strange to drop them in the wilderness to clear up our mess, but that was always part of the plan.

The flight took off again. This time I was the only passenger on board, and I saw Rick and Randy disappearing in a blizzard of snow as the engines roared and took us back into the sky. With the plane now empty the pilot and I flew onwards to the expedition group, where we would pick up everyone and their remaining equipment, and then continue on to the Magnetic Pole.

Flying onward we soon found the expedition just south of Cameron Island, at their appointed GPS position. There was an abandoned air strip on the island and as we flew over it we saw a neglected aircraft waiting silently on the ground, now swallowed up by the snow, only the tail protruding through the ice. Pen's party were camped on the sea ice, and I could see the colours of the tent against the white icy background as we circled overhead. The landing was the best yet – there were no pressure ridges or other obstacles. We landed on flat sea ice; once we stopped, I jumped out, eager to see them again.

I met Rob first. His face mask was completely encrusted in white and sugary lumps of frost. He looked a dramatic figure.

'Hi Rob!' I shouted from behind my own double mask.

'How are you?' he replied, 'How's the foot?'

'Fine.'

'Excellent. Gosh, fucking hell, am I glad this plane is here!' he said, as he shook my hand lightly.

Mark was quite close behind pulling a sledge. 'How are you?' I shouted, followed by, 'So you got to pull your sledge then?' He cried out as I shook his outstretched hand tightly – he was obviously suffering from cold hands. Pen was busy working on the komatik, and getting together a pile of things that he wanted to burn and leave there. There was a lot of equipment to fit into the plane and he didn't want to take anything that would weigh it down unnecessarily. We started a fire, using the last of the team's fuel, and set fire to all the items that we couldn't bring on the plane. This generated a light brown plume of smoke that rose and stained the clean air.

Eventually we all jumped into the aircraft and flew onwards to the destination of our expedition - the North Magnetic Pole positioned at 78.7N, 104.4W. It was a great atmosphere inside the aircraft – we all laughed and giggled. The others questioned me about what I had been up to, but there wasn't much to say in all honesty – I couldn't even make up anything interesting, given my inactivity in Resolute!

Geoff recounted how they had looked around the deserted air station on Cameron Island, which wasn't quite as deserted as expected – it was covered in wolf tracks - which he admitted had been a little unnerving. As Pen came back from the cockpit he shouted, 'Polar bear!' and pointed towards a window on the starboard side of our plane. I wasn't quick enough to see it as we hurtled through the sky.

We soon came upon our target, again guided by GPS, completing our journey that had begun some six months earlier in England. The Magnetic North Pole was off the north coast of Ellef Ringnes Island. It looked like anywhere else here, and was only here due to the activity of the molten magma, unseen far below the Earth's crust where we were about to stand.

The Twin Otter landed on the sea ice. The lack of current in the sea under the ice meant that no bumps had been formed in the ice, and the pilot glided along as we landed, gently applying the brakes. This would have been good, fast running ground on the skidoo, I thought – it would also have been easy ground to pull a pulk across. The plane stopped, and we were there. This time the pilot switched the engine off, perhaps because the ice was thicker and he didn't feel he might have to leave at a moment's notice. We all stepped outside. It had been cold in the aircraft because there was no heating or pressurisation, but stepping outside still took my breath away. The sky was huge and the view was as intoxicating as ever. The low rise of Ellef Ringes Island was in the distance to the south and a flat vista stretched out before us. Unlike the South Pole there was no pole to mark the location of the Magnetic North Pole.

'Where is it?' Geoff said, jokingly, as if he was expecting a some sort of sign, monument or gift shop, to signify the location of the Magnetic Pole. It was eerily quiet with the aircraft's engine off, and a light wind had picked up which caused the temperature to drop further. 'About minus forty-two,' Pen said knowingly, from behind his black bear-lined hood. 'Plus wind-chill,' he added, in response to the growing breeze which seemed to hug us with its icy welcome.

We obviously had to give our attention to finding something to represent the Magnetic Pole, and Bunny found a small icy hump approximately two feet high about a hundred yards away. He confirmed this with, 'There it is!' and pointed towards it with his glove outstretched. Being outside again we didn't hang about. I found that I had not forgotten the steps of the ice dance and quickly resumed them, and the others soon joined in.

I retrieved my flag from my pack and soon the Union Jack was flying in the breeze, hoisted on a ski stick, and flapping against a backdrop of the clear blue sky that I so loved up there. The red and dark blue of the flag looked powerful fluttering against the bleached white of the background. I stood briefly thinking about James Clark Ross, who had first discovered and found the position of the Pole in 1831.

Although the wandering Pole's position had moved by about 200 miles north west since Ross first marked it, I wondered whether he had shared the same sentiments as I now did when he stood at the Pole in his older materials much further from home than I. I felt for the later Franklin expedition stranded in this place in 1845, as their dreams of finding the northwest passage to China collapsed. It must have been dreadful for them, and the desperate feeling of isolation must surely have been overwhelming.

When Captain Scott and his brave party reached the South Pole on the opposite end of the world on a cold, lonely day in January 1912, they met not an unknown and empty ice field, but a tent and a flag already flying and awaiting their arrival. The flag displayed the colours of Norway, as it flapped uncontrollably at the command of the cold wind. 'The Pole yes, but – under very different circumstances from those expected.'

'We have had a horrible day,' Scott wrote in his diary. It's difficult to imagine the disappointment he must have felt as the bitter truth of Amundsen's arrival, weeks earlier, greeted him and his team. Even the desperate words written in his diary hardly convey his loss: 'Great God! This is an awful place and terrible enough for us to have laboured to it without the reward of priority.'

Unlike many modern polar adventurers who have since reached the South Pole, and are then flown back to civilisation, Scott's team had only reached half way, on their expedition. On reaching the Pole they then had to walk the whole way back again. It is almost impossible today to imagine what that was like. Scott's reputation and future would have seemed in jeopardy, as no one would be likely to remember the second team to the Pole. Honour and pride at the beginning of the twentieth century were perhaps more important than today, and they had driven him on to the Pole. It truly must have seemed an awful place.

The isolation of the nineteenth and early twentieth century explorers is difficult to comprehend today in our ever-connected world. There were no communications with home then. In contrast, even the astronauts stranded on Apollo Thirteen, apparently helpless in the vastness of space, and hundreds of thousands of miles from home, had the comfort of talking to their Earth-bound colleagues for reassurance and advice most of the time.

Evacuation for us was only a satellite telephone call away, so we always had the comfort and confidence of rescue behind us. It's difficult for someone, even a modern day 'explorer' to fully appreciate how men in past ages must have felt leaving home, on a ship, for any number of months or years, with an uncertain future ahead. For the same reason it must have been very difficult for those cut off from them and left at home. That age has now gone and more and more people are able to explore and survive because they have these better communications.

So I was actually there, literally in the middle of nowhere. This really was the definition of wilderness. To the north of us there were no towns, hamlets or any habitation. To the east and west much the same. Hundreds of miles of nothingness. You could almost feel the desolation. There was little or no sign of man there at all. I felt very humbled as few and fewer people, as our cities expand, will ever see or have the opportunity to be placed right in the heart of nature like this.

We took a few group photos and I brought out my blow-up sheep, the 'Love Ewe', given to me by my work colleagues. Blowing up the plastic sheep raised a few laughs. The sheep didn't last long, as the plastic became immediately very brittle and fragile in the cold air, causing a leg to snap off as I held it. I knew I should have put the sheep through my home freezer test!

After another moment's private thought I got my video camera out, and began filming the area around me before the camera batteries died in the cold. As soon as Pen saw me filming he immediately stepped up to the camera.

'Here we are at the North Magnetic Pole,' he stated in his best BBC anchorman voice. 'This is an historic moment for this British group, who have struggled against fantastic odds to get here. Their names are as follows: our leader Mark, followed by, in no particular order, alphabetic or otherwise: Peter – whose surname eludes me, Geoff, whose surname eludes me, Rob, Pen and err, at least two others, err, including our cameraman Mr. Duncan Eadie and...' The anchor was sinking fast. Peter could see Pen was struggling and shouted out from behind my video camera, 'Bunny!'

'Who? ah yes, Bunny. Bunny the Bastard,' Pen said. Peter shouted again from off camera, 'Bunny who broke everything.'

'Here's something for the camera.' Pen got his compass out and described to the lens how the needle was not locking onto north but aimlessly spinning. 'And it's being remarkably co-operative,' he said, as it willingly spun round for the video camera. It was true; all magnetic compasses in the world, be they held in ships, planes, military personnel or in boy scout's pockets, were right now pointing directly to the small group of cold men in this lonely moon-like environment. All points of the magnetic compass were effectively south from us right now. And our compasses were spinning as the text book said it should.

I took from my pocket the stone that my dad had given me from his green and shrub-laden back garden, and placed it onto the small mound representing the Pole. I thought of my family and wife, and wondered what they were doing right now. I also thought about the small boy who had a polar dream - that was now being realised.

This was one of my life's best moments, and I knew it.

13

Conclusion

'I thought, dear, that you would rather a live ass, than a dead lion.'

SIR ERNEST SHACKLETON; POLAR EXPLORER;
TO HIS WIFE AFTER DECIDING TO TURN BACK,
97 MILES FROM THE SOUTH POLE.

The lights dimmed in the packed room at the Royal Geographic Society in London, and the sound from the audience fell in unison. The growing darkness was pierced by a dim glow from the lectern, which also illuminated the face of Mark. Pen introduced the expedition. With images of the expedition projected behind him, Mark then spoke about what we had done and seen to the audience which numbered about a hundred people.

It was a proud day for us all, being in such a hallowed place with the bronze busts and nameplates of the great and famous explorers around us – such as Scott, Speke, Livingstone and many others. Mark's speech was sprinkled liberally with jokes that emphasised the camaraderie of the group, both on the ice and in the months of preparation for our expedition. The 1997 Oyez Polar Expedition had come to an end.

The Arctic makes and breaks men. Some it welcomes with a cold inviting hand, others it brings in only to destroy them with its icy breath of death.

All who survive are effected by it. Humbled or celebrated, the Arctic laughs at everyone.

Now that I have returned to the warmth of my world, life once again seems as normal. But it will never be normal again. My soul has been lifted by the experience that I had among the cold and empty wastes. Since my return there has hardly been a single day that I have not thought about the friendships formed and the sights seen – such is the power of the Arctic. They will live with me until my dying day.

A place that has still been largely untouched by travellers, has touched this traveller and left a permanent mark. In a world beginning to burst at the seams, the emptiness of the Arctic has a threatened beauty that must be treasured and preserved for eternity. More beautiful than any painting, more valuable than any treasure, the polar regions of this planet must be protected for the future. I feel privileged to have been there and feel a duty to such a place that it must remain untouched.

I would like to think I will return to the Arctic again one day, perhaps with my wife and maybe even a son or a daughter, who will share its marvels and will also feel an obligation to protect the Arctic for the future.

When people reply with the all too familiar 'Where!? But why would anyone go to the North Pole?' my answer is now more considered. Having now seen the magnificence of God's northern work, it is the simple and unexpected things that I now answer with : 'The stillness', 'The unimaginable beautiful blueness of the Arctic sky.' 'The purity and cleanliness of the cold.' These are things you may never fully understand until you too go there yourself.

Epilogue

*'If we don't have a go, we shall live the rest of our lives
wondering if we might have made it – and knowing that
only fear persuaded us from the attempt.'*

DAVID JOHNSTONE AND JOHN HOARE, BRITISH
ATLANTIC ROWERS, LOST AT SEA, 1966.

Duncan's toes regained their feeling and returned to normal after two months, once back in the comparative warmth of an English spring. Three years later he fulfilled his promise and returned to the Arctic when, in April 2000, he walked the last degree of latitude to the North Geographic Pole, again with Pen Hadow.

In May 2002 he returned once more to the icy wastes of the Arctic in an expedition and skied, unsupported, across the Greenland icecap, a journey of some 350 miles. Whilst not meeting temperatures as low as experienced at the Magnetic North Pole, '... only got down to -25, positively balmy,' he experienced no further toe problems.

His wife Niamh still loves her comforts and won't be tempted into the Arctic, at least not until tents come with running hot water and some of the luxuries that she requires to journey afar. They now have two beautiful daughters, Rebecca and Olivia. Duncan still dreams of going on 'one last' polar expedition...

Pen Hadow made a second attempt at walking from Canada to the North Geographic Pole, alone and unsupported in June, 1998. During this solo expedition he had a bad fall on his thirteenth day, and dislocated a knee. The pain of the injury left him temporarily unconscious and upside down on an ice block. He recovered consciousness, and then bravely continued for another twenty-seven days, until carrying on would have 'Left the realms of heroic and entered the realms of stupidity,' at which point he safely retired and was flown off the ice.

Five years later, on his third attempt, Pen achieved his life's ambition when he became the first person to walk alone and completely unsupported from Canada to the North Geographic Pole. This titanic effort was described by Sir Ranulph Fiennes as the 'greatest endurance feat left on Earth'. Pen travelled 478 miles over 64 days until he reached his goal in May, 2003. It is a feat still not matched, and one which has elevated him to be Britain's premier active polar adventurer. On his arrival at the Pole, he said he sank to his knees and shed tears having finally achieved his life's goal.

In 2004 Pen walked to the South Pole, guiding an ex-French Foreign Legion soldier who, at 63, became the oldest person to walk to the bottom of the planet – again totally unsupported. This last feat enabled Pen to enter the record books yet again, when he became the first Briton to have walked to both North and South Geographic Poles – without re-supply, and all in the space of twelve months.

Pen still runs the Polar Travel Company, now renamed the Pen Hadow Travel Company, and continues to actively lead expeditions of experienced and inexperienced adventurers to fulfil their polar dreams.

As for the status of some of the other expeditions encountered during the trip and mentioned in this book:

> David Hempleman-Adams and Rune Gjeldnes attempt to walk to the North Pole unsupported was abandoned after their sledge broke 124 miles into the expedition on day 53. They completed this challenge the following year.

The Penguin Relay team reached their destination. Caroline stood at the North Geographic Pole. Later, in 2000, with some members of her original Penguin team, she successfully walked to the South Pole and in 2002 walked all the way to the North Pole.

Sergeant Chapple, the Royal Marine, I met at Resolute, returned the following year for his attempt on the Geographic North Pole. This was unfortunately abandoned after his radio batteries failed. He has since become one of the Royal Navy's top polar experts and walked successfully to the North Geographic Pole. In 2006, he reached the South Pole by leading a team of Royal Marines, who became the first group of British naval personnel to reach the bottom of the planet since Captain Scott, RN, some 94 years earlier.

Rick and Randy returned safely to Resolute some days later with the abandoned skidoos.

It's not known how any of the other expeditions fared.

Acknowledgements

I would like to thank my good friend Graham Stanbridge, and my brother, Graeme Eadie, for spending their time editing my text, giving their advice and feedback, and helping to round my rough words into this book.

To Pen Hadow, for putting his balls on the line, literally! – there is no greater sacrifice to your fellow traveller. A true gentleman if ever I met one, and someone who gives me confidence that the British spirit of adventure still abounds.

To the staff of the Polar Travel Company, especially Mike, Nobby and Gary.

To Helen Thayer, whose exploits in travelling to the North Magnetic Pole in 1988, and her subsequent book *Polar Dream* inspired me to make this journey. To the sponsors of the expedition Oyez my grateful thanks.

My thanks to the pilots of Bradley First Air Resolute Bay, the unsung heroes of many a polar expedition's success, and the saviour of many a failed expeditions' members.

Appendix 1 - Expedition List

Duncan's list of expeditions, to date, consists of:

February 1995 - Expedition to Graham Land, Antarctica.

March 1996 - Ascent of Mount Elbrus, Europe's highest mountain.

April 1997 - Oyez Solicitors' Polar Expedition to the North Magnetic Pole.

April 2000 - Expedition to the North Geographic Pole.

April 2002 - Expedition to cross the Greenland Icecap.

Appendix 2 - Komatik Contents

Listed below are the principal contents of each of the expedition team's komatiks.

Komatik 1 - Pen

Food

Maps

3 cooking pots

Rifle & ammunition
Sleeping bag
Personal equipment bag

Komatik 2 - Duncan & Peter

2 pulks (Peter's and Duncan's)
14 ski sticks
1 radio (Spillsbury SBX-11A)
1 radio antenna
9 large fuel canisters for the skidoos
1 cooker
1 small bucket, 2 tent brushes & sugar
1 tent light (gas)
2 cooking trays
1 tent and ancillary tent equipment
1 spade
2 sleeping bags
2 personal equipment bags

Komatik 3 - Mark & Bunny

Polar bear scarer
3 pulks (Pen's, Mark's and Rob's)
4 large jerry cans of fuel for the skidoos
2 boxes of fuel for the stove
2 sleeping bags
2 personal equipment bags
Majority of expedition food

Komatik 4 - Rob & Geoff

2 pulks (Bunny's and Geoff's)
1 polar bear alarm
1 sack of spare clothes
4 large canisters of fuel for the skidoos
2 sleeping bags
2 personal equipment bags

Appendix 3 - Equipment and Clothing

Listed below are the equipment and clothing used by Duncan. The rest of the expedition team used the same sort of equipment and clothing, plus a few different items to suit personal preferences.

Most clothing items were made from man made fibres, mainly polyester, due to its quick drying ability. All Buffalo equipment is lined with a polyester pile, with a Pertex outer (100% polyamide).

Worn on the Ice

Head

Black bear fur-lined hood (attached to Pertex jacket) (natural)
Outer balaclava with Gore Wind- Stopper fabric and mouth gauze (Outdoor Research)
Inner balaclava (Blacks)
Neck gaiter (Blacks)
Ski goggles - orange lenses for low visibility conditions (Cebe)
Glacier sunglasses (Varney 2000)

Body

Underwear trunks (Lowe Alpine)
Underwear (worn over trunks) (Helly Hansen Windproof)
Long Johns (North Cape)

Long sleeve vest (next to chest) (Patagonia)

Light fleece (Lowe Alpine)

Pertex jacket (Mardale)

(Inner) Down jacket (Annapurna)

(Outer) Down jacket (Henry J Bean)

Pertex trousers Pertex fluff inner with braces and under crotch zip (Buffalo)

Hands

Cotton wristlets (to protect wrists) (Silvermans)

Fingered cotton gloves

Inner Pertex mitts (Buffalo)

Outer mountain gloves (Extremities Cyclone)

Feet

Inner socks (Thurlo)

Vapour barrier lining (Mountain Equipment)

Middle layer socks

Outer socks

Mukluk canvas boots (Sorel)

Worn in the tent (much of this was also worn during the day)

Neck gaiter (As above)

Trunks (As above)

Windproof underwear (worn over trunks) - (As above)

Long Johns (As above)

Long sleeve vest (next to chest) (As above)

Shirt (Lowe Alpine)

Middle layer sock

Pertex trousers with Pertex fluff inner with braces and under crotch zip (As above)

Pertex jacket (As above)

Worn in the Sleeping bag

Inner balaclava (As above)

Neck gaiter (As above)

Trunks (As above)

Windproof underwear (worn over trunks) (As above)

Long Johns (As above)

Long sleeve vest (next to chest) (Patagonia)

Shirt (Alpine Lowe)

Cotton wristlets (to protect wrists) (Silvermans)

Middle layer sock

Cotton liner (Rab)

Vapour barrier liner (Vango)

Pee bottle (Nalgene)

Lithium camera battery (Fuji)

Two insulated 1 litre plastic water flasks (Nalgene)

Insulated container for above (Outdoor Research)

General use / Personal equipment

Watch (Rolex)

Camera (Olympus Mjui)

Camera Film (Fuji colour 35mm 200 ASA)

Fragrant wet wipes (Tesco)

1 Litre metal flask (Vango)

Small magnetic compass (Suunto)

Insulated drinking cup (Outdoor Research)

Steel spoon

Steel fork

Plastic bowl

Small paper diary and lead pencil

Assorted plasters including zinc oxide tape to bind feet (Boots)

Diarrhoea tablets (Imodium)

Small steel mirror

Oral medical first aid kit

Paracetamol sachets

Whistle (pea-less) (R Perry and Co)

50ml honey based Whisky (Glayva)

50ml Sloe Gin (home-made by my dad!)

Blow-up sheep (? !)   Two inch thick foam sleeping mat

Sleeping bag (Ajungilak Denali)   Lip cream (Lypsyl with sun block)

Outer for sleeping bag (Gore-Tex)

Appendix 4 - Bibliography

"*Polar Dream*" by Helen Thayer.

"*Frozen in Time - unlocking the secrets of the doomed 1845 Arctic expedition*" by Owen Beattie and John Geiger.

"*Frigid Women*" by Sue and Victoria Riches, with Dawn French.

Appendix 5 - Data Chart

Temperature Conversion Table

Celsius	Fahrenheit	Comment
21	70	Comfortable room temperature
0	32	Water freezes
-1.2	30	Sea water freezes
-10	14	Fairly chilly!
-20	-4	Hairs inside nose freeze! However, when working its still fairly easy to break sweat - to be avoided in the polar regions.
-30	-22	Below this temperature, very cold, despite equipment
-40	-40	The two scales converge - It's cold, whichever way you measure it. Any exposed skin quickly freezes.
-45	-49	
-65	-85	Skin so cold it seems to have a burning sensation on contact with air

Wind chill Table

Wind chill on the body was significantly increased during the expedition as much of the travel was by skidoo. Running at almost full speed (estimated to be 30 mph) the additional wind chill generated is significant.

Ambient Temperature (°C)	Wind Speed (mph)	Wind Chill Effect (°C)
-25	30	-60
-30	5	-46
-30	30	-67
-40	5	-57
-40	30	-80
-45	30	-87

Location of the North Magnetic Pole

The chart below shows how the location of the North Magnetic Pole is wondering north west.

Year	Latitude °N	Longitude °W
1831	70	97
1904	70	96
1948	74	101
1962	75	100
1984	76	102
1988	77.26	102.43
1994	78.3N	104.0W
1997	78.7N	104.4W
2001	81.3	110.8
2002	81.6	111.6
2003	82.0	112.4
2004	82.3	113.4
2005	82.7	114.4

Source: Canadian Geologic Survey

Glossary

Celsius	A metric measurement of temperature. Water freezes at 0 degrees Celsius. The metric (Celsius) and imperial (Fahrenheit) temperature scales meet at -40. My own experience on the expedition is that, with the Arctic clothing worn, that temperatures:
	
	0 to -30°C is cold, but bearable with modern equipment.
	
	Temperatures lower than -30°C are very cold.
	    Fingers (even under 3 gloves) constantly freeze.
	    Feet are very cold and blood needs to be forced to circulate via the '*ice dance*'.
	
	Lower than -40°C is extremely cold. Exposed skin freezes very quickly.

Geographic North Pole	Known as 'true north'. 90 degrees north is the top of the planet. The most northern point on Earth, and the place where all lines of longitude meet. Situated in the middle of the Arctic Ocean (which is normally frozen over at this point all year round).

Ice Dance   The movement used by all team members to force blood around the body. As temperatures drop, the blood thickens, and it becomes more difficult for it to reach the extremities of the body: nose, fingers and feet. These become cold and the owner of these parts has to help blood movement by using the centrifugal force generated by swinging the arms and legs, to push the blood into these remote parts of the body to avoid frostbite. These swinging and rotating actions, somewhat violent as the temperature drops, were known as the 'ice dance' on the expedition.

Inukshuk   A stone pile left in the past by Inuit on top of hills to aid navigation amongst the seemingly identical white, rounded hills.

Inuit   The people found across much of northern Canada. Characteristics include dark hair and eyes, light brown skin and almond-shaped eyes. Inuit have been in Northern Canada for some 8,000 years, almost certainly arriving from Siberia via the Bering land bridge, before the seas rose as the last Ice Age retreated.

Komatik   An Inuit word meaning long or large sledge. Made of wood with wooden runners, even today. Too big to be pulled by a man. See pulk.

Magnetic Pole   The Magnetic Pole is the point on the Earth's surface where the magnetic field is directed vertically downward. This can be seen using a special instrument called a 'dip circle'. This will point exactly downward when over the Magnetic Pole.
Like a magnetic the Earth has two poles, a North and a South Pole. All the world's magnetic compasses point to the North Magnetic Pole. These magnetic poles are not fixed and move regularly. They are plotted on an annual basis, and knowing where the magnetic pole is, is an important part of navigation.

Mukluk   The Inuit word for a type of shoe made from skin. The modern equivalent, which was used on the expedition, is made of cloth and insulating fabrics.

Nautical Mile A nautical mile is based on the circumference of the Earth. It is used by all nations for air and sea travel and often by polar expeditions. A nautical mile is slightly longer than a statute mile, for example, 100 nautical miles is approximately 115 statute miles.

A nautical mile is calculated such: If you were to cut the Earth in half at the equator, you could pick up one of the halves and look at the equator as a circle. You could divide that circle into 360 degrees. You could then divide a degree slice into 60 minutes. A minute of arc on the planet Earth is 1 nautical mile.

Pulk A sledge. Typically five to six feet in length and pulled by man or dog. n this expedition each team member had a pulk. The top was covered in red fabric to protect the contents of the pulk. A central zip running the length of the fabric enabled access to the pulk's ontents.

Tundra Scrub land, often found in the northern part of the world. Typically found in Canada and Siberia. Often moss and grass-covered in summer, boggy, and harbouring hoards of mosquitoes. In the winter tundra is usually snow-covered. Often tundra ground is frozen to a depth of 2 - 10 feet.

Unsupported A term used to describe an expedition that once it has set off carries with it all the necessities needed. It has no outside logistical support until it reaches its destination, and is therefore unsupported. Arguments have raged in the polar community about the how detailed this is, for example - if you have contact with the outside world via radio - is this support? (It is certainly morale boosting.)

ISBN 142512215-9